Sean Condon is the author of *Sean & David's Long Drive* (1996) and *Drive Thru America* (1998), both published by Lonely Planet Journeys, as well as the novel *Film* (2000/2003). Any further biographical information here is more or less redundant because the book you have in your hands is, as its title suggests, all about him. His email address is: mydamlife@hotmail.com.

What they've said about *My 'Dam Life*

Booklist (American Library Association)
'Fans of offbeat travel literature rejoice! Condon, author of *Sean and David's Long Drive* (1996) and *Drive Thru America* (1998), returns with this hysterical, delightful, and (mostly) true account of his temporary residence in Amsterdam. … Chuckles abound. Stylistically and philosophically, Condon is as close to Bill Bryson as it's possible to be. He mixes fascinating facts with hilarious humor, peppers the book with an assortment of wild and wonderful supporting characters (Francis Ford Coppola and Monica Lewinsky, if you can believe it, make cameo appearances here), and keeps us thoroughly in stitches from beginning to end. This one's an absolute must-read.'

San Francisco Chronicle
'… a smart and funny book'

Chicago Tribune
'Sean Condon is a humorous chap from Australia who writes humorous books.'

'Condon writes about mundane things in a David Sedaris sort of way – dry and ironic with a skewed sense of the absurdity of it all. Whether trying to explain the idiosyncrasies of Dutch ways or just thinking about what to have for lunch, *My 'Dam Life* is an entertaining look at the life of an Aussie ex-pat. I just don't think the Dutch tourist board necessarily will endorse it.'

Australian Bookseller & Publisher
'Only a certain section of society (but I imagine, a fairly large one) will appreciate Condon's style of humour: self-deprecating, exaggerated, and not always politically correct. I love a book that makes me laugh out loud, and Condon's colourful adventures and witty observations certainly did.'

Sydney *Daily Telegraph*
'*My 'Dam Life* should be essential reading for anyone considering a move overseas.'

Sydney *Sun-Herald*
'Sean Condon is becoming a favourite among bookworms looking for some comic relief.'

Melbourne *Herald-Sun*
'He's managed to turn failure, self-doubt and minor disaster into an artform.'

'This book is like getting a series of entertaining letters from a friend.'

Luxury Travel
'Dry, whimsical and very funny, Sean Condon's latest memoir covers his three delightfully uneventful years spent in Amsterdam.'

'… a fun insight into both the author and the city of Amsterdam.'

My 'Dam Life: Three Years in Holland

Published by Lonely Planet Publications

Head Office:
90 Maribyrnong Street, Footscray, Vic 3011, Australia
Locked Bag 1, Footscray, Vic 3011, Australia

Branches:
150 Linden Street, Oakland CA 94607, USA
72–82 Rosebery Ave, Clerkenwell, London EC1R 4RW, UK

Published 2003, reprinted 2003, 2004
Printed by The Bookmaker International Ltd
Printed in China

Edited by Meaghan Amor
Designed by Daniel New
Map by Tony Fankhauser

National Library of Australia Cataloguing-in-Publication entry

Condon, Sean, 1965–.
My 'Dam Life: Three Years in Holland

ISBN 0 86442 781 6

1. Amsterdam (Netherlands) – Social life and customs –
Humor. 2. Amsterdam (Netherlands) – Description and travel.
I. Title. (Series: Lonely Planet journeys).

914.920473

My 'Dam Life

Three Years in Holland

LONELY PLANET PUBLICATIONS
Melbourne • Oakland • London • Paris

For Ray and Sally,
Both of whom deserve better.

Contents

Acknowledgements 8

Map 9

Introduction: False Starts 11

Handcuffed to a Ghost 23

In the Murder Park with Chickens 41

Assimilating with Fatty 62

Pitiful Figures 79

Bertie and Mrs X 97

Francis, Monica, Amopolo and Me 121

Four Hundred Years Too Late 133

2000: A New Millennium? 146

Trouble 156

2001: Another New Millennium? 172

Nothing Satanic 196

Me and EU 209

A Very Long Way Away 227

Epilogue: Collision 243

The author* wishes to thank the following for various forms of help, support and encouragement: Susan Keogh, Janet Austin, Meaghan Amor, Lauren O'Leary, Tony Hughes, Emily Schneider, Michelle Gauci, Stephan Beurskens, Sonia Harford, those Nigerian guys who keep asking me to share in multi-million-dollar bank transfers, Ken Wilkie, Amruta Slee, Fenella Souter, Eric Quennoy, Maria Englund, Alison Standish, Gary Walsh, Geoff Ingall, Kitty Flanagan, the Internet, Simonne Overend, Rowan McKinnon, Peter Morris, Amanda Lee Smith, Graeme Armstrong, Stephen Eastaugh, Lewis Miller, Mariana Donas, Winston Churchill, Leith Condon, Julie Condon, Diane Cummins, Simon Roberts, Italy[†], France[‡] and Belgium[§], Max Anderson, Christine Walker, Susan D'Arcy, the Greedy Beat Syndicate, Kelly and Elisabeth Phillips, Jenna Reed Burns, Inge Rietjens, Paul Sloper, Laen Sanches, Cedric Borghel, Manis, Sam, Claudio Macor, Jon Renard, Kate Sellars-Jones, David O'Brien, Michael Weldon, Pat Kavanagh, Frederika van Traa, Pieter Spanhoef, Niels van Laatum, and the Dutch, generally.

*Sean Condon. [†]All. [‡]Most. [§]Antwerp.

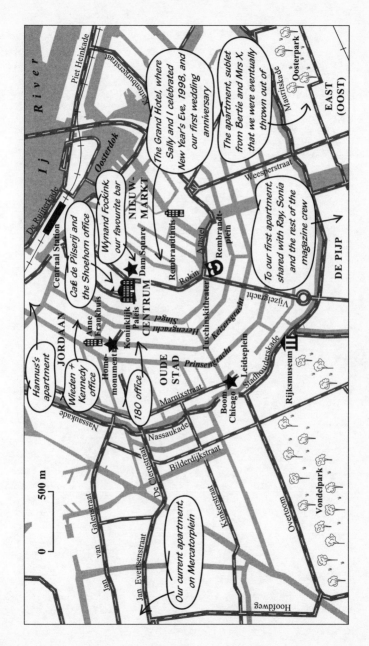

Ij River

Piet Heinkade

Kattenburgergracht

Oosterdok

De Ruijterkade

Oosterpark

EAST (OOST)

Mauritskade

Weesperstraat

The Grand Hotel, where Sally and I celebrated New Year's Eve, 1998, and our first wedding anniversary

The apartment, sublet from Bertie and Mrs X, that we were eventually thrown out of

Rembrandt-plein

Rembrandtsplein

Rembrandthuis

NIEUW-MARKT

Wynand Fockink, our favourite bar

Dam Square

Centraal Station

Café de Pilserij and the Shoehorn office

JORDAAN

Anne Frankhuis

Koninklijk Paleis

CENTRUM

Amstel

Rokin

To our first apartment, shared with Ray, Sonia and the rest of the magazine crew

DE PIJP

Vijzelgracht

Tuschinskitheater

Keizersgracht

Herengracht

Singel

OUDE STAD

Prinsengracht

S Leidseplein

Stadhouderskade

Rijksmuseum

Hannus's apartment

Wieden + Kennedy office

Home-monument

180 office

Nassaukade

Marnixstraat

Boom Chicago

Vondelpark

Nassaukade

Bilderdijkstraat

De Clercqstraat

Kinkerstraat

Overtoom

Hoofdweg

van Galenstraat

Jan Evertsenstraat

Our current apartment on Mercatorplein

0   500 m

Introduction: False Starts

Things would have been so much better for Sally and I if we'd arrived four hundred years earlier.

'Hi Honey, you're home!'

I kicked the PlayStation across the carpet and under the television, tried to look innocent and beamed up at my wife Sally. She's six feet tall and since I was sitting cross-legged on the floor, I was tilting my grinning face at close to forty-five degrees. It hurt.

Sally dropped her car keys and handbag onto a table. 'Have you been playing with that stupid thing all day?'

'No.' I kept beaming, tracking her like a tiny satellite dish as she moved about the room.

'What's that then?' she asked, pointing at my hand.

I tilted down; the coloured plastic controller was gripped firmly between my two fat, sweating little paws. 'Oh yeah. I only just turned it on.' *Seven hours ago.*

'Sit down,' Sally said.

'I am sitting down.'

'Not on the floor like a toddler. Go and slump on a chair like a teen or something.'

'Why?'

'I have some news.' I slumped as requested, wondering what the big, sit-down information could be. 'We're moving,' she said. I was relieved – not that I didn't hate moving house, all that packing and boxing and trauma just to end up in some other dump right around the corner from where you used to live. It's all such a . . .

'To Amsterdam,' Sally said.

11

'Oohhh . . .' I was excited, of course, but my very first thought was this: will the PlayStation work in Europe?

Sally had a good job as an editor at *Shoehorn**, an international cultural magazine whose editorial HQ was in Melbourne. I was trying to make a living by staying at home and doing the washing up, a little vacuuming and a lot of vacant staring. The only thing I absolutely *had* to do each week in order to earn some dough was write a few hundred words for a column which ran in one of Melbourne's Sunday papers. It was a pathetic existence without much of a future, and although there was no dental plan, I loved the hours.

By the middle of 1998 Sally and I had known each other for over ten years, had been going out together for five, shared an apartment for four and a half and been married for six months. We'd met in 1987, during one of the fifteen-minute periods when I'd tried to attend university. We'd gone on a few dates and it wasn't long before Sally discovered that I was something of an immature dick-head. We lost track of one another for five years during which Sally worked as a showgirl in Japan for a while and I attempted, with little success, to become an advertising man. Then, in the middle of 1992, Sally and I met all over again when her then-boyfriend, a record company rep, had dragged her along to see a hideous band with whom it was my sad duty to whack drums. In between sets I did my best to convince Sally that I'd grown up a little and that, despite its colourful dress sense, bright smiles and relentlessly sunny music, the band I was in was not a Christian rock outfit. Two good things came out of our meeting that night: I left the band and Sally left her boyfriend.

We had no children, no pets and no garden, feeling too young for the first, too old for the second, and not old enough for the third. Nevertheless, our lives lacked something. Or in my case, everything. We'd both grown up in Melbourne, a large, dynamic and beautiful city, but one with the poor luck to be located at the bottom of the world. Between us and the Antarctic was Hobart, a city never likely to be mentioned on perfume or cigarette packaging.

---

*Not the magazine's real name. Its real name was *Wanderlust*.†
†Also not its real name.

I realised that Amsterdam was not cigarette/perfume packaging material either but the idea of moving there appealed to me, partly because it might get us closer to where we both really wanted to live – New York City. To New Amsterdam via the old Amsterdam. It felt right.

'Well, what do you think?' Sally asked me, as I poured us both a beer.

'How many Dutch . . . whatevers to an Australian dollar?'

'Guilders. A little more than one,' Sally said. 'Around one twenty-five.'

'Hmmm . . . ,' I sipped at my beer and did a few swift mental calculations. 'Does that mean we get more or less?'

'Oh God.' Sally kicked off her Clergeries, leaned back on the couch and explained the international monetary exchange system to me one more time.

Half an hour later I nodded enthusiastically and said, 'When do we leave?'

In the six weeks before we left we tried to learn everything we could about our new home. Despite having had a Dutch father-in-law for half a year, I knew next to nothing about Holland. I was aware of all the obvious stuff – clogs, canals, windmills, Anne Frank, Heineken, raw herring and that the Dutch once had an armada that did some serious armading a few centuries ago – but the details, especially the practical details of what I could expect of life in Amsterdam, were entirely unknown to me. And I fear the unknown.

Since Sally's dad had emigrated to Australia in 1960 and hadn't returned to Holland (which itself was not a good sign, I felt), there was a great deal about contemporary Amsterdam he couldn't tell us. So about a month before we left, Sally and I had lunch with another Melbourne-based Dutchman I knew. Rob was a good choice because he had just returned from a visit to Holland. Rob could put us on the inside track Holland-wise straight away.

'First of all,' he began, 'the country is not called Holland. Holland is just two provinces in the Netherlands, but because Amsterdam is in the province of Noord Holland, most of the world seems to think that's the name of the country. Most of the world is wrong. Work is plentiful, but only for Dutch residents, so you can forget about that. Winter lasts six months, during the height of which it gets dark around four o'clock every day. It's a very cold city, a very crowded city, especially in summer when the already too-large population doubles. It's a very expensive city and you'll be damn lucky if you don't end up living in a tiny, overpriced hovel.' I nodded, as I wrote down the words 'small', 'expensive' and 'hovel'. While I had the notebook open, I crossed out the word 'Holland'. Rob hadn't finished. 'You can also forget about living in a houseboat – they're impossible to get and very damp and expensive anyway. Apartments overlooking canals are also impossible to get and incredibly expensive even if you can get one. Which you can't. So,' he asked, 'why are you going?'

'I'm not sure if we are any more,' I said. Actually, I kind of whimpered.

'Of course we are,' Sally said, not whimperingly. 'What've we got to lose?'

Rob smiled. 'That's the attitude! I'm very excited for you both. You'll have a wonderful time. Just hold your nose and dive in, it'll be a great adventure.'

That was easy for him to say, I thought. A Dutchman living in Australia – it doesn't get dark at four in the afternoon around here. After lunch, Sally drove to work and I went back to our enormous, inexpensive apartment where I pulled out the PlayStation and started work on 'SimCity', building a version of Amsterdam with extra canals and lots of affordable housing.

As potentially hostile as Amsterdam seemed, the fact was I'd always wanted to live overseas. I knew and envied a handful of people who'd done it. Many of them had ended up in London, a popular destination for younger, post-university Australians, mostly because it had been a popular destination for several previous generations of post-university Australians, which of course meant that London was full of other Australians, so nobody had any reason to feel too lonely. Or even too foreign. I also knew a couple who'd won a Green Card in the US Immigration lottery. Now they were both working in a bookstore in Seattle. Living in the United States was an idea that appealed to Sally and I greatly, but one which, it seemed, would never come to pass: we'd entered the Green Card lottery ourselves a couple of times before, with no success. On the other hand, I'd worked in a bookstore before and hadn't found that particularly appealing either. There were other people I knew, scattered around the world pursuing their destinies – spiritual, intellectual or corporate – and although I tried not to, I admired and resented them all. Even the ones who wound up in London.

The packing up of our lives seemed as though it would never end. It was a process which Sally had some firm ideas about. 'My Le Creuset pot is definitely going over,' she said, hunched on her knees and peering into a kitchen cupboard.

'But that thing weighs about fifty pounds,' I said.

'I don't care. It goes where I go. So does Stephanie.' Stephanie was a big orange cookbook who weighed about twenty pounds.

'What about the PlayStation?' I asked pointlessly.

Sally shook her head. 'No way. You've wasted enough time on that thing here. You're not going to Amsterdam to play.'

That was true enough, but what exactly *was* I going for? Coincidentally, I was at the exact age my father was when the flooring company he worked for transferred my family to Montreal for two years in the mid-seventies. It was coincidence, but not a parallel. He was the one being transferred – my mother, my two sisters and myself were just along for the ride. This time, my wife was the one being relocated and, once again, I was just along for the ride. But I didn't want it to be merely a ride, and while I wouldn't for a moment consider not going where Sally was headed, I wanted a reason of my own to go to Amsterdam.

In search of what I felt were appropriately Dutch vocations, I'd scoured adult education pamphlets looking for intensive clog-making or rollmop-rolling workshops. There were none. I tried to learn how to make Edam cheese – way too hard. I wrote to the Ajax Football Club asking if they needed an orange boy – they didn't. Might the Heineken brewery require the services of a skilled beer-taster, I wondered? We already have several million, they told me. I contacted a few Australian newspapers and asked if they would be interested in employing me as an Amsterdam-based correspondent. 'Nothing much happens in Holland,' was their reply.

'Actually, it's called the Netherlands, not Holland,' I told them.

I was out of luck and out of time. It seemed that the only

reason for me to move overseas would be to stay at home and keep the place nice while my wife went out and made an honest living. That the 'great adventure' Rob had referred to would be little more than a simple domestic relocation of several thousand miles. How wrong I was . . .

Amsterdam. Early September, 2001

It's an old truism in writing that you have to grab readers with your very first lines, and when I think of some of the greats, such as 'All this happened, more or less' or 'I come from Des Moines. Somebody had to' or even 'My appendix was killing me', I become almost certain that 'Hi Honey, you're home', while both brief and true, is not one of the greats. Unless, of course, my life bears a greater resemblance to some sort of sitcom than I care to admit.

I've tried other beginnings: garrulous, over-crafted ones full of peculiar detail and light comedy, principle characters (me and my wife Sally: tall, slender, fine-boned, believes the correct pronunciation of *solemn* rhymes with *golem*), establishing scenes and subtle adumbration. I re-read a couple and I hated them – too much simpering and whimpering. But the fact is they were written by me, albeit in a different state of mind, a different part of Amsterdam, a long time ago, in the crisp, chilly spring of 1999. I remember what motivated me to write in that jocular but uptight, middle-aged kind of manner, and I'm not proud of it. It was simply this: greed. I wanted to write – or at least try to write – a best-seller, along the lines of those books where somebody leaves their native country and sets up a home (usually a large one with a garden and a swimming pool) in a place with agreeable food and weather, like Tuscany or Provence. The difference with my book would be that the house would be a tiny apartment and neither the food nor the weather would be even close to agreeable. And so, as I began work on this book, I read a very popular travel book by and about a fellow in similar circumstances to my own: a life transplanted from one country to another. I read that book as a sort of guide, thinking that perhaps it'd give me some clues about the kind of thing that makes a travel bestseller, what readers want to know about some fellow's life in another land, how much and of what variety of swearing to include (none, it turned out), and that sort of thing. It was an absolutely horrible book – bland, lightly comedic rustic pabulum – but it sold a fuckload and I figured I'd have nothing to lose by not swearing and trying to come across all toothless and folksy. Hence, 'Hi Honey, you're home.'

It does the job – sets the scene, establishes the characters to some degree, engages in a bit of mild comedy – and it's pleasantly inoffensive. More than all that, though, is that it's all true*: Rob is real, Sally is real, the book named Stephanie is real and I really did spend staggering amounts of daytime with the PlayStation wondering what, if anything, would ever come along to change my sorry existence. Or whether it was in fact up to me to come along and change my sorry existence. But the lamentable truth is that I gave thoughts like that as much serious consideration as I did (and perhaps still do) to other troubling intangibles like quitting smoking, taking up some form of exercise or cutting down on booze; knowing, deep inside myself, that it'd take a doctor's dark diagnosis to inspire any real behavioural change, by which time, of course, it would be too late.

Three years ago, at almost thirty-three, I was a lazy, unmotivated ex-advertising man, ex-TV comedy writer who had worked on the unfunniest show on television, part-time newspaper columnist, twice-published author, layabout, scoundrel, wastrel, kestrel, cad, bon vivant and former good-time-Charlie who seemed to be going through a painfully attenuated phase of sluggishness coupled with an unshakeable feeling of disappointment (either with myself or everyone else), general ennui and a feeling of anxiety that felt like a clammy second skin.

I haven't changed much – I'm still uncertain of where I am in life, still looking to play games, still poor. Just half an hour ago I went downstairs to check the mail and ran into Jaap, one of our many neighbours in the large apartment block where Sally and I live. It's a renovated and quite fancy building from around 1920, designed by one of the Netherlands' premier twentieth-century architects, H. P. Berlage, and it looks like a cross between a minimum-security prison and a red brick factory built by itself.

---

*Except the stuff about contacting Heineken and Ajax and learning to make Edam cheese. None of that's true.

Our neighbour Jaap the bus driver was down at the entrance by the mailboxes, standing out front of the building, as he is often wont to do when not behind the wheel of a big blue bus. He was loitering there, the bright, cold sun hitting his pasty face, his manicured, stylised beard, his diamond stud earring (both features of which look sad and absurd on his jowly mid-forties face) – I mention this just so you get the correct mental picture of old Jaap, not to be mean, although I'd be quite happy to be mean about him as he's kind of a nosy, gossipy bore – waiting to collar some poor sap like myself into a brief but pointless conversation. Which he did.

There he was, hands in his pockets, rocking back and forth on his heels – the very cliché of a man of leisure enjoying semi-clement weather. 'Vhat's dat you write on de hand, John?' he asked. He thinks my name is John (which it sort of is).

Just before I came downstairs, I'd written the word 'truth' on the back of my left hand so I wouldn't forget to include the stuff about how, as much as I didn't care for the earlier draft of the beginning of this book, it was nonetheless the truth. 'Oh . . . nothing,' I said.

'Vhat for you write it, den?'

'Just to remind myself of something when I get back upstairs. It's nothing. *Niets.*'

Jaap stopped rocking and took a step towards me and looked at my hand. 'Truth,' he said, hardening the last sound, making a little spit out of it. 'Vhat is "truth"?'

A good question, and one which my mind had a quick answer for. *The truth, Jaap, is that I'd like to clip you over the ear for being such a goddamned busybody.* I sighed. 'It's um . . . when you don't lie to people. When you're honest.'

'I know dat!' Jaap said, a little scornfully. 'I know vhat de vord mean, but vhy you write him on de hand?'

Because I don't have any fucking paper with me! 'Because I don't have any paper with me,' I said. 'Have you by any chance seen the mailman while you've been out here?' I was waiting for a piece of potentially life-altering mail; an envelope that might change everything for Sally and I.

'Nee. Hoe gaat het met jouw Nederlands?' ('How's it going with your [speaking] Dutch?')

18

'All right. A little more every day,' I told him, only in Dutch: '*Prima. Elke dag een klein beetje meer.*' I'd told him the exact same thing every week for almost a year.

'It's nice dat you can conversate vid us in bit of Nederlands, but better you should be able to tink in de language.' He tapped the side of his head with a finger to illustrate his point. '*Snap je?*' I understood him all right, but I wasn't sure I agreed with him. Why would I want to think in Dutch? It's such a noisy, gnarled language that having it clatter around in your head would actually be a great impediment to thought. 'You going to buy the corner apartment for sale?' he asked.

'Whose apartment?'

'Fritz.'

'There's a Fritz here?'

'He always coming and going. Never see him.'

'How much is it?'

'Four hundred fifty . . . almost five hundred t'ousand guilden. It's a good apartment, big living room vid a kitchen in him, two odder rooms. Vhat you tink?'

What *did* I think? This was a very big question. Did I want to stay in Amsterdam, tied to property? (Yes; yes/no/I don't know/ probably, since the rent we paid was deadly.) As someone without a real job, would a bank give me a loan? (No, of course not.) Where did I see myself in a year, in five years? And doing what? (No idea/no idea/no idea.) Was my life of sufficient substance that I could give serious consideration to buying an apartment in a country where, only that very morning, I had sent off yet another application for a temporary residence permit? What would Sally, who probably *could* get a bank loan on our behalf, think about buying a place?

'Vell?' Jaap said impatiently, eager to get back to standing around doing nothing.

I told Jaap that I'd think about it (using English thoughts) and discuss it with my wife (using English words and phrases), then went next door to the toy store to see if there were any PC games going cheap.

In just a few weeks I will be thirty-six.

As I write now, I have been living in Amsterdam for just a little over three years. Sally has been at the office for less than five hours and, predictably, the apartment has already become a sty and I have watched several truly woeful TV shows, eaten what seems like kilos of fatty, sugary 'food', and begun to have long (and often very tedious) conversations with myself.

SC: When you get up in the morning, you follow a pretty set routine, don't you, Sean?

SC (quickly): Yes, I do. For the past few years, since I entered what I call 'the information age', the main thing that urges me out of bed is the unnatural excitement I derive from checking my email.

SC: Which is kind of ironic, isn't it, in that you often don't receive any email at all. Or just really dull stuff from the Postbank or Blokker on line.

SC: If that's irony, then yes. Anyway, I get up, check the email, take a shower, put a pot of coffee on so it's bubbling away while I get dressed – a time-saving measure, you see – usually flick on BBC World Service in order to keep in touch with what's happening and then come here and sit at the computer.

SC: Where you do what, exactly?

SC: Oh y'know, reply to emails.

SC: If you get any. Which is not all that often. I mean you haven't heard from any of your friends for quite some time, isn't that correct? I'm talking about people like David O'Brien, with whom you've travelled before, James whom you might recall from high school and Michael, whom you'll no doubt recall from a former place of employment. And let's not even get started on your mother and sisters. Or your father – whom you might remember was recently diagnosed with bowel cancer.

SC: Nice one. Are you trying to shock me? I already knew he had bowel cancer.

SC: But you haven't given it much thought since you've been aware of it, have you?

SC: No, I haven't. But I haven't spoken to my father for over three years. And before that, I hadn't spoken to him for about five years. We're not close.

SC: So how did you find out?

SC: My sister Leith told me. In an email, as a matter of fact. Can we move on?

SC: In a moment. How is he now, your father?

SC: Last I heard, from a telephone conversation with my mother, he'd had the cancerous stuff removed and had given up smoking. She made some dry and derisive comment about how that was typical or something. How the only thing that would make him do something like give up smoking would be to be diagnosed with cancer. She herself quit when she was in her late thirties and she never shuts up about other people smoking. Me especially.

SC: It's twelve-thirty – how many cigarettes have you smoked so far today?

SC: Four. What's that got to do with anything?

SC: Character is detail, so they say.

SC: What will you be having for lunch today?

SC: I think fruit, to make up for yesterday and last night.

SC: And you think that eating an apple and a banana once every two weeks will help you evade bowel cancer, unlike your father?

SC: No, I don't, but . . .

SC: Because it won't.

SC: I *know* it won't.

SC: Are you happy, Sean?

SC: Not particularly. Sometimes I'm happy, when I feel happiness is warranted.

SC: Why are you unhappy?

SC: Because I'm always worried about dying or being killed. And not just from cancer, by the way. From anything. From everything. From being in a train wreck on the way to Reims to cover a story about champagne manufacture.

SC (sarcastically): 'Cover', I like that. It makes you sound hardy and intrepid. Which is very far from the truth . . .

And right then, at the exact moment I was writing 'very far from the truth', a friend called to tell me that apparently a plane had crashed into one of the World Trade Center Towers. I turned on CNN and, as I saw what was happening, I worried about my friends who lived in Manhattan. I worried about Sally at work. I watched history skew right before my eyes and I worried about everyone, all over the world.

Handcuffed to a Ghost

A man lies in a filthy, dirt-floored room on the thin and crooked Kalverstraat in central Amsterdam. The Augean hovel stinks of manure, animals, smoke, blood, pustular excretion and the oily ordure of mortal despair. The man is gravely ill, close to death, and receives the Holy Sacrament from a visiting priest. Immediately afterwards the man regurgitates the Host in a torrent of bile. A woman attending to the pyrexic man throws the vomit into a fire, which is kept burning throughout the night for warmth. The next morning, while raking the ashes, the woman finds the Host, clean, white, whole and unharmed. Over the next few hours the Host changes colour several times and begins to slowly move of its own accord. The dying man recovers and soon the entire clergy of Amsterdam descends upon the house on the Kalverstraat to see for themselves the evidence of this great wonderment. Amidst a procession the Holy Sacrament is taken to the Oude Kerk. There are banners, flags, songs of praise and great thanks.

This well-documented incident is called The Miracle of Amsterdam and it happened on March 15th, 1345. I'd been in Amsterdam for less than a month when Sally, her colleagues from the magazine and I all felt like doing a bit of vomiting of our own. The reasons were fivefold.

First, there were far too many of us living in the small one-and-a-half-bedroom apartment the magazine had provided for us. Sally and I shared a single mattress in a tiny, airless chamberlet we called The Cooler. We were lucky: Bernard, *Shoehorn*'s nominal publisher who did little other than engage in long arguments with the magazine's executives before passing out around seven o'clock every night, slept in a swag on the living room floor – with

23

his girlfriend. Terry, a wry and softly spoken New Zealander who was the magazine's art director, slept under the dining room table on a piece of green foam roughly cut into a shape resembling his own, right down to the grey moustache he'd favoured for the last thirty years. 'We should have moved to Paris,' Terry said almost nightly. 'It's more roomy. And so much more French.' In the main bedroom (which we referred to as the Penthouse Suite because it had a window) were Ray, the magazine's senior editor, and his journalist girlfriend Sonia. Ray was – and remains – the closest I have ever come to knowing a real-life Henry Blake (TV version) crossed with the endearingly rumpled and slobby Walter Matthau of *The Odd Couple* and *The Taking of Pelham One Two Three*; he is a relentlessly kind, generous and affable fellow as well as being a very sentimental and lovable drunk. 'But,' in his own words, 'I'd rather be tall, thin and witty. And sober.' If Ray was Henry Blake, then Sonia was his Radar. They were a perfect match in loyalty, companionship – and size. Of course even the most devoted and suited couple could implode under these circumstances: over-crowding, smokers cohabitating with non-smokers, too much alcohol and general filth. Fortunately, a cleaner came in once a week to dispose of cigarette-butt mountains and head-high stacks of empty Grolsch cans in the living room, created by Bernard, who lacked the domestication, and sometimes the intellect, of a cat. Or a man dying in fourteenth-century Amsterdam.

Many locals commented to us, 'Oh, seven of you live in a small apartment in the south-east. Yes, it is far away and not a nice area. You are very lucky.'

The roots of Amsterdam's housing crisis go back to the mid-seventies. Well, I suppose they really go back to about 1200 when somebody stumbled upon a marshy swampland and thought that it would be a nice place to build a city. But it was hard for me to blame that person as they were probably unaware that eight hundred years later I'd be showing up looking for somewhere fancy to live. So I was forced to blame the following groups for my domestic restlessness: city planners, *krakers* (squatters), police, property investors and fat men in tracksuits.

Early in 1975, plans were announced to raze a large section of the Nieuwmarkt neighbourhood to make way for a metro line connecting the city with a huge housing project/ghetto called the Bijlmer (where, in 1992, an El Al jumbo crashed into an apartment block, killing dozens of people). Unhappy with the eradication of a historic city precinct, a large group of *krakers* occupied the mostly derelict Nieuwmarkt and turned it into a fortress. Then on 'Blue Monday', March 24th, the *krakers* were forcibly evicted by the police, many of whom were injured (probably from cutting themselves on broken porcelain skull bongs or from slipping on lentils). This incident inspired the shocked city council to set about renovating inner-city buildings and providing affordable housing around the canal belt. Suddenly everybody realised that everybody else wanted to live in beautiful old buildings next to beautiful old tree-lined canals, and such property was promptly targeted by investors. The problem was that investor interest then shot the prices of these places through the roof, to the extent that they were no longer affordable and often remained vacant. This irritated plenty of people who decided to occupy the empty places illegally – and freely. This would have been fine (unless you were a vacant-property owner) except the city council responded in its usual vexing and foolhardy manner. In March 1980 the police employed tanks to evict a large group from a building near the Vondelpark. Cops with tanks is an impressive, unusual and disturbing sight and so attracted hundreds of demonstrators to the area, which quickly threw the city into chaos. After the tank-assisted eviction, the building was immediately re-squatted and the entire movement gained further support by the riots which occurred on the Queen's Coronation Day a month later.

Defeat, humiliation and expense forced the city council to reconsider its tactics. Meanwhile, however, the property investors, lacking a police force and a ready supply of armoured vehicles, sent in their own eviction forces – the *knokploegen*, or 'fat men in tracksuits'. These fellows worked on a more personal and intimate level than the cops; basically a *get out or we'll break your legs* approach which doubtless proved very effective against the squatters, many of whom were probably enfeebled by veganism and bong-smoking. The riots continued and culminated in a three-day festival of shouting and burning trams in 1982, following evictions from Lucky Luyk, an expensive villa in the very lovely museum district. As a tram went up in flames, a state of emergency was declared.

A year later the city had a tough new mayor called Ed van Thijn who employed tear gas against the *krakers*. By 1984 the last important squats had fallen to make way for a Holiday Inn, and the *krakers* were no longer a force to be reckoned with. However, the legacy of the squatters, the cops, the city planners and the property investors remained – by late 1998 it was damn near impossible to find anywhere decent and cheap to live.

Second of the vomit-inducing factors was that the Netherlands is very flat. It's not so much that I like mountains and hills – although I have nothing against them – it's just that without some sort of topographical variety, I get nauseous. I'm quite used to flatness; Melbourne is pretty flat, but what I'd seen as my plane had flown over Holland a few weeks earlier was truly nauseating. The entire country looked as though it had been steamrollered then heavily vacuumed so that not even mounds, hillocks or bumps remained. When we landed I was pretty sure I could see a guy in Belgium waving from a stepladder.

If a cultural landscape can be defined as the point where Man and Nature come together to fight it out – Man's urge to shape and civilise and Nature's natural inclination to be natural – then the Dutch, in their struggle against rivers and the sea, can perhaps claim a Pyrrhic cultural victory. The necessary cost to the physical landscape has been dramatic: tidal and river flood defences and agricultural functionality have reduced much of the Netherlands to geographical monotony (the fine work of seventeenth-century Dutch landscape masters notwithstanding). This sense of order has extended to other forms of civic planning as well: sterile train stations, straight, reliable roads, model villages and razor-sharp parcels of land all seem to be simple copies of each other – neat, homogenised and often bland. (But, it would seem when viewed from above, excellent inspiration for Piet Mondriaan.) Compared with the unruliness and diversity found just over the border in Belgium (where dangerous roads twist and wind into tangled forests; where houses look ragged, built by hand rather than delivered by truck), the Dutch appear somewhat constipated and anxious in their desire to preserve and maintain orderliness in all things. On the other hand, Holland's, again necessary, system of canals, watercourses, dikes, polders and drainage areas is impressive, if you like that sort of thing. And living here, you're obliged to like that sort of thing because without it Amsterdam, several metres below sea level, would be better known as the Atlantis of northern Europe. The inhabitants are therefore proud of their battle against the sea and sum it up thusly: God created the world, but the Dutch created Holland.

Third: the weather was utterly abysmal – cold, wet, grey – and it wasn't even winter yet.

Fourth: my research, undertaken by peering at restaurant menus and increasingly stomach-churning wanders through cookbooks, showed me that, among other treats, traditional Dutch dishes consisted of sautéed cabbage, buttered leeks, baked endive, fried parsnips, beets with nothing done to them other than being put on a plate, sugared potatoes, *Tante Lorna's Vroege Zomer Aardappelen* (Aunty Lorna's Early Summer Potatoes), Gouda balls, gin balls, apple balls, bitter balls, soup balls, oil balls, rabbit curry, braised rabbit, thrice-baked rabbit, *karnemelk* (buttermilk), beef with salt and pepper on it, codfish tail, raw herring, fish pudding, eel (in any form), *drop* (a mouth-wizeningly tart combination of liquorice and salt) and *hangop* (buttermilk poured into a pillowcase or stocking and left to hang for about twelve hours). I like food, quite a lot as it happens, and to say that I was dismayed by my discoveries is putting it mildly. I was, in fact, repulsed, even a little insulted. How could a country so close to France show such contempt for cuisine? Have such a stodgy, utilitarian approach to matters of the palate and stomach? Then I remembered – England wasn't far away and Germany was just next door.

Last on the vomit list was the fact that *Shoehorn* magazine – the reason we had relocated from Australia to Europe – was having some troubles. There was an enormous amount of tension between Bernard and DOA, the magazine's parent company. In order to save costs, the parents insisted that the magazine's children (the staff) move into an already established office block in the unattractive far outskirts of Amsterdam. But the kids – especially Bernard who was intractable on the matter – wanted to work in the attractive inskirts of the city. To this end, an arrangement had been

struck with two young entrepreneurs who owned and ran a successful bar called Café de Pilserij. It was on the top two floors of
this establishment, the former office of *De Telegraaf* newspaper,
that the magazine had decided to set up office. As Bernard put it,
'I didn't come all the way to Amsterdam to live in fucking Utrecht
and work in fucking Amstelveen.' Meanwhile, though, nobody
was being paid . . . 'Ah, don't worry about that,' he would say,
over his lunch-time beers. 'I'll sort it out when I meet with the
boss in Germany. He loves me like a son.' In a few weeks we
would all learn that that term was almost accurate – just three
small words were missing at the end of 'son'.

Unfortunately, I'd arrived just in time to help with the dusting,
scrubbing, polishing, furniture removal and general renovations
required to make the office space usable. And in a 300-year-old
building, that was quite a lot. In return, however, I was given a
large room at the back of the fourth floor in which to do whatever
it was I was going to do with my Amsterdam life, which consisted
mainly of staring at a stapler and wondering what to have for
lunch other than meat, cheese and fluffy white bread.

De Pils, as we referred to it to save time, was what the Dutch
call a typical 'brown café' – an old, dark, woody place lit almost
entirely by candles and typified by what Amsterdammers call
gezelligheid or 'cosiness'. The café (which in this case means bar,
as opposed to 'coffee shop' which means marijuana café) was
located right in the centre of town, just behind Dam Square, and I
was thrilled to be there in amongst the *dringen en stompen* of life
in the winding, cobblestone streets and alleys of the Centrum,
where at any time of any day you might see a crackhead scoring
some crack, somebody eating a tulip, or a bicycle being stolen
right before your very eyes. We loved the place; it was historical,
European and surprisingly cheap – everything a bunch of Down
Under New Worlders could want. We were right behind the
Koninklijk Paleis (royal palace), which as far as European palaces
go is not very nice, largely because it began life as the town hall
and is now absolutely filthy from pollution and centuries of
municipal neglect. Apparently even Queen Beatrix Wilhelmina
Armgard – a big-smiling, big-faced woman who favours flashy
oversized hats – hates it, which, while understandable from an

aesthetic point of view, seemed rather ungrateful from a seven-people-living-in-a-tiny-apartment point of view.

It was through the noise of his hammering on the floor below mine one morning that I met Keith Finney. I went downstairs, perfunctorily introduced myself to him then asked the question I asked of everybody I met lately. 'Do you know anywhere cheap and nice to live around here?'

'You got more chance of bein' 'andcuffed to a ghost than finding summing like that, mate,' he said, looking me up and down. 'You wearing that shirt for a bet, or wot?' A moment fluttered between us as he waited for my reaction. I looked at my shirt – hot pink polyester. 'It's no good standing there like one o'clock 'alf struck, mate, *do* summing,' he said. So I laughed. I had to do *summing*.

Keith was a small-framed, tanned and extremely fit cockney (almost a caricature of one – he even pronounced his name 'Keef') who did everything with great urgency – he ate urgently, walked urgently and spoke urgently, almost as though he believed every passing second to be his last, or that he would die of boredom like a still shark if he slowed down. He'd been living in Amsterdam on and off for the previous twenty-three years, working at a staggering variety of jobs, everything from refitting houseboats to cleaning Delft porcelain to transforming charming country cottages into charming marijuana hothouses. He claimed that he'd come over from London in 1975 when he was twenty-eight to visit a friend who'd been hit by a truck. She'd been looking the wrong way in traffic – something I'd imperiled my own life by doing more than once, especially after a few drinks – and was severely injured. ''Er 'ead was in three pieces and it looked like 'er face'd melted,' Keith told me vividly, somehow almost melting his own face. He'd stayed in Amsterdam 'because there was nuffing else to do. An' I was staying in a pension over by the zoo, run by a woman and her three lovely daughters and I got to know the eldest rather well. And I never 'ad anywhere else I could call 'ome. This is as good as anywhere. What I like about Amsterdam is not 'avin' to dress up to go to any bars. You can get by 'ere if you dress like a slob like me.' He was wearing thick tracksuit pants and flat, paint-spattered runners. 'And you can always find work 'ere. I'm a bricklayer by trade, but I can turn me 'and to just about anything. Specially if it's not quite legal, innit?' Just then, he seemed to be practicing as a not-quite-legal plumber.

'Can you turn your hand to being a real estate agent?' I asked.

'Prob'ly not. Meantime 'ave a squiz at *Via Via*.' He picked up a wrench and disappeared beneath a sink. 'Mind 'ow you go, then.'

Mindful of how I was doing it, I went back upstairs. I had, as a matter of fact, already had a look at *Via Via*, a horribly yellow paper, appearing yellowly every Wednesday, in which Amsterdammers advertise anything they want to sell, hire or rent – including apartments. A couple of nights earlier I'd called a creepy character named Karel, who answered the telephone in hushed tones and spoke in halting Euro-English, describing his advertised property as a big, top-floor apartment, overlooking a canal, right in the Centrum for only *f*1750 per month. 'Okay, we'll drop by at ten Monday morning,' I said. He ummed then aahhed and finally reluctantly said that would be all right. (I had yet to learn that the Dutch like to sleep in until Tuesday on Mondays.)

'We can't afford that,' Sally said, after I relayed the details.

'I'm sure I'll find work soon. Something excellently paid.' (Exactly why I said that, I cannot say.)

The following Monday morning, a rainy bastard like all the others, Sally and I found ourselves on Kloveniersburgwal, at a four-storey eighteenth-century building in a great location near the Hotel De L'Europe. We were beside ourselves with excitement, imagining the inside of the place: high, beamed ceilings, old wooden floors, a fabulous view of the canal and the row of tall, skinny buildings opposite. We waited around for Karel, wondering what a real estate agent named Karel would look like, until finally I realised that he wasn't *coming* to meet us at all, that he was most probably up there in the apartment. *His* apartment.

We rang the buzzer, Karel burped a greeting into it and said that he'd be down 'in three moment'. At least ten moment later, the front door was opened by a grimy, sleep-stained guy around thirty; thin, blond and wearing a tatty green jumper and plastic sandals. '*Kom op*,' he beckoned after staring at us for a while. Behind the huge outer door was a small interior courtyard with a winding marble staircase leading off it. We followed Karel up into the darkness. It didn't matter if he got too far ahead of us – we might lose sight of him, but we would never lose smell of the guy. In keeping with the building he lived in, he had a very historical approach to hygiene. Many winding flights later we came to a small blue door of navel height. Karel slunk through the doorlet and motioned us to follow. We got down on our hands and knees and crawled in.

The view from the broken window was wonderful – oak trees, a canal, an elegant row of buildings opposite and classically central Amsterdam, virtually unchanged in three hundred years. On the inside of the window, however, things weren't so appealing. This ƒ1750 per month apartment was a series of scummy, tiny rooms with wet, sticky carpet the colour of cat's vomit and low, cracked ceilings which flaked paint on to Sally's hair as it brushed the plaster. The furniture, Karel explained, pointing to a steel cot, two broken chairs and a deck of cards, was included in the price. There was also a sinister smell about the place, but that may have been Karel himself. To cap it all off, the apartment featured no bathroom, no kitchen and absolutely no toilet.

'What you think off it?' Karel asked, scratching at his arm.

I was just about to say that while there certainly *were* some lovely features, such as outside, it wasn't quite what we were after, but Sally got in first. 'I wouldn't live here if you *paid* us ƒ1750,' she declared, leaning right into his face, 'you little prick.'

Besides being undignified and cramping, seven adults living in such close quarters was also apparently highly illegal and soon after the Karel episode we were reported to 'the authorities' by our cleaner, a German woman named Marlene. Apparently 'the authorities' simply appeared at your door at any hour and demanded to know who was living there. Under no circumstances were Sally or I to admit to being in residence, we were warned by Bernard. But what exactly, I couldn't help wondering, would these authorities do if they found out there were seven of us in a domicile built for four? Even a jail cell would have more room than the ridiculous place we were in. (I'd never really appreciated Australia's space back when I was in it. I do now, though. Australia, I salute your size and emptiness.) Nonetheless, as a precautionary measure, a bookcase was placed in front of the door to Sally's and my bedroom. I felt like Anne Frank but with different hair.

We were heading south by train to visit relatives. Courtesy of her half-Dutch lineage, Sally had an *oom* (uncle), a *tante* (aunt) and a *neef* (cousin) living in Venlo in the deep south of the Netherlands, on the German border. I hadn't realised that I'd already become so Amsterdam-ised until I left the city for the first time. By Amsterdam-ised, I mean that my idea of a tall building was one more than five storeys high; that my idea of a great open space was a cobbled public courtyard about one hundred metres square; that if I found myself sitting on a tram for more than ten minutes, I considered it a long trip and worried that I didn't have my passport with me. My sense of Australian space and time had virtually disappeared, replaced with more finely calibrated 'Euro-measurements'.

'When you're in Amsterdam, you get the impression that there are no tall buildings anywhere in the Netherlands,' Sally said, looking up from the *Vogue* magazine she was reading. 'That the Dutch headquarters of IBM is in some little basement on Keizersgracht.'

'God, this place is flat,' I said, looking out at the flatness. 'Look, there's a windmill. Boy, if I could see someone in clogs eating cheese and smoking a joint after they'd been to the red-light district, all this country's clichés would come together at once.'

After two hours of flat greenness broken only by windmills and bridges over swollen rivers (no cheese-eating clog people), we came to the town where Sally's father grew up, the apostrophically challenging 's-Hertogenbosch. Even more challengingly, it is pronounced 'set-hogenbosh' or, more commonly, 'den bos', which means forest. I was too frightened by the look and sound of the word to notice the actual town and decided I'd have a more thorough peer through the window on the way back. One thing I could be pretty sure of though, was that the town was flat.

I liked Joep!, who was married to Sally's cousin Marielle, immediately because he kept saying, 'Yeah right!' about everything. It was endearing and exciting, brightening up even the most ordinary comment or observation, of which I made plenty because I am an ordinary person and because I loved hearing Joep! say, 'Yeah, right!' After being introduced to Joep!'s baby Imme (who dribbled on me) and his wife Marielle (who didn't), we sat down to a traditional, non-fancy Dutch lunch in Joep! and Marielle's kitchen. Lunch consisted of a pile of bread, a selection of sliced meats including (but by no means limited to) *boterhamworst, boterhamworst dik, paardenworst, gebraden gehakt (met* and *zonder uitjes), gekookte worst, rookworst, reclameworst* and about eight different varieties of ham, as well as slices of Holland's two principle styles of cheese – old and young. Based on many previous lunches, I thought this would be a normal, run-of-the-mill self-making sandwich fest and was about to start slapping together pieces of everything between two slices of bread, when I noticed Joep! and Marielle (and the quick-learning Sally) all placing meat and cheese on to a single slice of bread then cutting it into bite-sized pieces with a knife and fork before daintily swallowing them. *There were no lids on the sandwiches.* I followed suit so as not to appear too foreign or greedy, however because I need a hell of a lot of starch before I'm full, I had to do the single-slice-half-sandwich stunt about twice as often as everybody else. It was pretty embarrassing, so in order to divert attention from myself, I made frequent witless remarks so that Joep! would keep saying 'Yeah right!' This tactic had the twin advantages of making me seem interesting and allowing me to eat without being scrutinised. I hate to eat whilst under scrutiny.

But the lunch weirdness wasn't over. The Dutch like to finish things up with a kind of dessert sandwich involving a product called *Hagelslag.* Take a piece of bread, smother it with butter, pick up a box of *Hagelslag* and pour onto bread. Bread is now covered with tiny logs of brown and white chocolate sprinkles – the sort of stuff I am accustomed to seeing on top of little cakes or on sandwiches at parties for the under-eight crowd. Then you cut that into tiny morsels and chomp away chocolately – unless you want to spread on this gloopy, sewage-coloured apple syrup stuff which is also very popular, but to my mind too disgusting to even look at, let alone eat. Then again, where I come from, people eat Vegemite.

After lunch it was off to Oom Henk and Tante Doortje's newly renovated house. 'We moved in on April 9th, 1961,' Henk told me, with an exactitude I found alarming. 'Now we finally have new windows last week.' Sally had earlier advised me that it was customary to admire household renovations and improvements, so I commented on how large, lovely and clear the new windows were. Henk also mentioned that they'd had new locks put on the doors. I inspected them and made further appropriate remarks. Somehow the subject of smoking came up (probably because I asked if anybody would mind if I did) and Henk said, 'I gave up smoking on October 4th, 1979.' The old guy was like a brilliant machine for dates. Either that or an idiot savant. 'But you are most welcome to smoke,' he said. A brilliant machine, I decided.

In addition to dates and renovations, Oom Henk was obsessed by his neighbour, whom he did not care for. 'He has a roof with silver tiles,' Henk announced, dismissively pointing through the new front window at the opposite house.

'Cool,' I said, leaping off the couch and peering out the new window. I looked up and saw nothing even shiny, let alone blinding. 'Where?'

'He does not have a roof with silver tiles,' Joep! said. 'It means he has a big *hypotheek*.'

'*Hypotheek* is a mortgage,' Marielle explained. 'Silver tiles mean he has a heavy mortgage.'

Henk waved out the new window once more. 'He's sticking his hand into a wasp nest.'

Without getting up this time, I looked out the new window and saw absolutely *niets* – no guy, no hand, no nest and no wasps. It seemed that Oom Henk spoke either in vague, mysterious parables or with absolute precision – like a molecular scientist telling a children's story.

'He is also such a liar I can feel it in my wooden shoes,' Henk said. I looked at his feet – slippers.

Later, as we left, Henk shook my hand and cautioned, 'Don't stand in the sun if you have butter on your head.'

'No,' I said, deeply confused by what I took to be yet another obscure Dutch proverb. 'I certainly will not.'

Joep!, Marielle, Sally and I took a walk around the city centre of

Venlo (small, pretty, flat), during which I was surprised to hear from Joep! that despite his enthusiasm for just about everything, he greatly disliked Amsterdam. 'It is an unfriendly place. The people are rude. You will like the southern Dutch much more. Good, friendly people. No drugs and prostitutes. Also, we have a better dialect. Yeah, right!' And then, placing his hands on my shoulders and looking me square in the eye, he shared a strange, almost Zen-like morsel of wisdom: 'Amsterdam is not Holland.'*

Apart from referring to the Netherlands as Holland, the strange thing about Joep!'s comment was that half an hour later, as Sally and I waited at the station for a train back to the wicked city, we saw in the falling light two youths huddled by the tracks cutting up some heroin. Venlo may be tiny and two hundred kilometres away from Amsterdam, but clearly, nowhere in the Netherlands is really all that far from anywhere else.

'What was that butter comment of Henk's?' I asked Sally. 'What does it mean to not stand in the sun with butter on your head?'

'My dad used to say it to me and my brothers sometimes. It's about telling the truth, keeping a clear conscience.'

On the train, there were two bald Germans sitting diagonally opposite us, both slouching ostentatiously, both dressed entirely in black, both speaking without looking at each other – speaking forward, in front of themselves – each maintaining a mean sneer on his lips. 'I vant to do a chob that I luff,' one said.

'Yesss, money isn't everyding,' said the other.

As we passed through 's-Hertogenbosch once again, Sally pressed her face against the window, calling, 'Daddy!? Daddy!?' Her father lived here during the Second World War and I remembered him telling me that there were German tanks in his front yard. In some ways, the memory of the war is still very strong with the Dutch; mainly the ones over sixty, but some younger people as

---

*This disaffection for Amsterdam felt by other parts of the Netherlands is hundreds of years old. In the middle of the seventeenth century the city was at the peak of its power and influence and little could happen elsewhere in what was then the Republic without Amsterdam's assent. Seats of power tend naturally to breed mistrust and resentment from outside, which is why I have personally sent many letters of agitated sentiment to Canberra, Washington DC and Microsoft.

well. At soccer matches between the Netherlands and Germany, Dutch fans will often chant 'Give us back our bikes', a reference to the thousands of bicycles which were stolen when the Germans evacuated in 1945. A bitter memory, but one expressed with the good humour I was becoming fond of in the Dutch.

After the train pulled out of Utrecht, a husky, pallid, unshaven young man who looked like he had only ever eaten potatoes began walking up and down the middle of the carriage and, without making eye contact with anyone, placing plastic, water-filled key rings in the shapes of dolphins or bears or tulips in front of every passenger. Underneath the key ring he slipped a piece of paper which said that you had to pay ƒ5 if you wanted one. I turned the paper over: on the other side was the alphabet represented in sign language. Was the guy deaf or just pretending, I wondered. Part of the sales pitch of pity? Whatever the truth, it was an awful way to make a buck. Jobs and money, two of the biggest challenges in any life – even German ones, judging by our fellow passengers. I rolled the watery dolphin around my palm, acutely aware that I still had no idea of how I was going to make a living.

'What do you think's gonna happen to the magazine?' I asked Sally. 'D'you think Bernard will persuade the bosses to pay you when he goes to Germany?'

'I don't want to talk about it,' she said.

Gee, that's not a good sign, I thought to myself. *I wonder if I should –*

'Shut up,' Sally said. Boy, she knew me well.

Nearby, one of the Germans said, 'I like de liddle bear. I take him.'

In 1626 a Dutch explorer named Peter Minuit bought the island of Manhattan from the native American inhabitants for $24, which even back then was not a lot of money. This was without doubt the greatest real estate bargain in history and highly indicative of things to come for the Dutch. The first half of the seventeenth century was a golden age for Amsterdam: the city was the financial centre of the known world; three great canals (Herengracht, Prinsengracht and Keizersgracht – collectively known as the Canal Ring) were built; Rembrandt van Rijn was busy becoming a fat, influential genius; the Indonesian archipelago was colonised, beginning the lucrative spice trade. In 1629 Dutch sailors on the *Batavia* discovered Australia and, even though they claimed to find nothing of value there, decided to name it New Holland anyway. ('I heard there was supposed to be a fancy white building and a big bridge somewhere 'round here,' one sailor remarked to another. 'There's nothing but fine weather and strange pieces of *vertical* land. What a dump!')

Then, literally in the case of the *Batavia* and metaphorically for Amsterdam, the boat sank: the Stadhuis burned down; a maritime war with England began in 1652; Rembrandt died; the French, with superior forces (and vastly superior cheese), attacked south Holland; and then, in 1674, the Dutch *gave* Manhattan to the English, without doubt the biggest real estate blunder in history. I like to think of my own fortunes reflecting those of historical Amsterdam, except that I've never gone through anything like a golden age, so I identify quite closely with the decline. But while Amsterdam quickly recovered from its late-seventeenth-century trials to become a quietly thriving and wealthy city, my situation, as well as that of Sally and her colleagues, was about to get a lot worse.

I continued to go to my 'office' at De Pils each day, but I had nothing to actually *do* there . . . I thought about becoming a busker. Amsterdam is full of them; the usual scraggy hippie types wrenching out Bob Dylan or Grateful Dead tunes with the aid of a broken guitar; goblin impersonators in colourful caps juggling soft balls; and those idiots who spray-paint themselves silver and pretend to be robots. Boy, those guys had it made, just standing there all day not twitching a muscle until somebody threw a guilder into their hat, after which they'd make a buzzing sound and bend over slightly. Besides the indignity, humiliation and bad hairstyle required to join the International Brotherhood of Buskers, I had no actual skills to busk, unless I could somehow get people to pay to watch me watching TV, eating, sleeping or sitting at a desk. And these are not so much skills as hobbies.

One afternoon I was flicking through *Esquire* magazine and imagining what my name would look like in big letters on the cover (the same, but big), when a small classified ad caught my eye. 'Work your own hours! Make lots of $$$!! Be your own boss!!' it said, above a picture of an unsavoury-looking cartoon fellow who looked like he'd been badly beaten up. 'Become a private eye!! Send for FREE information.' Even though I wasn't sure if the bruised cartoon guy was the investigator or the subject, I decided that being a PI (as we call it in the trade) would be exciting, glamourous and lucrative, plus I liked the fact that they were giving away the secrets for FREE. So I wrote to the company – Streetwise PI Inc., of Bond Street, London.

Dear Sir,
I saw your ad in a recent issue of *Esquire*. I have long dreamed of being a 'private eye' and would be very grateful if you would send me the FREE information pack.
Yours sincerely,
Sean Condon
PS Who do you prefer – Sam Spade or Philip Marlowe? Also, what's your feeling on the term *gumshoe*?

Two weeks later I still hadn't heard back from them. I'd always known that English people didn't much like me, but now it seemed as if they'd decided to go to war with me. Perhaps they thought I was Dutch and that this was 1652. I wasn't sure but either way I couldn't afford to wallow over the dispiriting silence of my fellow Commonwealthers – I had to get some money fast.

Making money was on my mind so much because money can be very convenient to have and because making money is something that the Dutch are extremely good at, and in which they place a great amount of stock (no pun intended).* It's a pastime they have turned into a passion and a passion they have elevated to an art form. The Netherlands is the world's sixth largest exporting country (the third largest in food exports) and is ranked fourteenth in gross domestic product. For a small watery nation, these are extremely impressive achievements. The Dutch own almost everything that the Americans and the Japanese don't: Philips, Shell, Unilever and the cake-making chain, Multi-Vlaai. Many of the Dutch people I know – most of them younger than me – own

---

*Actually intended.

their own apartments, businesses and boats. They are well-educated, hard-working and justifiably proud of their achievements, and therefore make me bitterly envious and a little sick. Even worse, of all the people in the world, the Dutch are the least showy in their collective and individual wealth. Sure, there are plenty of latest-model Mercedes, BMWs and Audis zooming around Amsterdam, but they're all driven by people wearing old jeans and T-shirts. They don't own enormous houses with swimming pools. Admittedly, due to the lack of space, they can't (and in this climate a swimming pool might be used twice a decade), but even if they could, they wouldn't. They will always drink beer or *genever* in preference to champagne, unless it's a special occasion like making their first million – of the year.

'What are you without money and a job?' asked my friend Jeroen, who at twenty-eight had already set up and sold his second business and was then employed as an IT guy at Heineken. He also owned his apartment, a Saab and two boats. Despite all that, I liked him very much – his blues eyes looked as given to melancholy as mischief and I like that sort of duality in a fellow.

'Poor and anonymous,' I answered, feeling acutely both. 'So how *do* you people spend all those guilders you work so hard to earn?'

'I have been to Africa three times, next week I am going skiing in Austria and in April I'm going to Fiji for three weeks. I'm also thinking about going to Australia in October.'

The modern Dutch aren't financially conspicuous but, like their armada-based forbears, they sure like to travel.

'It's your shout, Joey,' I said. (I called him Joey as it is easier on my tongue, and although I can now say 'Jeroen' with ease, the name has stuck.) 'Let's have some champagne!'

'Why?'

A truly exciting thing about being a recent arrival in a foreign place was that I found myself far more open to new experiences and new people than I'd been at home. There was something very liberating about not having roots or connections webbing stickily throughout the city, seeing people you half-know (or do know but wish you didn't) and having to nod at them or smile or get into some stiff conversation about how you used to work or sleep together. Being anonymous had set me free. (Being poor had hampered me somewhat, but what the hell.) It had also become much easier to like groups of strangers in bars (or at least not dislike them so quickly) because I couldn't understand what they were talking about. Back in Australia I was always standing in noisy groups overhearing conversational excerpts that made me want to eat glass. *'You gotta live in London if you wanna make it in finance, mate. They've got the Footsie.' 'Sydney Melbourne, Melbourne Sydney, what's the difference? Mate, they're both full of Aussies.'* Up here they were probably talking the same crap as down there – drunken idiots are pretty much the same the world over – but it sure was nice not to be more directly exposed to their blatherings. Life in a foreign land with a strange tongue. It was very exciting – *anything* could happen!

Something did – Bernard returned from his meeting with *Shoehorn*'s bosses in Germany with the interesting news that the magazine no longer existed. Just six weeks after we'd arrived, we were stuck in Amsterdam with nothing to do, handcuffed to the ghost of the idea which had brought us all here.

In the Murder Park
with the Chickens

As thousands of ruined livers, failing kidneys, distended guts, weakened hearts, annihilated brain cells and early deaths can attest, Amsterdam is a great place in which to get drunk (even back around 1365 an impressive 2500 tons of beer was being imported to the city every month); in addition to being the home of two of the world's foremost beers – Grolsch and Heineken – there are irresistibly inviting bars on just about every block throughout the entire country. The night the magazine disappeared (and with it, our apartment, which we were told we had to vacate in two weeks) we pilgrims had a very good reason to be in a bar, of course, but not much reason to be in a bar in Amsterdam. Nonetheless, we were getting drunk with the assistance of the Benelux countries. We drank Grolsch *pils* and Heineken Tarwebok, a strong, dark beer brewed especially for the winter misery that had come early for us. We drank Hoegaarden, a white, cloudy, sweet summer beer made in Belgium. Moving back to the Netherlands, we drank Columbus and Amstel Oud Bruin. Over to Belgium once more we drank De Konick, another very dark, very strong, very dangerous beer. We were all in stupor and in shock, trying to numb ourselves to the dreadful uncertainty of the future. And the more we drank, the better it worked.

I had been introduced to alcohol long ago and had become quite fond of it, as my no-longer-girlish girth could attest. But my introduction that night to the Dutch spirit *genever*, a kind of oily gin, was a landmark. The fateful introduction was made at a seventeenth-century bar called Wynand Fockink, just behind Dam Square, where we had been forced to move after De Pils ran out of beer. Fockink is tiny and lopsided, with just enough room to hold about twenty keen drinkers; the low wooden bar has been worn smooth and is richly stained from over three centuries of spilled booze, despite the traditional method of serving *genever*, whereby the spirit is poured into a stemmed shot glass until it forms a bubbled meniscus, making picking up the glass both foolish and wasteful, unless you're the sort of person who doesn't mind standing in a crowd and sucking your fingers. (Personally, I quite enjoy that kind of activity, but the arch traditionalist in me ensured that I embraced the proper method of drinking *genever*. Plus it's kind of expensive and I didn't want to waste any.) In order to get the most out of your booze dollar, the way to drink *genever* is to stand at the bar, put your hands behind your back, lean forward until you make a right angle and sip at the glass from this position, like one of those drinking birds with the red butts. After you've sucked the meniscus right off the glass, you can pick it up and down the remainder. Repeat process until you become stuck at a right angle.

I was stuck at a right angle after a dozen shots of *genever* (and a dozen beer chasers) when I met Hannus, a typically tall and typically good-looking Dutchman. Because of his height and my low angle, I first met his knees and worked my way up. By the time I reached his square, black glasses and curly blond hair (he looked astonishingly like Gary Busey being Buddy Holly), he'd agreed to sublet his place for one month. He was able to do this, he told the top of my head, because he was temporarily moving in with his pregnant girlfriend, the excellently named Patricia Kockelkorn.

'Howmushisi?' I asked his shoes.

'Two thousand guilders per month,' Hannus said. 'You like the *genever*?'

'OhIlovethstuff,' I told him, then fell over into a very welcome 180 degrees.

Several days later, when I could stand up straight again, Sally and I moved in. And because Hannus's place was expensive, and everybody's finances were stretched, so did Ray and Sonia.* But

---

*The day after the magazine collapse, Bernard had flown back to Melbourne, his girlfriend decided to tour Europe, and Terry went to Paris for a month 'to see if there was any room'.

this joint was a stark comparison to our previous small, suburban flat. Hannus, a veteran squatter, lived right in the middle of town, in a converted schoolroom on Korte Prinsengracht, a long way north up the road from Anne Frank's old place. Hannus's space was enormous – 25-foot ceilings, 15-foot windows covered by bright orange curtains, a great mezzanine above the rear of the room with a small sunlit bedroom leading off it, a well-equipped kitchen and a whole lot of space left over in which we could run around, recline, work and play. At last we were in the real Amsterdam – the only niggling question was, Why? We decided to ignore it. Besides, how could we remain unhappy when our new landlord had taken the trouble to lay out four bathrobes for us when we moved in. What a gesture, I thought. What a lovely thing to do, just like a hotel. But I soon found out the real reason.

As wonderful as Hannus's place was, it had one major fault – no bathroom or toilet. At least nothing we could call ours, or to put it more exactly, nothing *I* could call *mine*. And if there's one thing I like to establish ownership over, it's a bathroom. Sure, I'd gradually and reluctantly grown used to sharing my shameful intimacies with the others in the old place, but this was a whole new story. The ablutionary facilities here were located at the far end of a long, cold hallway – and were shared by *everybody* who lived on the fourth floor. And while I wouldn't have minded a bit if the curvy actress who lived next door wandered down to the shower every morning wearing nothing but a Band-Aid on her ankle, she sure as hell wouldn't want to catch sight of me similarly attired. In fact, she'd probably prefer to see me bandaged up like a mummy. Hence the bathrobes.

But a dress code for the can wasn't the only new thing to get used to bathroom-wise. It was here that I first experienced a typical Dutch toilet, one that came with what Sally termed 'the inspection shelf'. The inspection shelf is a porcelain platform which sits above where the waterline in a normal (by which I mean scatologically sane) toilet would be. I don't want to go into too much detail here, but what this means is that, because, umm . . . 'it' just sort of . . . sits there, it's available for . . . errr . . . detailed . . . inspection before being dispatched off to where it belongs – which is anywhere but sitting on a shelf right in front of you. I can see no possible reason for this cultural phenomenon, except that the Dutch are notoriously liberal when it comes to sex and drugs, and I suppose that this attitude extends to . . . other things as well. 'Oh, the humanity,' Sally moaned when she was first confronted with the results of the inspection shelf.

There were surprises in the shower department, too. While the rest of the world has embraced the combination of excess water, a drain and gravity, the Dutch don't seem to buy it. They have drains and they have water, but instead of slightly angling the shower floor and letting basic Newtonian physics do the work, they prefer a flat surface and some furious, post-shower sweeping of water with a rubber broom. Apart from building up a poorly timed sweat, the sweeping makes an awful screeching noise, a sound not dissimilar, in fact, to that made by people nearby as they turn and face the brutal horror of the inspection shelf. Mornings can be noisy in Amsterdam.

It was our first Friday night in the new place and we'd decided to have a small but fancy dinner party (just the four of us) in celebration of our large and fancy new location. The kitchen was a warm bustle of activity – the others were all down there preparing dishes while I sat up on the mezzanine enjoying the aromas and looking out at the boats on the canal. Boats are nice. Ray was putting the finishing touches to beef vindaloo and chicken masala; Sally was punching and rolling paratha dough, while Sonia chopped dozens of vegetables for a curry. I continued my boat-staring, every so often reminding myself that back where I come from, I enjoyed neither canals nor servants. Even though I had no good reason to be here I was beginning to like where I was.

Around six there was a furtive rapping at the door, as though a nervous bird was pecking at it. I looked down and saw Keith Finney's head appear through the crack. The rest of him followed. He wouldn't speak and rushed about downstairs making a big show of looking for something – picking up cushions, opening cupboard doors, peering under the bed – all in complete silence, like a bad mime.

'There you are, you dozy git!' he shouted when he finally

saw me, then scurried up the stairs. Looking all squirrelly and conspiratorial, he lowered his voice to a hush and said, 'Can you look after summing for me?' I hadn't seen Keith for a few days. I felt he needed a haircut.

'Sure,' I said. He looked askance theatrically then pulled two rectangular bundles from the inside of his jacket. He handed them to me, then poked his head over the mezzanine and peered down at the others. I followed his glance; Sally was 'advising' Ray on how much garam powder to add and 'suggesting' to Sonia the best way to chop carrots. I looked at the smallish packages in my hand. One was a heavy cream-coloured cloth bundle, the other was a rubber band full of hundred-guilder notes divided into thousand-guilder lots – ten of them.

Keith tapped me on the shoulder. I looked up. 'You got some-where safe to put this?' he said, evidently for the second time.

'Yeah,' I answered, dropping both bundles into a large card-board box and covering them with old newspaper.

Keith looked at the box then at me. 'That'll do nicely.' To my surprise, he said it like he meant it. He concluded our business by saying, 'If you don't 'ear from me by Mond'y, you won't be 'earin' from me for a while.' Then for the first time since he'd arrived, he calmed; he'd been panting and hopping from foot to foot the whole time. He looked me up and down, as though in appreciation of the smart suit and tie I was wearing. 'What's goin' on 'ere? You look like a pox doctor's clerk.'

'We're having you over for dinner.'

'Luvly, I could eat an 'orse and 'alf the saddle. What we 'avin'?'

As we ate, Keith told us that he'd just returned from the Loire Valley where he alleged he had been eating horse meat (no sad-dles), drinking wine and knocking down an old stone barn (with his bare hands), before towing a 1971 Benz back to Amsterdam (presumably with the aid of another car).

As soon as I could, I dragged Keith away from the others and began some furtive whispering of my own. 'What's going on with this dough?' I said. 'Are you gonna be all right? I mean, is anybody *after* you or anything?' I was trying to be cool about the whole thing, but it wasn't coming across too well – my voice kept breaking into these little squeals of excitement.

Keith nodded and smiled a bit. 'I'm expectin' a knock on the door some time tonight and I thought it'd be better if me and the bread an 'oney wasn't around.'

'A knock from who?'

'The filth, you berk.'

'Oh. Why?'

'Coupla months ago I brought ƒ4 million into the country, for this firm I know. Today I got a call from an associate in the nick telling me that the firm'd been done.'

'And that money's your percentage for doing the job, right?'

'Summing like that, yeah.'

'You could go to jail.'

'Somebody once said, "If you can't do the time, don't do the crime".'

'Yeah, I know. It's in practically every crime book I've ever read.'

'This ain't no book, son.' Keith went back to the table where he literally licked his plate clean, holding it up to his face and tonguing it like a dog. For a man almost on the lam, he had a very healthy appetite. I was impressed.

Later that night, after Keith had left and Ray and Sonia had gone to bed, I told Sally what Keith had given me to look after. 'It's about ƒ20,000, I'm guessing, if the first bundle's anything like the other one.'

She burst out laughing and pointed her finger at me, saying, 'L.O.C.'

'What?'

She pointed hard. 'Life Of Crime. That's you.'

'D'you want to go and look at it?' I asked.

'Of course,' she said.

Upstairs at my cardboard-and-paper safe, I showed her the open wad. She swore with healthy admiration. I extracted the cloth – a money-belt, I could see now – and unzipped it. Inside was *another* ƒ20,000 and a great wodge of English ten- and twenty-pound notes, adding up to ƒ1650. We were stunned and couldn't help laughing. This was more money – actual *money* – than we'd ever seen. Then I noticed another zip on the money belt. I opened it and saw a thousand-guilder note, a rare and beautiful thing of deep, shining emerald and spearmint high-lights. Behind that note were more of them – *seventy-four* more. Sally refused to touch any of it. 'Prints, man. I don't want my prints on it.'

We were in possession of well over ƒ100,000. Sure, we were only looking after it as a favour to a friend, but who, apart from Keith, knew that? And just how good a friend *was* Keith any-way? A slew of film noir style fantasies crossed both our minds, but too often Sally and I ended up on the run and finding our-selves at the Bates Motel. It was awful – all this cash literally at our fingertips, yet untouchable. (Well, touchable, but there are more attractive qualities to money than the merely tactile.) We stared at it for a long time, wondering whether or not to tell Ray and Sonia, before dumping it back into the box. We decided not to tell the others – it would be a rudely sobering shock for them. Besides, if 'something' happened to Keith between now and Monday, we didn't want the dough being split four ways.

Then we started wondering what we'd do if something actu-ally *did* happen to Keith: a post-breakfast heart attack; looking the wrong way and being crushed by a tram; drowning in the deadly filth of a canal (*sleeping with the bicycles* as the Dutch Mafia call it); or us hiring a hit man to whack him – the irony of which was that the only person we knew who could actually put us in touch with a trigger was Keith himself. It was a strange thing to consider: would you *seriously* wish somebody you knew dead for the sake of ƒ100,000? The answer was, of course, yes.

I mean no. But it was a hard notion to keep completely out of our minds. In a strange, but very real way, the fact that we'd both thought in precisely the same grubby moral fashion on the mat-ter made me glad that I was married to Sally. It also made me glad that I was not a rich husband.*

---

*If we were a film noir couple, Sally and I would have split with the money in the deep dark of the next available stormy night – leaving by stolen boat only to turn on each other just before we crossed the border to somewhere – but in the real world, where it is my obligation, if not inclination, to live, Keith showed up a week later, thanked me for being his short-term banker, slipped me a hundred guilders and left with my dough. I mean his dough. I mean whoever's dough it actually was.

Having a coffee – the right way.
November 11th, 1998

At the moment Amsterdam is quite beautiful. And when I say 'at the moment', I mean right at this very moment – 3.28 p.m. – because at any moment it could change from cold, crisp and eye-wateringly clear and bright, to dark, cloudy and nose-runningly icy. So I've decided to go for a short walk and have a coffee and a cognac in a small, woody, *gezellig* bar called Café t'Papeneiland at the intersection of two canals, Brouwersgracht and Prinsengracht. It's a wonderful place with a low, exposed-beam ceiling, a tiny staircase leading up to a tiny toilet, wood-framed windows and a panel of antique Delft porcelain allegedly discovered in the basement during renovations fifteen years ago. The bar has been here since 1641 and comfortably holds no more than thirty people. The ornate, twin-spouted beer tap is about one hundred and fifty years old and has a garish but charming woodland scene featuring two typically majestic deer painted on it. The whole place is heated by a single man-sized upright stove. Covering every wall are dozens of dusty framed etchings, paintings and photographs of the bar, seen from every possible angle. It's fabulous and exactly the right place to go when you're feeling as low-down and blue as I do, right now; worrying about the usual matters – where to live, how to live, what to do with my life. That sort of thing and whether or not Dutch director Paul Verhoeven will ever be able to repeat the artistic triumph of *The Soldier of Orange* and the box-office success of *Basic Instinct.*

The barman, a guy around sixty with a face like a wry and maudlin dog, greets me with a nod, which I return before asking in fractured Dutch for a *koffie verkeerd*, which translates as 'coffee the wrong way', deemed wrong because it has *melk* (milk) in it. After I order a cognac, the barman spurtles another sentence at me, and thinking that he is asking if I want anything else, and pretending to be Dutch but unusually short in stature, I say '*Nee, dank u wel*,' ('No thanks') and shake my head, feeling semi-bilingual and semi-proud over this brief transaction.

'I'm sorry,' the barman says, 'but I asked what sort of cognac you'd prefer – Courvoisier, Rémy or Martell?' He speaks English perfectly.

'Ummm . . . Rémy Martin,' I reply, not leaning too heavily on the French accent. He nods, not patronisingly or anything, just a run-of-the-mill barman's nod. But I need to regain some dignity fast, so I change my coffee order to an espresso and I think I see him smile.

The trees are leafless, grabbing at the low sky with thin fingers; there are birds' nests in the tops. Boat and bicycle traffic is heavy, but obviously doesn't cause the road rage that automobile traffic does. This languid corner of the city – far away from the tourist shopping street Kalverstraat and the red-light area on the other side of Dam Square – feels a bit like a school at the end of term: empty, yet full of wistful memories. I see a paperboy on his bike straining up the small cobblestone bridge, *De Telegraaf* in sacks bulging over his back wheels. Riding a bike here, the icy wind on your scrunched-up face, makes you look as though you've been crying. The bright, gold sun hitting the facades of a row of chocolate-bricked five-storey houses. Coats, earmuffs, scarves, gloves and hats, and a Smart car zipping across the bridge. A tiny crimson, three-wheeled delivery van with a big plastic peanut on top. A mother pedalling a bicycle with a sleeping child folded across the handlebars.

Unfortunately the whole ambience of quiet solitude is ruined a few moments later by a pair of middle-aged English tourists (the male of whom is wearing one of those watches with the thick leather strap that snaps over the face – a 1970s weightlifter's watch) who sit nearby and proceed to complain about the lack of Belgian chocolate shops around here and the 'rotten' trains. When they've finished bagging the Netherlands, they move on to Germany, Austria and Switzerland. I wonder if they know that I can understand everything they say (the barman too, only better than me). And if they did, would they give a sodding toss?

But all this – even the whingeing Poms and my whingeing self – all this, I realise after my third cognac, is why I came to, and plan to stay in, Amsterdam. Because it is a long, long way from home.

Through a friend of somebody's acquaintance's associate's neighbour, Sally found a permanent (but only semi-legal) flat for the two of us to move into. I was very relieved except for one thing: the actual moving. I hate moving. And driving. Amsterdam is not a city designed for automobiles. It's full of rivers, canals and dykes and it's been my direct and unhappy experience that cars tend to sink when negotiating waterways (Edward Kennedy would agree with me, I'm sure), even if they *seem* frozen. Clearly, the city's transportation ethic was developed with floating in mind. Floating, cycling and perhaps riding horses, but nothing bigger than a Shetland pony. However, quite apart from the tininess, often one-wayness, frequent blockedness and always slippery cobblestonedness of its numerous *straats, wegs* and *laans* (all varieties of the basic road), there are many other reasons not to drive in Amsterdam. In order of dangerousness, they consist of the following:

Trams. Amsterdam's trams are enormous, twin-carriaged, articulated behemoths which have right of way over everything and stop for just about nothing. The very basic braking system seems to consist of a concrete-block anchor and is only employed in the most dire of circumstances, such as for a group of old women in wheelchairs carrying boxes of kittens across the road. And even then, the look of undiluted hatred that kitten-carrying old ladies would receive from the tram driver would make them wish they were dead anyway. So always carry a box of kittens when strolling around Amsterdam and, if possible, try to be old. And a lady.

Bicycles. There are approximately two million *tweewielers* (two-wheelers) in this city, but it seems like more. A *lot* more. They're absolutely everywhere, silently bearing down on the idiot pedestrian (me) who has wandered into the bicycle-only lanes in order to get a better view of an old, skinny building, or weaving in and out of traffic with a glare and a swear at whom- or whatever has caused the sudden stoppage (me again, this time by standing in the middle of a road staring up at another skinny building). In addition to their plague-proportion numerousness, they are a danger to vehicles because cyclists despise cars and will do everything they can to irritate, confuse and imperil the lives of their drivers. This is because drivers hate cyclists and will do everything *they* can to irritate, confuse and imperil the lives of cyclists. The whole city is therefore full of cars and bikes screeching to head-on stops, or drivers and cyclists screaming at each other to sell their car/bike and buy a car/bike. (And Dutch, not a particularly pleasant language in the first place, as many of the Dutch themselves will attest, is simply horrible when it's loud.) It's dangerous and it's noisy.

Cars. Despite all the water, bikes and tiny streets, Amsterdam is nevertheless full of cars. And other cars are a danger to cars. Especially the sorts of cars which are most practical in a city of canals, bicycles and alley-sized roads. They are, fittingly, small cars – with names like the Renault 'Twingo', the Nissan 'Micra' and the Toyota 'Sub-Atomic Particle'. The danger with small cars is that their drivers (especially the male drivers) tend to compensate for the puny size of the vehicle by driving them as fast as possible along the twenty or so metres of clear road available at any time in Amsterdam. I have been a passenger in a small car (a BMW 'Flea') driven by Keith and it was extremely frightening – although I was very glad not to be a cyclist at the time.

Another problem is that the Dutch have completely disavowed the use of the indicator when turning, overtaking, changing lanes and any other potentially fatal manoeuvres. Apparently they think it's too much trouble to move their hand a quarter of an inch to flick it on and avoid an accident; or they think that it's some sort of instrument to be employed in moments of autovehicular celebration. 'Oh look Piet, here comes Queen Beatrix. Quick, turn on one of those orange flashing lights.'

Canals. Every year more than fifty cars are pulled out of Amsterdam's canals.

Pedestrians. Every year more than one hundred pedestrians are pulled from the city's canals.

Taxis. Like in most major cities, taxi drivers think they own the roads. The difference here is that they do: the taxi companies in Amsterdam are run by the Dutch equivalent of the Mafia, who also have a very big 'interest' in road construction. They are allowed to drive on tram tracks but show even less respect for human (or kitten) life than trams. The only reason they stop is to pick up passengers – but even then they kill them with the fare as they are the most expensive taxis in Europe.

Coffee Shops and Prostitutes. It doesn't matter whether you're 'into' these *divertissements* or not because, like bicycles, they're everywhere. You might just walk by a 'coffee shop' and accidentally inhale some marijuana smoke billowing from the doorway and before you know it, you're sitting behind the wheel of your Fiat 'Bambino' – *absolutely stoned out of your brain!* Never a good way to drive, but especially dangerous in a city full of bikini-clad women sensuously combing their lustrous curls in full-length windows and winking at you. Driving under these influences is just asking for trouble.

Ultimately it's this simple: when in Amsterdam, just say no – to bicycles, drugs, winking women in windows and, most of all, cars.

By the middle of December, Sally and I had been living alone together for two weeks. We'd spent all day and all night, every day and every night, together. When we left the house to face the fog, mist, rain, hail, snow, sleet, extreme cold, general dampness and face-cracking iciness (and combinations thereof), we did it together. We ate together, watched the Dutch chat show 'De Kip is Klaar' ('The Chicken is Ready') together, slept together and stared out the window together. It certainly brought us together but I couldn't help thinking that if either or both of us didn't soon have something more in our lives than hanging around the house wondering what to do, being together would drive us apart.

The novelty of establishing a new home – buying old furniture, peeing into corners, etc. – soon passed and we needed to have normal, regular lives. The sort where you both left the flat for work in the morning, went off and had a terrible time working for eight hours, returned home in a crummy mood, ate something, watched television, then went to sleep in preparation for doing it all over again the next day. What we did instead was rise at ungodly hours (late in the morning) because we went to sleep at ungodly hours (early in the morning) then sit around wondering what to do. I would lurk in the spare room and watch planes from all over the world fly into Schiphol (an addictive, mesmerising and somehow poetic pastime, I thought) while Sally, when she was not doing freelance editing for a tourist magazine, read detective books. 'Shhh, I'm solving crimes,' she would say if I disturbed her.

I decided to attempt to make us a pair of legitimate Dutch residents by applying for residency status with the Foreign Police (who, ironically, all seem to be Dutch). They sent me a booklet full! of exclamation marks and personal! questions to answer. 'The date the Police Foreign Department receives the application will be the application date!' It also warned that in the case of passport photos, 'both eyes must be visible (no dark glasses!)'. But what if you've only got one eye? And should Ray Charles just forget his dream of becoming a Dutch resident?

I worried about the staggering and fragile construct of lies we'd had to invent in order to move into the flat. The original renters had bought a house in Zaandijk, but wished to hang on to the apartment so they could double the rental price and ease the strain of their mortgage. Sally had explained that she was a free-lance editor for about fifty magazines and I'd said something about being CEO of Shell but they hadn't printed the cards yet. As well as copies of our passports and DNA samples, we'd had to give our landlords a huge *borg* (security deposit) and *over-naam*, the uniquely Dutch arrangement whereby new tenants must offset the cost of existing 'improvements' made to a property by the previous tenants. *Overnaam* covers anything from heating and lighting to walls and a floor, all of which I like to have in the domestic environment.

Our flat was in an area called the East, so named because it is east of the city's centre. (Most Amsterdammers – the cool ones, anyway – had a somewhat disparaging attitude towards the East and tended to nod slowly then look away when we told them that we lived 'out there'. Amsterdam is quite a small city and any-where further than two minutes' bike ride from Dam Square is considered at least suburban, often rural. We were about six min-utes by tram from being cool.) The East is an odd area. For a start there are no canals – there's a dyke, and even though dykes are more indicative of the Netherlands as a whole, rather than just Amsterdam, local hipsters dismiss them as a poor, functional cousin to pretty little canals. From a certain angle, faces pressed hard against the glass, we had a view of a dyke from our front win-dows. On the far side of the bridge that ran over the dyke was a florist's shed, one of half a dozen along our stretch of Linnaeusstraat, a *straat* of healthy retail competition featuring four chemists, three supermarkets, three *slagerijs* (butchers), over a dozen bars and two solaria, both of which I could see from one window. The Dutch love a year-round tan.

A little further east of the East is a large Turkish and African enclave. The dividing line between the near-east and the far-east is the Dappermarkt, a market full of cheap vegetables, cheap meat, cheap clothing, cheap flowers, cheap toothpaste and cheap pets (including shop-soiled kittens available for hire if you needed to cross busy roads). The market suited Sally and I very well because, through necessity, we too had become cheap.

Our third-floor flat was roomy and spacious – mainly because we couldn't afford to put much of anything in it to alter its spaciousness. Except a television. A house is not a home without a television, no matter where in the world you live – even where the chat shows are called 'The Chicken is Ready' and you don't have a clue why. Buying the television at the nearby BCC electrical goods emporium was a wildly humiliating experience. After wandering around the overheated store for a while (winter in Amsterdam is the peak season for hypothermia – freezing outside and sweltering inside; go in and out of too many stores too quickly and bang, you're hypothermic) and finally selecting a modestly priced, non-brand television, I handed over my credit card, trying not to vomit with excitement when I realised this was the first time in my entire life I'd bought a brand-new television, one completely unwatched by anybody else's eyes. It was pretty busy in BCC and things moved rather slowly. They became downright sluggish when the salesman took my credit card out of the swiper, cut it in half, yanked the television off the counter, asked for some further ID from me, and called security. After proving that the credit card was definitely way over its limit but definitely not stolen, and that I was – reluctantly but inevitably – definitely me, the security hump released me and I borrowed some cash from Sally and red-facedly (a nice match with my financial condition) handed over a wad of guilders. I was deeply thankful for the fact that Sally had recently picked up some freelance work and was able to buy the television; I was embarrassed, emasculated, desperately broke, generally wretched and a poor husband – but without a television, I don't know if I'd have been able to cope.

The most horrifying thing about our new flat was the non-existent hot water pressure in the shower. Turning the taps on full released a lukewarm leak which was not unlike having a very old person standing on a stepladder and dribbling on your back. And in a decision of perhaps questionable hygiene, the Jazz Age builders of this apartment elected to rubberise the floor, whack in a door and put the actual shower in a long room directly off the kitchen. Every morning, after a depressingly ineffective period of being trickled on, we had to employ the old rubber broom method to urge the shower water from the bathroom floor towards the plug hole. But at least we no longer had to share it with a bunch of strangers with tinea any more. The podiatal infections and moulds were ours alone. As was the dreaded inspection shelf of the toilet. (I suppose it was another sign of my creeping Amsterdamisation that I wasn't unhappy to see Mr Shelfy, his proud porcelain chin jutting up at me when I first looked in the new can.)

In another move of incipient Amsterdamisation, Sally and I announced our intention to be long-standing residents of the place by having a little nameplate made. Glued on to the front door of the building was a black and white block which read 'S. P. Van Es – S. P. Condon' in small sanserif letters. Right below that was a faded metal plate which said 'M. van Dijk' and below that was the cryptic, almost mystical 'Wiggers'. This nameplate business is a strange one, but absolutely everyone in Holland has one, so we figured we'd better not rock the houseboat and happily shelled out f15 for our own. What most confounds me about it is the initials element – first names have no place on the plate. However, since you pay by the letter, it's probably a cost-saving measure for the keenly penny-pinching Dutch, in which case 'Wiggers' must live in the thriftiest of all possible worlds.

The first sign that Christmas and the New Year period were approaching was an odd and very striking poster. Set against a black background, bold red type exclaimed 'Bullfighting!' above the words 'X-plosive night!!'. Below the headlines were large colour photographs of the bullfighters – six in all, three white men and three black men. Hoekstra was an angry fellow with no hair but plenty of muscle; Tijden looked as though he could scare viruses to death; Drijfhamer was screaming with rage, his thick neck straining so hard it seemed as though he might tear through the paper he was printed on; Elektra would probably be able to hold his own in a stoush with God; and the other two had these looks on their faces that seemed as though they disliked me personally. They were all standing there shirtless, in their trunks, their arms raised protectively up and out – squared off in the classic boxer pose, ready for action, ready to kill. I was greatly relieved not to see anybody called Wiggers.

My first thoughts as I stared at the poster were that boxing must be making some sort of comeback in Amsterdam, and that maybe I'd like to go because I'd never been to 'the fights' and it could be interesting watching a couple of Dutchmen beat the crap out of each other. But just as I was wondering how I might get some tickets, I noticed that none of the bullfighters had any hands; their arms ended in bumpy, knobbly wrists. Every one of these guys was an amputee. I continued staring a while longer, a little nauseated, and soon the reason that the event was called bullfighting became clear. It was because when they were held up above the head as weapons, all those handless arms looked like bulls' horns. The thoughts that flew through my head were many. Where do they get all those handless guys in the first place? How do they convince them to become bullfighters? How do they train them in the art of same? And what exactly do they *do* to each other with those stubby ends of bone and scar tissue? All this became too much and finally I tore my eyes away, disgusted and sickened.

'How fantastic!' exclaimed Sally. 'D'you wanna go?'

'Hell, yeah.'

There were other signs of the Yuletide season – it had begun snowing, lightly at first but then with greater enthusiasm, as though somebody up there was warming to the idea. It was a good idea: Amsterdam, already a very pretty city, is just beautiful when dusted in white. Every four years or so the canals freeze over and the people of Amsterdam whip on their ice skates and glide up and down Herengracht, Keizersgracht and Singel, which must be nice.

Then there was the sudden appearance of temporary vans selling traditional Dutch *oliebollen*. 'Oil balls' are deep-fried batter, a direct cousin of the donut (probably an even more direct relation to the heart attack), only without the hole (although how something can be without something that's not actually there escapes me). A good *oliebol* should be about the size of a tennis ball, slightly crispy on the outside, doughy on the inside and golden yellow in colour with a hint of white from icing sugar, most of which should end up around your mouth and all over your nose, depending on whether or not you can swallow them whole. But because of their highly addictive nature, the *oliebol*'s most important quality must be its availability. Consequently there are *oliebollen* vans set up every twelve feet to ensure that the Dutch are never short of a sugar-and-oil high. The vans are usually operated by corpulent youngsters with greasy skin and greasy hair and greasy hands and greasy clothes, which ought to serve as some sort of warning against overindulging in fried fat and icing sugar, but doesn't. *Oliebollen* are too delicious, so I thank the god of retail legislation that they're only sold for around a month.

A week or so after we saw the first one, we encountered another in the series of bullfighting posters, and it led us to a very different conclusion on what they were actually all about. This time the poster was much larger, pasted up on a billboard below a railway bridge near our apartment. It featured the same dense black and red type headline, this time simply saying 'Beverwijk', the name of a small town fifteen kilometres away. The picture was of a hand, the thumb sticking out as though hitching a ride. The hand had no fingers, just bloody stumps of crimson flesh with a small grey bone in the middle of each. It was fascinating, repellent, compelling and obscure. Sally and I concluded that this poster and its bullfighting cousin were part of some extreme art installation project made by a crazy Dutch person who had a thing for missing limbs and digits. My admiration for the anonymous terrorist/creator began.

'I wonder if they did it on a computer or took actual photos in a hospital emergency room,' I said. 'I wonder if it's even legal.'

'I guess we're not going to see any stumpy Joes fighting it out,' Sally said. 'Bummer.'

Late one night we were in a taxi and we passed the third of the bullfighting posters. This one, again following the same design treatment as the others, showed a *Vlaamse frites* (Belgian fries) container – the paper cone so popular in the Lowlands – full of dismembered fingers. A cone of torn-off fingers, all with filthy blackened nails, sitting there like so many . . . torn-off fingers. This image was accompanied by some Dutch text, the only words of which we could understand were 'illegal' and 'Belgian'. Sally quickly concluded that it was something to do with illegal Belgian workers coming to Amsterdam, a reasonable enough assumption based on what we could read, but one which I failed to see connected with all those lonely fingers sitting in that paper container. I asked our cab driver exactly what the words on the poster meant. He nodded and cleared his throat. 'It warns to beware of illegal Belgian . . .' He paused and I thought of the other posters we'd seen, wondering what he was going to say next. Hitchhikers with no fingers? Boxers with no hands? *Vlaamse frites* with knuckles? The driver continued, 'Vhat you say in English . . . eeeh . . . firevorks.' It was an advertising campaign – an excellent one.

The cab driver went on to explain that illegal Belgian fireworks were a big problem every New Year's Eve in Amsterdam. Dozens of people lost all sorts of body parts (especially fingers) because of them, and that there was a large burns hospital in Beverwijk, hence the fingerless hitchhiker on the second poster we'd seen. Worse though, was that not only the purchasers of these foreign fireworks were at risk – the driver told us that during the festive season it was customary to throw the explosives at anybody nearby, perhaps as some sort of expression of dangerous Dutch *joie de vivre*.

Despite these alarming developments, I was so pleased to have the bullfighting mystery put to an end that I tipped our informant ƒ10 and enthusiastically shook his hand (glad that he had one) as I climbed out of the back seat, happy to be the proud owner of eight fingers and two thumbs – all of them clean.

'I can't wait for New Year's Eve,' Sally said.

I didn't say anything, but planned on staying inside wearing some heavy protective gear.

Dutch advertising is unlike any advertising I've ever seen. Its chief difference from the ads of other nations lies in the fact that sometimes it's clever, sometimes it's crazy, and sometimes it's both. One of the first examples of the crazy style I saw was an enormous AWA delivery van which had proudly emblazoned on the side in sign-written type, the following strident message: 'Who the fuck is AWA?' Who the fuck are their advertisers is what I want to know. And while I'm on the subject, who the fuck are the advertising standards representatives in this country? And do they give a fuck?*

Just plain disturbing is the hand-painted image above a coffee shop on Weteringschans. The work of some deeply insane person, it shows a dog, a Labrador I think, in repose puffing on a cigarette with the aid of a very long cigarette holder. This would be accept-able – just – if it wasn't for the fact that the smoking pooch has human legs and is wearing a garter belt and black stockings. If that's the kind of vivid picture which comes to mind after a visit inside the premises, then just say *nee*.

When Sally wasn't working (I'd like to say bringing home the bacon but strangely, for a country keen on flesh in all its forms, ed-ible and otherwise, there appears to be a moratorium on the King of Meats here), she and I took walks around our new neighbourhood, part of a small-scale program we called 'Getting to Know You, East Amsterdam'. Our first stop was the Koffiehuis de Meer, which, even though it called itself a *koffiehuis*, was neither a 'coffee shop' (marijuana café) or a coffee house (coffee house). It was a very small bar seemingly managed and frequented by former criminals and their recently escaped or paroled associates. We went there because the beer was cheap and the people were, as is the case with virtually all the Dutch, very friendly. They were full of questions about why we'd come to Amsterdam (especially why we'd come to the *east* of Amsterdam), what we did for a living and why the hell we'd left Australia to come to cold northern Europe. In the height of winter, these questions were difficult to answer. Nevertheless we tried our best to convince everyone that it was actually possible to become, if not sick of, then inured to and perhaps even jaded about warm weather, blue skies and wide open spaces.

*Perhaps 'fuck' has a softer quality when it's buried amongst the agitated growls and splenetic discharges of Dutch. I recently saw an espisode of 'The Simpsons' screened at the kid-friendly TV hour of 5 p.m., where the words 'screw Flanders' were subtitled in Dutch as 'fuck Flanders'.

'Oh you must be crazy,' said fat Joost with the ponytail. 'I would love to go in Australia.'

'We love Amsterdam.'

'Really?' asked tattoo-knuckled Liselot behind the bar. 'Really you mean dat? You like all de snow and de cold?'

'Well, not so much the cold, but . . .'

Insulating ourselves against that cold with puffy jackets, mouth-covering scarves and gloves, we also liked to wander through a vast (by Amsterdam standards anyway) tangle of forest we called the Murder Park. There was an abandoned glass factory which sat on a large island in the middle of a lake in the centre of the park. And there were dozens of wild chickens. Not just regular old hens, these were special, fancy chickens with bronze feathers who strutted about with a slightly self-important, magisterial air. These were very European chickens. Why they were there, who fed them and where their coop was (if they had one) was a mystery to us. Apart from the *kippen*, we very rarely saw any signs of life in the park and every time we went there we fully expected to discover some human remains loosely covered by branches and rocks. Fortunately (or perhaps unfortunately for anecdotal purposes) we never did. Sally hated walking on icy ground and often clung tightly to my arm, afraid of slipping and becoming dead herself. She said something to me and even though her mouth was close to my ear, her thick scarf muffled the words and I didn't know what she was saying. I pulled her scarf down.

'What'd you say?' The small words came out in dry puffs that disappeared.

'Would you cover me with rocks if I died right here?'

'Yeah, baby, I'd cover you with a few rocks then go home with one of those chickens and call it Sally. Nobody'd know it wasn't you.'

'You would not. You'd call it Sean. Didn't you name a cat Sean once?'

'No, my friend Tim did. But it was named after me . . . What are we gonna do?'

'How do I know? We're not going back, though.'

'I know we're not going back, we've come way too far. But what are we going to *do* here?'

'You mean what are *you* going to do.'

'No, I mean us. We. What are *we* going to do? What are you going to do? And, more importantly, what am I going to do?'

'What would we be doing if we were still in Melbourne?'

'I guess the same. Living, working, chasing our dreams.'

'The only chasing you did was on PlayStation, my friend.'

'At least I'm not doing that any more. My new idea of fun is a brisk walk in a desolate body dumping ground surrounded by arrogant chickens trying not to break one of four ankles I'm responsible for.'

'Why don't you write another book?'

'What would I write about?'

'This.'

'What this?'

'Everything this – what we're doing now.'

'Exactly what we're doing? Like right now – in the Murder Park with chickens? *This* this?'

'Yes. And don't make anything up. Just tell it how it is, no tricks.'

'Without embellishment?'

'Yes.'

And right then was when we discovered the body . . .

Assimilating with Fatty

December in Amsterdam is exhausting; there are so many official and unofficial excuses for drinking, dancing, eating and talking to excess. Officially, the Dutch like to recognise several Christmas-like events, beginning with the night before Sinterklaas. For maximum confusion, Sinterklaas is the name of both the event – the feast of Saint Nicholas on December 5th – and the name of a Santa Claus-like figure who struts about the country around that time. By early December, Sinterklaas (the guy, rather than the event) has been in Holland for a couple of weeks, having arrived by boat 'from Spain' (the Dutch equivalent of the North Pole, but with better weather and food) back in the middle of November. When the bearded, mitre-clutching Sint arrives, he rides a white horse through the *stads* and *dorps* (cities and towns) accompanied by Moorish 'Black Petes' (the Dutch equivalent of elves but with heavily racist overtones) who distribute sweets to the good children and allegedly put the bad children into sacks and haul them back to Spain, thus providing the youngsters of Holland with material for a lifetime of horrific nightmares, terrified as they are of having to live in a land of sunshine, merriment and flavoured food. Due to the already-mentioned racist aspects of having a tall white man with a white beard on a white horse being attended to by a number of small black helpers, attempts have been made by the relevant Dutch authorities to turn the Black Petes into multi-coloured Rainbow Petes, thereby offending persons of red, yellow, blue, green and cerise descent. However, every year it's been tried, it fails and next time round Black Pete the Bag-Carrying Enforcer is back. But the problems don't stop there. Amsterdam has a substantial Muslim population and they have their own reasons for eschewing Sinterklaas, chiefly that he is seen as a

Christian infidel and a dangerously Westernising influence on Muslim children. So who exactly is this troublesome fellow?

As older readers will recall, during the Middle Ages saints were an important part of life, being called upon to win wars, protect ships, locate lost items and assist with not getting the plague. Even school children had their own patron saint, Saint Nicholas of Myra (modern-day Turkey), about whom a number of (possibly unreliable) stories sprang up. One such tale concerns three young boys who sought shelter from a storm at an inn where the innkeeper and his wife cut the lads into small pieces and preserved them in a barrel of brine to be served as a meal for the next guest. The next guest, however, was Saint Nick, who, after a mouthful or two of pickled kid, realised what he was eating and promptly brought the youngsters back to life then delivered a stern lecture to the hotelier and stripped the inn of its Michelin star. Another story, this one less likely than the other to traumatise and nauseate, is about the three daughters of an impoverished nobleman. Being poor, the girls (who were probably good-looking, but nobody knows for sure) had no dowry and therefore no suitors and were about to turn to prostitution when Saint Nicholas, then a young priest, heard about their sorry circumstances and began showing up at night and tossing money* into their bedroom through an open window. On the third night the girls' father collared Saint Nick and demanded to know what was going on. 'Throwing coins into your daughters' shoes,' Saint Nick told him (although I'm paraphrasing). The father demanded to know why. 'Because I think it could become a nifty tradition.' (Again, I'm paraphrasing.) Then he disappeared, the only trace of him a gingerbread man on the floor. (Here I am not so much paraphrasing as simply inventing.)

And so it did become a tradition; seventeenth-century Holland was a place brimming with people leaving secret gifts in shoes and suitors placing gingerbread men on doorsteps as signs of their intentions toward maidens. These days, on December 5th, people suffering hangovers from celebrating the night before still exchange small gifts hidden in footwear, as well as poems, specially written by Sinterklaas himself, mercilessly

*Possibly a metaphor.

lampooning the recipient. It's also customary on this day to eat seasonal comestibles such as *speculaas* (a horribly sweet cinnamon gingerbread) and, for reasons I cannot fathom (or even invent), chocolate capital letters of the person's first name.

'I'm sick of chocolate. What I'd really like is some mutton,' Terry said as he walked in the door with Ray and Sonia. 'Mutton made me what I am.'

'And what's that?' I asked.

'Sheepish.'

Sally and I were having a small Sinterklaas party at our flat for the above-mentioned people and Kevin, a friend from Australia who was staying with us. Kevin, a television comedy writer/producer working on what was then, through no fault of his own, the second unfunniest show on TV, had very long, dirty-blond hair and large black spectacles, a look he had favoured for many, many years despite spending much of his professional life surrounded by television stylists.*

It was great to catch up with the gang again as we had not seen them since the previous night, when we'd all gathered at Café t'Papenieland to drink mulled wine and eat *oliebollen*. The next evening nobody was feeling too good and the plates of *speculaas* and alphabetised chocolate did not have the appeal to a bunch of hung-over adults as they might have had for a bunch of excited children. But we were determined to assimilate and therefore did things strictly by the Dutch book, and the Dutch book of December is full of alcohol and sugar. So we exchanged gifts, teased one another in verse and consumed so much sugar and alcohol that pretty soon we were less like a bunch of hung-over adults and more like a gang of excited children (for about ten minutes until one of us became over-stimulated, began bawling and had to be put to bed).

Astute readers will have noted a distinct similarity between Sinterklaas and Santa Claus in both physical description and general

---

*Kevin would later go on to do Emmy-winning work in New York. He would also finally have his hair cut to a reasonable length and begin wearing contact lenses, proof of the powerfully transforming effects of life in a new metropolis.

disposition. This is because they are basically one and the same, although Santa Claus is fatter. But how did this Turkish/Spanish/ Dutch concoction come to be so Americanised and eventually a (presumably unpaid) representative of the Coca-Cola corporation? It began in New York (formerly New Amsterdam) in 1822 (formerly 1821) when a theologian, Dr Clement C. Moore, listened to a short, chubby, white-bearded, rosy-cheeked Dutch friend telling stories about Saint Nicholas back in the old country. Taking inspiration for the physical details from his Dutch friend, Dr Moore wrote popular verses about a creation he called Santa Claus. Further development came in 1863 when a cartoonist, Thomas Nast, pictured him in *Harper's Illustrated Weekly* in a fur-trimmed suit. The rest – and indeed the preceding material – is history. However, it's worth remembering that no matter what the good saint is called – Jule-nissen, Sankt Nikolaus, Sint Nicolaas, Santa Klaas, Father Christmas, Petit Jesus, Pere Noel, Kriss Kringle, Krist Kindlein or Kris Kristofferson – his name is a synonym for the spirit of selfless giving. And Coke.

Following Sinterklaas is *Kerst* on December 25th then *Tweede Kerst* (second Christmas) on Boxing Day, both of which also demand celebration, and therefore alcohol. Add to this New Year's Eve, a couple of birthdays and two or three 'bon voyage' do's for people leaving for a week in Rotterdam, and you've got a year's worth of excess and indulgence packed into a month. By the end of December I was ready to die.

December 21st, 1998

Appendix about to burst. Liver about to fail. Heart about to stop. Lungs near collapse. Teeth loose, skin clammy, eyes red/yellow, breath faint and sour. Have been walking around the flat gingerly, like an old person. Or an old cat with sore paws. Weekend of extreme indulgence catching up in very definite fashion. Feel quite unlike self: dizzy, woozy and soft. More like that guy who vomited up the Miracle of Amsterdam. Sally is the same. Friday night we went to a friend's party, held at an anti-*krak* joint*

---

*Anti-*krak* places are buildings awaiting refurbishment, whose rooms are rented out for short, definite terms at deflated prices to ensure that they will not be squatted.

on Oudezijds which was formerly a university science building, so people were drinking out of beakers and test tubes, which may account for how especially horrible I feel. The amazing thing is, my hair looks terrific.

The following day I rolled out of bed at the crack of noon and constructed an *ontbijt*, the Dutch breakfast staple consisting of a pig pen's worth of ham (I'd have used bacon but when you can find it, it's too expensive here. I don't know where the Dutch think bacon comes from, but judging by the price they must believe it's part of a unicorn or something), a henhouse of eggs, a dozen slices of bread and a full wheel of cheese. The whole thing was as big and round as a truck tyre and, since I overcooked it, tasted a bit like one as well. Sally, eating half a grapefruit and some strawberries, looked at my plate and said, 'You'll die.'

'I'm *trying* to assimilate,' I panted. 'It's a classic Dutch dish.'

'Well try and assimilate with the living Dutch, not the dead.'

Kevin stood in the kitchen doorway. 'Good God . . . You could have a heart attack just looking at that thing.'

The reason I was trying to kill myself with breakfast was that that night was Keith Finney's birthday party and the thought of more drinking made me suicidal. 'I believe Van Gogh spent an entire summer drinking in order to create his famous yellow colour,' I replied to Sally, somehow convinced that my remark was relevant.

'So?'

'Well . . . he was Dutch.'

'I think you better go back to bed.'

'I'm fine,' I said, then threw up on the floor.

Kevin pointed at the puddle. 'Well done, Sean. You've created Van Gogh's yellow without the aid of paint.'

But there was no time for more sleeping; Sally and I felt obliged to do a few touristy things so that Kevin might leave with a greater appreciation of our new home. And, I figured, it would certainly do me no harm to see something of Amsterdam other than yet another bar. First we decided to visit the former home of Rembrandt, Amsterdam's favourite son and bearded person.* I always like to

*The fact that he was born in Leiden notwithstanding.

see how the other half live (even if they lived over three hundred years ago) so we all happily forked over ƒ7.50 then read the sign inside the Rembrandt Museum adjacent to the Rembrandt House that said that the house would be closed until next September. 'Dey putting in a new staircase,' the attendant told us.

'Why does he need a new staircase?' I said a little louder than I meant to. 'He's dead.' Sally and Kevin hurried away while I continued my rather angry discussion about renovations, concluding with, 'And just how big is this staircase that it's gonna take nine months to finish?' I was pretty annoyed. But that's the Dutch for you, they'll advertise the hell out of something like the Rembrandt House, take your dough and only then tell you that you can't go in. I trudged upstairs to the museum and took a desultory look at some of Mr van Rijn's etchings. They were okay. But they were no *house*.

We followed our non-visit to the Rembrandthuis with a canal cruise, reasoning that taking a cruise on a rainy, dull, overcast day was an excellent idea because the bleak weather would mean that there would be fewer people in the boat along with us gawping up at skinny buildings and bridges. It was not an excellent idea – there were plenty of other people and the rain on the glass roof of the canal cruiser meant that we couldn't actually see any skinny buildings and bridges. Still, there was a baby crying loudly to help us take our minds off everything we were missing out on.

'What language is that child crying in?' Kevin asked. The reason he said it was this: in order to accommodate and inform tourists from all over the world, our guide, a young woman in her mid-twenties, had to give her spiel in six languages – English (of course), Dutch (naturally), German (just like Dutch, only bossier), Italian (for the crying baby's parents), French (very pleasant) and limping Korean (impressive). The result of this multilingual babble was that by the time she'd finished telling everyone what we were seeing (Amsterdam's skinniest building; seven bridges in a row; the smallest hotel in the city, the New York, which has only three rooms, outside of which was an ambulance removing a guest who'd died of claustrophobia), we were long past the subject, not that we would have been able to see it anyway because of the rain and fogged-up windows.

As we puttered down Herengracht, Miss Manytongues told us that the green iron bars bolted into the concrete at the edge of the canals to stop cars from rolling into the water were placed there not by the City of Amsterdam, but by the city's insurance companies. This fact I found extremely Dutch on many levels – all of them financial. The only other interesting thing we heard about during this damp and rather tortuous hour was three buildings in a row which leant to one side because of their rotting wood foundations. She told us that they were called the 'Dancing Buildings'. Presumably they were going to be more accurately called the Leaning Buildings, but that tower over in Pisa had heard about it and slapped a writ on them quick smart.

That evening, after a few Bloody Marys (and a few Hail Marys), I was well enough to be introduced to Keith's sister Jenny, who referred to him as Frank (because that is in fact his name) and shared with me many of the tall tales he'd been telling about himself ever since she could remember. For years he'd claimed that his sister was a prostitute; that he couldn't read until he was ten; that he was brought up by one-armed nuns in Stepney Green. None of this was true. Indeed, when I'd first met him, he told me that he was fifty-one, but there I was, along with many of his friends and family who'd flown over for the occasion, at his first and only fiftieth birthday.

'So his name is Frank and he's fifty years old,' I confirmed. 'He is not a fifty-one-year-old man named Keith.'

'Yes, that's right,' Jenny said.

'Are you really his sister?'

'I am, yes.'

These revelations brought to mind some of the other stories Keith* had told me over the past few months. My favourite concerned a fat druglord/gangster in his sixties who had come to Keith in search of a solution to a problem. The problem was that the gangster had bought a very large house just outside Amsterdam and paid cash for it. The tax department wanted to know where the cash had come from. The gangster told them that the money was loaned to him by a friend. The tax department

*Frank.

wanted to know who the friend was. 'He's Austrian and he's . . .
dead,' the ageing don had told them.

'Then,' Keith continued, 'the almighty, all-powerful, all-seeing,
all-conquering tax department says they want to see a death certificate. That's when Fatty the gangster comes to see me. I was
talkin' about it in some boozer on Nieuwezijds and this
Yugoslavian bloke I was with says there's plenty of dead people in
Bosnia, so why not go there? And this was at the time when they
was exhumin' all them graves for the war crimes tribunals – '96 or
'97. So anyway, me and Fatty and Jonny the bank robber 'ired a
Mercedes and drove down to Belgrade where they told us –'

'Who are "they"?' I remember asking.

'Never you mind,' I remember Keith telling me. 'They told us
that everywhere outside Belgrade was terrorists and militia and
armies and whatnot so we'd best not stop for any roadblocks and
carry plenty of ammo and US dollars. Fatty 'ad about a 'undred
thousand guilders but no guns and no greenbacks so once we was
outside Belgrade, we didn't stop until we got to Split. An' when
we got there, it was fuckin' chaos. Thing is, you can buy just
about anything in a war economy, but you got to know who to ask
and it was my job to do the asking. So I found this civil servant
type fella who said he could give me a death certificate of a
croaked Austrian but we had to formally identify the body in
front of witnesses. Jonny and Fatty didn't want no part of that so
the next day I 'ad to go to this mass grave, me face covered with
an 'ankerchief 'cause you never smelled nuffing like that, and the
first body I seen, I said, "Yeah, that's him. That's Wolfgang or
Hans or whoever the fuck. I reconise 'is scarf." And then they
'anded over the certificate, only the civil servant wouldn't let me
take it out of the country because it 'ad his signature on it. So we
paid him 'alf the money there and had the thing delivered to
Amsterdam by a Yugoslav associate of the civil servant's. All
went smooth as you like. Couldn't've gone better. Only thing
was, four weeks later Fatty had a fuckin' coronary and fuckin'
died. The wanker.'

True or not (and even though he was not raised by nuns, Keith
assured me that it *was* true), it was a good story. And as I stood
there recalling it, I couldn't help thinking that if December kept on

the way it was going, I too might have a fucking coronary and fucking die.

Another thing which was sending my blood pressure skyrocketing around that time, apart from my excess in the alcohol and *oliebol* departments, was getting used to the Amsterdam Retail Experience, hereafter referred to as ARE to save time (which is pretty ironic, considering that the ARE is all about wasting time).

Ever since the seventeenth century, Amsterdam has been famous for its lack of customer service (even Rembrandt complained about the café/gift shop in his house), and the city's retailers have been refining their sluggishness, rudeness, hostility and general disregard for people who give them money ever since. This in itself is also highly ironic when you consider the almost hysterical over-formality of Dutch social interaction. Even the most basic exchange is peppered with curiously Victorian formalities. Say for instance you've just popped into the *tabac* (newsagent/tobacconist) for a *strippenkaart* (tram ticket). After waiting in line for fifteen minutes in the tiny shop while the tobacconist and a regular chat about herring and Sumatran cigars, you say, '*Een strippenkaart, alstublieft.*' ('A tram ticket, please.') The *tabac* guy hands it over, muttering a desultory '*Alstublieft*' as he does so. Then, when you hand over your dough, you have to say '*Alstublieft*' as well. Mr Gelukkig (Happy) gives you your change – again with a reluctant and miserly '*Alstublieft*' – and you accept with a final '*Dankuwell*' (thanksverymuch). Then you miss your tram.

Curiously, in contrast to this wealth of civilities, there seems to be only one word for sorry (*sorry*). On the rare occasions I heard it used, it was always said in an insincere and extremely sarcastic tone, as though preceding a beating.

While the busy Christmas season exacerbated the ARE problem, at other times of the year it was not the least bit unusual to spend twenty minutes waiting to buy a pen at a HEMA, the low-end department store chain, or to while away half an hour at a grocery checkout purchasing a leek, or up to ninety minutes doing anything at a post office or train station. Already I conservatively estimated my time spent staring at the back of somebody's head in Amsterdam's retail outlets at what felt like – indeed what could actually have been – a month; one of the ones with thirty-one days in it. But your problems are far from over even when it's finally your turn. A visit to the post office was a salutary lesson.

'Hello,' I said to the slumped, grey figure before me. 'I'd like two stamps and two envelopes, please. *Alstublieft.*'

With the charm and alacrity of a corpse the guy slid the two stamps toward me then told me that they didn't sell envelopes.

'This is a post office,' I reminded him.

'Neverdeless, we do not sell envelopes,' he reminded me. Then he pointed in the direction of Belgium and said, '*Tabac.*'

I went to the *tabac*, queued up for seven minutes, bought three envelopes, went back to the post office, took a number, sat down and read mail-related pamphlets in Dutch for three-quarters of an hour until my number came up, went to the dead postal worker and handed over my spare envelope. 'Next time somebody shows up and wants to buy an envelope – and that time *will* come, my friend – please give them this. It's on me.'

Not having a job gave me plenty of time to think about what I wanted for Christmas – what I wanted to give and what I wanted to receive. But since I had no job (see previous sentence) and therefore no money, I spent less time thinking about giving, more about receiving. At the top of my list was some Self Respect (available in a lotion from chemists or in three-kilo bags from most supermarkets), closely followed by A Sense of Purpose (available from better department stores and practically all churches, although with the latter, conditions of use may vary) and finally Lots of Dough (available from banks, however the cost can be high: five to ten years if you get caught). Any of those things would do, but I'd also have been quite happy with some socks and handkerchiefs, which in the event was what I got, but not in that order.

One evening in the middle of the festive wasteland between Christmas and New Year's Eve, Sally and I used the tickets Ray and Sonia had given us for Christmas and went to see Cirque du Soleil, the French-Canadian/International troupe of lithe people. Despite the fact that there were no bears and very little nudity, it was a wonderful night of human-based entertainment – even though the whole thing was loosely held together by this pretty hokey story of a child's imagination, so you get all this naiveté and wonder and innocence floating about everywhere. And unless you're an imaginative child full of naiveté, wonder and innocence, that stuff can be pretty hard to take. Anyway, they had a terrific live band, some clowns, a master of ceremonies who did some pretty funny things with a coat stand and his nostril, a bunch of musclemen and musclewomen, people balancing on things (mostly each other), and other general stuntery.

The highlight for me was a group of four Chinese girls aged about eight, all dressed like the Tin Man from *The Wizard of Oz*. They spun wooden tops on ropes and threw them in the air and to each other while flipping themselves around the stage like crazy kids with ADD who'd drunk too much red cordial. It was an incredible display of precision physics at work. I was grinning like such a fool that I thought my face was going to fall off. The funny thing was, at the same time I was also on the verge of hysterical tears, sick with the thought that one of the kids would drop a top, or snap a rope or a hamstring or something. Laughter, tears and excitement – it was a giddy combination.

As I gazed at some of the less dynamic acts (a fat guy in a tutu sucking a lollipop), I couldn't help thinking how wonderful it would be to run away and join the circus. What sort of a life must these performers have? International travel, the adoration and admiration of millions, daily adventure, nightly fun and probably excellent health coverage. Then I got to thinking that since I didn't actually have any kind of proper job or sense of purpose, why didn't I go and see about joining the Cirque du Soleil – after all, I had lived in Montreal for *deux année* when I was a kid, so I was halfway in already.

During the intermission I left Sally at the bar and skipped off through the sawdust and peanut shells in search of the cirque's ringmaster. I found Franco somewhere out the back, poring over a ledger. Disappointingly, he wasn't wearing a top hat or carrying a whip; jeans and a pocket calculator seemed contemporary ring-master gear. I knocked on his tent flap and asked if I could have *un moment* of his time. He motioned me in (very theatrically) and

I sat down. Franco had thick curly hair and a kind of weary look, as though he knew what was coming. 'Can I 'elp you?' he asked.

'Yes,' I told him firmly. 'I want to join the cirque.'

He rolled his eyes (very theatrically) and sighed. 'I see. What can you offer us?'

'Enthusiasm, *monsieur*. Lots of enthusiasm,' I said, enthusiastically.

'Can you leap?'

'Not leap, exactly, but I can jump.' I raised my hand a good three feet off the ground by way of demonstration.

'Perform any feats of strength?'

'I've been able to open some pretty difficult jars for my wife. But feets of clay is more my area.' I laughed a little to assist my joke.

Franco didn't look too impressed. 'Can you sing?'

'No – tin ear.'

'I see.'

'And throat.'

'Can you have a lithe young woman dressed only in a flimsy leotard hang off your neck while you yourself dangle by one foot from a rope forty feet above the stage?'

'You cannot imagine how much it pains me to have to tell you no,' I said. 'But no.'

'Well, what can you do?'

'I can be as irritating as any of your best clowns,' I said, screwing up my face and pretending to cry (very theatrically). 'I'm fairly . . . husky, I look okay in a tutu and I like lollipops. Only, on my passport, would I have to put that I'm a clown?'

He told me to leave. I did, and was unsuccessful in my attempt to slam the tent flap on my way out.

Heading back to the big top I passed the 'concession stand', selling a staggering array of Cirque souvenirs and mementos. They had everything: T-shirts, sweatshirts, hats, caps, leather jackets (ƒ450!), CDs, videos, keyrings, postcards and umbrellas, right down to an official Cirque stopwatch. But I guess that's the reality of the modern circus: leaping is all very well, but the financial backbone of today's circus is clearly merchandising. It's more about balancing the books than each other.

I enjoyed the second half of the evening but couldn't help wishing I was any one of the people doing absolutely anything in the ring – except the high-wire stuff obviously, which is just foolish and dangerous. And I supposed the other gymnasts would have a pretty difficult time tossing me about after all the hot dogs, peanuts and fairyfloss I'd been eating. And I'm no dancer, that's for sure, so I forgot about flopping around the stage in a pair of tights. As for the juggling, I'm strictly three oranges, and that just doesn't wow the crowds as much as it did back in primary school. And the closest I come to fire-breathing these days is lighting a cigarette. But a boy could still dream, couldn't he?

And then, at long last, I saw a guy doing something that I just knew I could do as well, if not better, than him. Practically the whole crowd had left, but there he was doing his thing – not for applause and cheers and whistles, but just because he loved it. He was sweeping the stage; a regular guy doing regular sweeping. Not some clown with an oversized, coloured broom, just an ordinary Joe pushing an ordinary broom. And I figured maybe that's how I could begin *my* life in the circus. Hell, it's a start and perhaps eventually I could work my way up, maybe all the way up to merchandising. Then I thought that if I did join Cirque du Soleil and only ever ate sandwiches, my life really would be all bread and circuses. Which could be nice. Sitting in the tram on the way home I asked Sally how she would feel about being a circus wife.

'As opposed to what?'

'The wife life you have now.'

'I don't have a wife life,' she said, screwing up her face slightly. 'What the hell's a wife life?'

'I don't know – one where your husband's kind of a loser, I guess. And you're the wife. And that's all you've got.'

'You're not a loser, baby,' she said, then kissed me on the forehead. 'You're an idiot.'

Just before the end of the year more of our things arrived from Australia, freighted over courtesy of my friend/personal warehouse manager Anthony Kitchener (who will appear 'in person' and more fully described later). Almost all of it was clothing, including a lovely Brooks Brothers tuxedo with dull olive lapels.

Exactly what sort of life I imagined I'd be living in Amsterdam which would require me to own such an item escaped me, especially since I wore the same drab pants, dull T-shirt and tatty jumper combo just about every day. I suppose that back in Melbourne a few months earlier, I'd figured that somehow I was very likely to meet Queen Beatrix or the mayor and would be pretty heavily booked for rather smart social engagements where cuff links and olive green lapels were essential. This was not the case. And even if it had been the case, I probably wouldn't have shown up to any of these occasions in a tuxedo anyway, because I found that any time I left the house a variety of events conspired to ruin my clothes. In my first week here I had dressed in a beautiful vintage (1962) suit for dinner at an Indonesian restaurant, only to have a waiter pour satay sauce all over the jacket. The restaurant paid for the dry-cleaning, which was the least they could do – and in some ways the most, since the operation cost ƒ30. At other times when I was outside and suited up I would be acid rained on; mud spattered by some Euro-car fitted with a puddle-detector; I'd step in one of the several billion lurking mounds of dog shit that blight the streets year-round; have the creases in my pants flattened by the fierce Siberian winds which blow through the city; or would be stared at in outright confusion by the citizens of Amsterdam. They would stare because the Dutch, as a rule, just don't 'dress up'. ('Dressing up', in this case meaning merely wearing a matching top and bottom of any fabric other than denim.) In my first months in the city I saw no more than six people wearing ties, and in fact I wouldn't be surprised if it was the same guy on six different occasions wearing six different ties. The truth is it just doesn't make any sense to dress smartly in Amsterdam, unless you're friends with Queen Bea or the mayor. And who knows, perhaps even they get about in jeans and a parka, just to avoid being glared at.

Quite apart from the sartorial uselessness of the matter, the cost involved in shipping my tuxedo, three more suits, several pairs of shoes and a number of shirts, as well as a Cornish Blue salt shaker and a small jar of saffron threads (both Sally's), was astronomical. On top of the initial ƒ503.30 just for shoving a suitcase and a box into the cargo bay of a plane, at this end the Dutch, in their much-loved tradition of nickel-and-diming you to death, charged me the following:

- Customs: ƒ21.00
- Shed hire: ƒ37.50
- Admin.: ƒ19.50
- Advisory/Assistance: ƒ10.50

And while I cannot deny that for twenty-four hours my luggage sat on a shelf at Schiphol airport (Shed hire) and a customs guy creased up my clothes diligently searching for drugs and wombats (Customs) and another guy with a hand-rolled Javaanse Jongen cigarette hanging out of his tight mouth stapled some papers together (Admin.), at no point during my two-hour ordeal in the sprawling concrete industry-scape of vast, looming sheds, shimmering walls of Avgas fumes and Brobdingnagian forklift trucks did I receive anything resembling advice or assistance. On the other hand, I didn't get hit by a plane and that's always nice.

December 30th, 1998

Tomorrow is Sally's and my first wedding anniversary – the popular paper anniversary. Sally has woken this morning with a pain deep in the left of her chest. I have begged her to ease off on the cigarettes for a while but she refuses, telling me lovingly to 'get lost' and reminding me that I am not a doctor. So I get lost and worry like a layman. What if it's lung cancer? What if my beloved wife is dying? Right on our anniversary. These thoughts are too horrible so I try to take my mind off my potential grief by having a cigarette myself and concentrating on my ever-ready hypocrisy. It works and soon I have developed a slight pain of my own in the same spot but I decide not to tell Sally because she always thinks I'm 'getting in' on her illnesses. Maybe it's just a cracked rib – God, I hope so.

It's a pretty nice day today – sunny, crisp, bright blue – and, apart from a wife on her deathbed, I have very little to complain about. Not much to complain about, but plenty to worry about. Especially the matter of what to get for Sally for our paper anniversary. What immediately springs to my rather literal mind is a piece of paper, but it seems somehow an inadequate expression of my feelings toward her. As does a newspaper (even a subscription), a paper bag, a paper ring (good song, though), some papier-mâché or a paperweight (which wouldn't count anyway, as it is only paper-related, not actual paper). Right now, Sally herself is off shopping in the Jordaan buying something paperish for me. And they sell really nice stuff in the Jordaan. It's become a fancy area. God, what'll I do? I want to be a good husband and there's only twenty-four hours until P-hour.

All day, since about eight this morning, it's been bang! . . . Pop! . . . Rat-tat-tat-tat!!!! . . . Ker-pow! . . . BOOM! . . . Pffffffssssstttttt . . . clack! etc. due to the fireworks. Whistles and blasts, the whole day long. It's like living in a war-zone with nobody panicking about anything. It's dark now (at only 5.10 p.m. – good Lord!) and there is still a great deal of booming and banging as the local delinquents continue testing their fireworks in preparation for tomorrow night's finger-losing festivities. Not too many showers of coloured sparkles, though; these seem to be merely noise-makers. Earlier today, a small store which sells fireworks across the street was so crowded that people were oozing out the front door and into the street. The excitement was all the more thrilling because these stores aren't allowed to sell the coveted items until immediately before NYE. The Dutch are absolutely crazy about fireworks (and bylaws), a national characteristic I had formerly thought to be exclusively Chinese (same with the bylaws).

And on a completely unrelated matter, looking through the window, I can see two moons because of the double glazing. How very poetic. (Note to self: must remember to get drunk soon and stare out double-glazed windows to see four moons.)

Around seven on New Year's Eve, Sally and I met in the living room to pop a bottle of Moët and give each other paper anniversary gifts. Sally is one of those gift-givers who gets so excited about the gift she's giving that it's often difficult to tell who's the luckier person out of you and her. She hops around the place urging you to tear off the wrapping and get into the gift straight away. My first ever first anniversary present was a fancy stamp of the letter *S* to stamp into my books. Simple, superb, surprising. In return, I gave her *Food* by Waverley Root, a book (made of paper) which she was absolutely mad about. So much so that she didn't want to go out any longer, just wanted to stay home and read. This was a very satisfactory reaction, but inappropriate as I'd earmarked two of my fingers for possible loss that night.

By the time we'd finished the champagne it was eight o'clock and we'd missed the very last tram into town. Yes, this sophisticated, international city shuts down its public transport system at 8 p.m. on New Year's Eve – and I thought Melbourne was a burg.

So we were forced to take a taxi to the Grand Hotel, where we had a reservation at Café Roux, where Albert Roux (one of the brothers Roux who'd invented the roux) was reputed to have personally chosen the drapes as well as the style of cuisine. They were very nice curtains, so I was expecting a lot from the food. Sally looked beautiful, tall and elegant as she strode through the dining area. I looked okay, I suppose, but probably sounded a little foolish shouting 'Wait! Wait for me!' as I struggled to keep up with her.

Around three, after puffing on fat cigars and sniff-sipping fine cognac (come on, it was our first ever wedding anniversary and if Sally wanted to act like a big shot turn-of-the-century banker, who was I to stop her?), Sally and I left the hotel and began walking through streets of snow, red-tinted from the paper wrapping of fireworks. Cabs were nowhere to be seen so we decided to walk back to the east. It was icy cold and Sally held on to me tightly. 'Are you sure you know the way home?' she asked.

We'd been in Amsterdam together for fourth months but in that time we'd covered a lot of ground. 'Yes,' I told her and confidently led us in the direction I would find out only much later was west. 'I know the way.'

Pitiful Figures

For a week after dawn broke on January 1st there was nothing but deep grey skies and thickening rain. The temperature hovered around four degrees and the frosty air seemed heavy with doubt and uncertainty – about the Y2K bug, the looming Euro and more. The only thing anyone was sure of about 1999 was that for the next twelve months, no matter where in the world you were, you could count on hearing a lot of a certain Prince song.

January 15th, 1999

9.07 a.m. *I was dreaming when I wrote this so forgive me if it goes astray . . .* Wake up and thump bedside radio alarm clock. Stare at ceiling. Hate self for not waking up eight minutes earlier – self-respect quotient for the day ruined. Have shower. Do washing-up from two days ago. Make coffee. Look in fridge for milk. Completely milkless. Put on shoes and walk down three flights of stairs then around the corner to buy milk at the Dekamart, the Dutch supermarket chain whose specialty is not having anything you want and making you queue up for hours to get it. Buy milk.

Wander back to apartment thinking about the word 'milk'. In Dutch it's called *melk*. In *A Clockwork Orange* it's called *moloko*. Wish that I wrote *A Clockwork Orange*, then recall that Anthony Burgess had to get drunk to write the book because it was inspired by the horrific abuses his wife suffered at the hands of a bunch of American soldiers stationed in England during the Second World War, and consequently brought back too many painful memories. By the time I am back up the three flights of stairs I am glad that I didn't write *A Clockwork Orange*, although it would have made a fine excuse for my frequent drunkenness. Make coffee (with *melk*) and check email. No email. Poke head out front door and check regular mail. No regular mail. Feel isolated and unpopular.

10.45 a.m. Time for work. Spend a while trying to decide what to work on – an article about the quotidian details of my fascinating life which I could try to foist on some unsuspecting part of the world where they don't hold the English language in very high esteem, or a book about the same thing but with a much more discerning audience in mind. Flip a coin, but just as coin is about to land on desk I notice that it is after midday and I have not yet decided what to have for lunch. Coin hits desk but I don't even bother to see whether it's heads (article) or tails (book).

12.05 p.m. – 12.55 p.m. Think about lunch: what to have; how much of what to have to have; where to have whatever I have in whatever amount (at desk or in living room); what to do while having it (read a magazine or stare out window on the off chance that something exciting will happen for me to write about), etc.

2 p.m. Baked beans on toast and new issue of Dutch *Esquire* ('Clogs are *still* not back!') out of the way, I am now completely ready to begin writing. Coin advises me to work on an article about my Amsterdam life. Toss coin three more times just to make sure it's sure. It is – comes up heads four times in a row. Which reminds me of that scene in *Rosencrantz and Guildenstern Are Dead* where the coin comes up heads (or tails) about fifty times in succession and how, as a youngster, I always wondered how they managed to keep the coin coming up heads whenever they put the play on. (I was not a mentally lively kid.) Decide to see how many times in a row I can make my own coin come up heads – a disappointing seven after a full hour's tossing (not counting the original four).

3.15 p.m. Write short piece about the 'tossing qualities' of Dutch coinage. Not my best work, but not my worst either. Since money is always on my mind (especially when tossing coins then writing about tossing coins) I wonder if I might be able to sell the piece to a coin-collector's magazine, if such things exist. Put on shoes and head off to the AKO newsagency to investigate. No magazines about coin collection – plenty about stamps, but you can't flip stamps.

4.30 p.m. Only ninety minutes to go before I can knock off. Will feel terribly guilty if sum achievement for the day is the coin piece, so I begin urgently writing, because my motto is 'A writer writes – always' (a handy little piece of advice I picked up from the 1987 De Vito/Crystal vehicle *Throw Momma from the Train*). Soon tomorrow's shopping list is spellchecked and filed away. Then I knock over a schedule for this evening's television viewing, but am unhappy with both the indent (five inches) and the typeface (Arial medium) and start again. Continue searching for appealing font until 6 p.m. then quit in preparation for another day at the intellectual coalface tomorrow.

January 16th, 1999
Pressure too much. Take day off.

I tried, through a combination of whimsy and sheer idiocy, to put a brave, palatable (and therefore saleable) face on it, but the truth was that I was having quite a hard time. I really *was* worried about a lot of things. Money, employment, our residency status in the Netherlands, our residency status in our flat in the Netherlands, and my fading sense of self-worth were all part of it, but there were other things like the fact that my career as a doctor had failed to materialise, largely as a result of my not having gone to medical school. (Same with my law, banking and architectural careers.) I also continued to worry about mortality (mine, everybody's), usually at a mercifully vague level, but that had changed a few days earlier when Sally and I had gone into the Centrum to see a movie.

We'd hopped off the tram at Muntplein and walked down Reguliersbreestraat toward the ornate and beautiful old Tuschinski Theatre. We were nervous about going back there, the scene of our first Dutch cinema experience with which we had numerous problems – price, the ceaseless and loud conversation between other patrons, and the pause they shove in the middle of proceedings to allow people to stock up on popcorn, beer and fresh conversation topics to be loudly discussed during the second half of the film. The cinema is unfortunately located on a thin and busy tourist striplet of food joints, sex shops, gambling houses and souvenir shops leading down into Rembrandtplein (named after the artist Rembrandtplein), a lovely square ringed by open-air bars, cafés and hotels where there are large street fights every Friday night.

As we got to halfway down Reguliersbreestraat we were blocked by an enormous fuss: a line of trams butted up against one another; a couple of ambulances; a throng of rubbernecks; two police horses standing head to head, reined in by a policewoman; and paramedics pumping the chest of a dying man, his face every bit the descriptive cliché that is 'ashen'. (I'd never seen a dead or even dying person before and I found it astonishing how that phrase 'ashen-faced' popped straight into my head; it was grey and sagging, like cardboard left in the rain.) We edged through the crowd, trying not to become part of it by staring at the drama for too long, but it was hard. After a short while, we tore ourselves away and wandered up the cinema stairs and bought our tickets at the window then turned around as the paramedics were stretchering the man into an ambulance. He was around fifty, shirtless, wearing big leather boots and had his hands folded neatly over his lower stomach as though he were already dead and on display in his coffin. As is usually the case when you get a crowd like this – anywhere in the world, not just Amsterdam – there was one particular guy, a big, Lenny-type with a buzz cut who pressed his face against the ambulance window staring stupidly in at the paramedics as they pounded the guy's chest. I couldn't take my eyes off this big lug – making me some sort of rubberneck rubberneck, I guess – and the longer he stood there the more I grew to hate him. When at last the ambulance drove away and Lenny was left with nothing more to gawk at he turned and I could see his face – lip-licking and crazed with excitement, even a kind of joy. The policewoman made her horses form an L-shape around where the work on the dying man had taken place, an area littered with dozens of discarded hypodermics and pieces of plastic and paper, all of them white, blue, sterile and serious. Her partner was on his knees picking up the mess of life-saving equipment. When he stood up, my mouth dropped. It was Steve Martin – lumpy, smiling face, thick grey hair and twinkle-filled eyes. I had strange thoughts – where were the cameras filming this elaborate, vérité movie scene? Where were the crew? Were Sally and I extras? I stared at the actor, his head tilted back slightly, his mouth open, about to say something. I moved a step closer, eager to hear what it was – *Can we do another take? There was a fly on my ear.* – something that would explain this strange business. I could practically hear his creaky, drawly voice even before he said a word. And then he spoke. Dutch. It wasn't Steve Martin. The scene wasn't for a movie. It was real. And the fellow in the ambulance was dying, maybe even dead.

'Look at that guy,' Sally said, belting me on the arm. 'It's –'

'Steve Martin, I know.'

'It's incredible. I wish we'd brought the camera. But we'd look like a pair of assholes taking photos of all this,' she said. 'Wouldn't we?'

Even as Sally said the words, an older man had placed his arm around the shoulder of Steve Martin, now holding his horse's bit, and was having his photograph taken by his wife, who was standing near Sally and I. He thanked the policeman/actor then walked toward us. I was very keen to ask the gentleman whether he'd had the snap taken because of the cop-on-a-horse angle or because he thought the guy was Steve Martin. But I didn't. It would have been too hard to explain, even in English.

At home there was a letter, apparently opened by mistake by our downstairs neighbours, slipped under the door with a scribbled (but, I imagine, quite insincere) apology. The letter was addressed to the occupants of our flat – us. From what we could make out it was a scary letter: words like 'rent', 'apartment', 'housing authority' and 'eviction' all have a kind of internationally fearful ring to them. I rang my friend Jeroen 'Joey' Witteveen, who answered his mobile phone on a highway somewhere between Amsterdam and Utrecht. 'I am in search of a new muffler for my Saab,' he told me. After the auto-report, I read the letter out in halting, but flashily accented Dutch and Joey translated for me. Basically it said that according to the Amsterdam Woningdienst (housing authority) the originally listed people were no longer living in our flat (which was true) so what the hell was going on? Answer this letter soon or we'll evict you. It wasn't a good letter. More disturbing, however, was the fact that it had been opened and presumably read by our downstairs neighbours – a family of angry ceiling-bashers, who, I felt certain, would be only too happy to turn in a couple of illegal *buitenlanders* (foreigners). After all, it was a Dutch person, not a German, that fingered Anne Frank.

I called our British landlords – the originally listed tenants from whom we were subletting – and explained the situation to them. 'Oh dear, that does sound serious,' said the English woman. 'Yes, quite serious.' Then she started calling out to her Scottish husband. 'Bertie! Bertie! Those people in the flat in Amsterdam seem to have received a letter that seems to want them to leave.' I could hear her and Bertie discussing the matter. 'Are you there, Sean?' I was. 'Yes, Bertie agrees that it does indeed seem a serious situation . . .' And? 'But we neither of us know what to do. Bertie! *Bertie!* The cat seems to be stuck behind the television set again. Do something please. Do you have any ideas, Sean?' No. 'Well we don't want to give up the flat.' I'm sure you don't, doubling the rent the way you are. 'And I don't imagine you two wish to move. This is Amsterdam, after all.' True – doubled as its rent was, the place was still cheaper than anything we'd ever seen. 'Bertie! Take that ice lolly out of your mouth and think of something!' Yeah, Bertie! What are you, six years old? 'I'll call you back in a few days, Sean. Bertie – the cat!!'

'What did they say?' Sally asked me after I put the phone down.

'Our landlords seem to be a pair of idiots,' I told her. 'I'm sure we'll seem to be fine.'

'What are we gonna do?'

'I have no idea. That horse cop really did look a lot like Steve Martin, though, didn't he?'

'Yes. And?'

'Nothing. I'm just saying is all . . .'

It is with shame and regret that I confess that in the middle of February I visited a prostitute. However this *is* Amsterdam, so I suppose that in one way or another such a thing was probably inevitable. But, I hasten to add, Sally knew about my carnal adventure. And she knew because she joined me in it.

It all began a couple of weeks earlier when Terry and his moustache took me to meet a man named Michael B., a former showbiz dentist/acid dealer/jailbird turned natural healer whom Terry had met at a Christmas party. Michael, a gentle and entertaining fellow who has retired from dentistry and crime in favour of less painful pursuits like art and natural therapies, mentioned that he was good friends with Xaviera Hollander, the Happy Hooker herself. My ears pricked up immediately and I expressed some interest in meeting her. Michael told me that he'd see what he could do, but couldn't promise anything, especially not free sex with the other Deep Throat of the mid-seventies. (Not that that's what I asked for.) To my surprise, however, Ms Hollander herself called me the very next day and told Sally and I to be at her house the following Monday at 8.15 and to bring a bottle of white wine. 'A *good* bottle,' she warned. 'And something to eat.'

I have to admit that I was pretty excited by the whole prospect of dining at Happy's place – I'd known about her since I was seven or eight years old, when, through inchoate, youthful notions of her calling, she opened up the whole idea of sex for me. As a kid, when I thought about 'doing it' I thought about doing it with the Happy Hooker, or someone very much like her – anyone from *Bilitis* or an *Emmanuelle* movie, ideally Emmanuelle herself.*

'What'll we bring tonight?' Sally asked from the kitchen, on the afternoon of our visit.

'Cash,' I said.

'No, you foolish fool – to eat.'

'Plenty of condoms.'

'To eat!'

'Fetish gear. There's probably a pretty big fetish scene happening there. You got any latex?'

And while I tried to wrench myself from my psychosexual seventies dreamland, Sally made a frittata.

Ms Hollander lives in a house in the south of Amsterdam – and the fact that it is a house rather than an apartment makes it the Amsterdam equivalent of a mansion – which is fitting for somebody who has sold over ten million copies of her book, *The Happy Hooker*. However that was some time ago. Early 1999 found the happy, hooky one rather adipose (she was a member of Overeaters Anonymous) and quite dull (she kept telling everyone that she was a member of Overeaters Anonymous). She answered the door in a muu-muu, shook our hands and immediately grabbed the frittata –

---

*Sylvia Kristel (as opposed to Emmanuelle Arsan, the actual Emmanuelle).

we never saw it or the plate it came on again. As ordered, we had also brought a bottle of wine – a *good* bottle – but needn't have bothered because she doesn't drink and, judging by the fact that the bottle disappeared immediately after the frittata, discourages others from doing so as well.

There were about fifteen people at the soirée, many of whom, like us, didn't really know Xaviera or had met her only briefly a long time ago, probably during one of the tens of thousands (by her own calculation) of sexual encounters she has engaged in. She thinks of herself as a 'collector' of people, an expression and a habit I find extremely objectionable. Persons she collected that night included a very short English copywriter named Alan who told me about a new ad agency that had opened up on Keizersgracht, and a hawk-faced, balding window cleaner named Jerzy, who knew the HH through a 'world-famous' gay S&M master who lived in Amsterdam. 'Even though I'm not gay,' Jerzy hastily added.

'And not into S&M?' I asked.

'Oh yes. But only a little bit. Only when it is still a game.'

There was also an Israeli named Eldad who invented toys and was in Amsterdam to finish his PhD in perceptive psychology. There was a handsome older woman called Analise, who carried a fan with her because she was entering her menopause and getting hot flashes or flushes. Analise was there with her boyfriend, whose name I didn't catch but whose face I did – he looked like a Satanist. Or the subject of Satanic worship. There was Benjamin, the horrendously stoned, drunk and generally whacked-out sometime chauffeur/butler/lover with sad eyes like John Hurt who looked after the HH's mansion in Marbella, Spain. Benjamin was in his early fifties but sounded as though he was closer to seventy, with a rough voice swimming in phlegm and ire. Benjamin stooped and skulked. Benjamin depressed me.

Xaviera's living room was almost entirely decorated with photographs, pictures and other representations of herself in her premuu-muu days. Any spare wall space left was covered in erotic art of one tacky kind or another: phalli in clay, steel, copper or plastic; porcelain muffs; a bronzed pair of stiletto heels; and something that looked like a vacuum cleaner crossed with a uterus but may have actually just been a vacuum cleaner. As I stared up at a wall of two-dimensional representations of her, the actual, very three-dimensional Xaviera pulled me aside and whispered loudly how she was now in a lesbian relationship *and* screwing her nephew, a part-time gigolo, on the side, which I found charming and irrelevant. I watched her schoolmarmishly ordering some other guests around – 'Change the CD!', 'Turn it down!', 'Turn it up!', 'Bring me some food!' – and tried to see in this bossy, self-obsessed woman, some hint of the person who, a quarter of a century ago, was known far and wide as 'the greatest fuck in the world'. It was tough. Still, twenty-five years is a long time. What will I look like when I'm sixty? Old. Fat. Dead? And I sure won't have a reputation like hers behind me.

The thing that I was most disappointed about was that, apart from being made to watch – in enforced, respectful silence – a ridiculous 'art' video made by Andres Serrano of chicks refusing his commands to blow a horse, the evening contained no adult situations or nudity. Hardly even any swearing, except for me wandering around muttering, 'Shit this is boring. I want to see some breasts.' I vowed never to visit a (or the) prostitute again.

'I hate to think what that fiend did with my frittata,' Sally said as we left. 'Can you imagine her with a mouthful of egg and potato?'

'I can imagine her with a mouthful of c –'

'No!'

An almost-six-month review of life in Amsterdam for Sally and Sean. March 1st, 1999

Sally just checked our bank account back in Australia and found to her enormous distress that we have exactly $365 in it. No more, no less. Three hundred and sixty-five measly bucks. 'It's Europe on a dollar a day,' she said, but there was a dismal tone to the joke. '*Australian* dollars.' I thought about telling her that she looked pretty, whether maybe that would cheer her up, but decided against it. *I* may be that simple, but my wife isn't.

I wonder in what ways our move to Amsterdam could have been more difficult. Nobody has a job. Terry has nowhere to live; tomorrow he's coming here to stay in the spare room for a few days. Or weeks. Ray and Sonia have found a dingy, woody, Western-themed flat (which they call 'High Chapparal') near the Jordaan to rent in one month's time. For the next four weeks they're moving to the flat right next door to Hannus's, formerly occupied by a gay concert pianist. Money is thinning for everyone.

Sally and I have spent virtually all our dough setting ourselves up in this flat – from which we may shortly be evicted because we are not Dutch, not registered with the Woningdienst and therefore not deserving of living space (which, if I were a deserving, registered Dutchman, I would think completely fair enough. However, I am an anxious, displaced Australian, so I do not). I am trying to convince myself that something good will happen soon but in my heart of hearts (I have several) I believe that the good things in life are reserved for merchant bankers and A-list movie stars. Regular people, like Sally and I, are condemned to a life of uncertainty, struggle and doom. On the plus side, we do get to watch as much television as we like.

In order to see if he could help with her recent anxiety-induced insomnia, Sally was hypnotised by natural therapist Michael B. yesterday. She came home pretending to be a chicken every time I said the magic word, which, because it was 'the', caused a lot of squawking and arm-flapping on my wife's part. Of course, she was only kidding around. I hope it works, but since the condition is worsened by distress, I'm not confident. On the other hand, if she *wasn't* kidding around with that whole pretending-to-be-a-chicken deal, maybe she'll start laying eggs. That'd save us a little money.

It's not that either of us is unwilling to get a job in order to extricate ourselves from our penury, either. (Although that being said, I didn't notice that Peter Mayle doing a single minute's work in his Provence books.) We are not allowed to work because we don't have permits. And the Dutch are such a fearful, law-abiding bunch that even mentioning working illegally ('working black', they call it, but not in a racist way – I think) gets them all squirrelly.

I have the flu – or *a* flu, I'm not sure. Symptoms include general enfeeblement (especially physical and intellectual), hostility, sensitive skin and soul, headaches, nausea and an unusual affection for Greek folk music. (Joey Witteveen has the same thing, only he calls it 'a small pneumonia' and leans toward the Dutch pop of Marco Borsato rather than Mikis Theodorakis and his bouzouki.) Today is the first day of spring and it's raining like a bastard. Amsterdam greets the new season with rotten weather and the launch of a new television station, Fox, which is broadcasting shows like 'Jake and the Fat Man', right from the very first episode (the seven William Conrad fans scattered across Holland are rejoicing; the rest of us just have one question: why?). As I've already mentioned, TV here is crazy but at least there's thirty channels of madness to choose from. 'Murder She Wrote' is just called 'Jessica Fletcher', even though there are Dutch words for 'murder', 'she' and 'wrote'. 'NYPD Blue' is called 'New York Police', and the broadcaster, Nederland 1, has even gone to the trouble of re-touching the police ID badge that appears at the beginning of the show so it no longer says 'NYPD Blue' but 'New York Police'. It bothers me and I thought about calling and asking why, I really did, but what stopped me momentarily was this thought: *shouldn't you have more important things to worry about, Sean?* The word *No* rattled around my brain as I reached for the telephone.

Many days later, nothing was getting better. Sally's insomnia was in fact getting worse and making her even more unhappy. During a telephone checkup, hypnotherapist Michael B. had been telling Sally about some long-past group sex incident at Xaviera's. 'We'd just all lie in bed having fun, then some slave or another would arrive and begin servicing and it would start all over again,' he said. 'So how's your sleeping pattern?'

'Pretty fucked.'

'Well then we must have another fuck . . . er, session soon,' Michael said.

If that ain't the Freudian-est slip of all time.

By way of thanks for sharing our house with him, Terry bought us a CD of Dutch ambient music which he described as sounding 'like a small group of Tibetan monks chanting over a bird's nest next to an autobahn'. It was fun having him stay with us, the fact that he talks to himself while doing the washing-up with cold water notwithstanding. 'I think I might move to Paris,' he said dreamily, hauling his suitcase towards our front door. Not maliciously, I reminded him that he had neither work nor automatic residency status in France. 'I'm a New Zealander, Sean. We're welcome anywhere.' He then shook my hand and kissed Sally goodbye, off to be welcomed where and by whom, I was not sure.

That afternoon I received an alarming local bank statement: my personal total worth in the world was ƒ1131.49. This was very worrying and it looked even worse in euros – a paltry €513.49. Then again, absolutely nothing looks good in euros. It was a dangerous, upsetting sight, that pitiful figure staring up at me.

Soon after I made a call to the advertising agency I'd heard about at Xaviera's party. For many reasons – all of them very moral, none of them very financial – I had not planned on even trying to get back into advertising, so I also had to call my former art director/partner, Cambez Pitt, back in Melbourne and ask him to send me what passes for my folio. After working for almost seven years in the evil industry, the work I'd produced ranged from the appalling to the unremarkable (with a couple of *hmmm . . . that's interesting*s in between), so I expected to be humiliated soundly some time over the coming weeks.

Just as I recovered from my tussle with influenza, Sally and I were invited to a building-warming party one Saturday night. A building-warming is like a house-warming, only the person has bought the whole building – in this particular case, all three and a half storeys. As well as celebrating the purchase of a beautiful property on the enviably located and lengthily named Utrechtsedwarsstraat, just by the Carré Theatre, the party was to mark the buyer's thirtieth birthday. When I put these two elements together (thirty years old + being able to buy a very large building) I wasn't in much of a celebratory mood but did my best to pretend by getting quite drunk. Which wasn't hard, as I'd come to really appreciate the Dutch tradition whereby when you give a party, you supply all the booze. It's a good tradition and one that ensured that it was a long while before Sally and I threw a party in Amsterdam.

In keeping with the city's very international population I met an Irish lady horse trainer; a Scottish accountant who worked for Greenpeace; an epicene-featured Estonian guy (or gal) who told me repeatedly that Estonia is not in Eastern Europe, although where it actually is he (or she) declined to mention*; a young fellow called Dieter from Germany who told me that the two lines in the dollar symbol were binary and had something to do with our lives being controlled by financiers (I pointed out that Dutch currency used the € symbol rather than the dollar sign and he walked away, convinced I was some sort of fool); and, on a wooden bench in the kitchen, I encountered a pale-skinned, pale-haired guy called Christof who insisted that he was Ghanaian, that his parents were black and that he too, despite his almost translucent whiteness, was black (an hour later, he caved and admitted that he was Norwegian). And in the spirit of the very international evening, I drank alcohols from all nations – Polish vodka, Greek ouzo, Dutch beer, French wine and some viscous green stuff which may have been Estonian.

As well as making it my business to change the CD every time someone put on '1999', I also said 'Where's the ice?' a lot. At every party I'd been to in Amsterdam, they didn't have ice. They all had that goddamned Prince CD ready to go but none of them had ice.

'Where's the ice?' I asked.

The hostess informed me that she couldn't get any.

'In any normal country you can get ice,' I told her. 'Ice is not a difficult thing to get, y'know. It's just ice!'

She looked a little upset and I began to think that perhaps I wasn't completely recovered from the flu and that the hostility symptom I'd developed during its course was still very much in my system. But was it the flu or was it being in the Netherlands that was the cause of it? I hoped it was the former because, despite the hardships, I was beginning to really love my new land.

'Ah, don't worry about it,' I suddenly blurted to the hostess. 'It's only ice.'

---

*Just a few months earlier I wouldn't have really cared exactly where Estonia was (if it existed at all) but now that I was living in Europe, I felt a greater responsibility to be aware of its constituent elements. It's a bit like the Australian obligation to remember that Tasmania is part of Australia.

March 23rd, 1999

The Oscars were held last night. I did not win Best Picture. Apart from that I have just one comment: Gwyneth Paltrow as best actress – come *off* it!

Through a new friend, Erin – an Australian woman originally from Mount Isa, whom we know from going to her club, Vegas – Sally has an interview with a comedy theatre company called Boom Chicago. Erin, a very kind, funny and daringly dressed red-head, works part-time in the box office there. If Sally passes muster, she may too. For my own part, I have an appointment with the creative director of that advertising agency on Keizersgracht. But who am I kidding – my work is dreadful and I have a bad attitude. I ain't got a chance. I'm mainly going because I like seeing inside canal buildings and I might get a free cup of coffee.

It is somewhat saddening that our standards and expectations of employment have been lowered to the point where the smallest thing like Sally getting a job that's beneath her (or even a step backward) or me considering the possibility of re-selling my soul to Satan fills us with a sense of Roberto Begnini-esque joy. And this is Oscar week!

A couple of days later I went for my interview at the agency, 180. They were not called 180 because they were located at Keizersgracht 180. They were not located at Keizersgracht 180. They were called that because they were part of a trend in advertising to call your agency something very much other than the last names of the partners. Notables included Mother and St Lukes, both in London, Australie in Paris, and the truly wacky Strawberry Frog here in Amsterdam. Coming from a J. Walter Thompson, Young & Rubicam, Leonardi & Curtis type background, I was highly suspicious of this trend. I felt that it could come to no good.

To my horror and disappointment, and against all the odds, the creative director at 180, Larry Frey, was a very likable, extremely intelligent guy who did not keep me waiting in reception for half an hour before glancing at my work, throwing up and then dismissing me. He was thoughtful (asked me if I'd like a coffee), attentive (made the coffee) and constructive (suggested I might like sugar in my coffee). And kind of handsome, too: he reminded me of George Clooney crossed with Robert Forster. On top of that, he'd written and/or art-directed some of the most famous commercials of recent years, for clients like Nike, ESPN and Subaru, and worked with people like George Plimpton, Michael Jordan and Bill Gates. All of which made me want to work at 180, crazy name or not. But as I left I felt sure that my outdated folio of inferior work would ensure that that would not happen.

The sun was out that afternoon and so was practically everybody in Amsterdam, crowded into every available bit of liquor-licensed sunshine. Rembrandtplein was packed with the tourists who don't know any better; all the bars on Leidseplein had released their outdoor furniture, and the square was packed with al fresco tourists who knew a little better; Vertigo, Het Blauwe Theehuis and all the other cafés and bars in the Vondelpark were packed with locals and smarter tourists. Every canal-side table was crammed with eager drinkers. This was a weekday, a working day for those with jobs, so what, apart from dry-cleaning and beer-production, was keeping the Dutch economy afloat while all the locals were out drinking in the sun in the secret, non-tourist places? I'll tell you what – the fact that the economy is so buoyant and healthy that everybody in the entire country could afford to take a week off if they felt like it and there'd be no harm. Except for the air-traffic controllers at Schiphol, I guess. Then there'd be some harm.

Sally received word from Boom Chicago that they wanted her and that her first shift in the box office was scheduled for the following week. While pleased that she finally had some regular work, she was nonetheless unhappy about where her career as an editor was going; on the other hand, when she was seventeen she'd done work experience in the box office of the Church Community Theatre in Hawthorn, so she had the theatre in her blood.

Under the stewardship of its founder and cast member, a bright, witty guy named Andrew Moskos*, Boom Chicago had

---

*Andrew's father Charlie, Professor of Sociology at Northwestern University, was an advisor to Bill Clinton on military manpower issues and coined the term 'Don't ask, don't tell'. I met Charlie at a wedding about a year later and asked Moskos senior about his phrase. 'Don't ask, don't tell was a great compromise,' he said. 'But I know it worked because it pissed everybody off.'

been lampooning the Dutch and the Americans for more than five years, and the company was quite a success story, playing to packed houses just about every night. I was keen for Sally to remain in their employ because staff received a whopping discount on booze at the theatre's bar and I planned on spending a lot of time there basking in the scintillating company of actors and throwing back cheap drinks. One such actor, by way of introducing himself to Sally, said, 'Who's the new meat?' Theatre people – they're so *on*!

March 28th, 1999

I'm bushed from helping Ray and Sonia move for the fifth time in seven months this afternoon. I was specifically asked to come over and assist with Ray's prized television set, an enormous Sony job. There's something kind of depressing about moving a very impressive television which belongs to someone else. But I guess removal and delivery guys live with that particular anxiety their whole lives.

By way of celebrating our slowly and slightly changing fortunes, Sally and I went out for dinner last night with Joey Witteveen to an *eetcafe* called Blauwhoft on the outskirts of Prinseneiland. As the three of us were eating and chatting, two guys at a table behind us suddenly jumped up and ran out the door. I was convinced it was the old dine-and-dash, but the words quickly flying round the whole place were *fiets* (bicycle) and *dief* (thief) – and they weren't talking Italian cinema classics. The two dashing diners had glanced outside, seen their bikes being tampered with, and run outside just in time to see a girl taking off on one stolen bike and a second thief on his own (or 'his own') bike pedalling off with the other stolen bike in his hand, speedily and dextrously guiding it away like a wheeled calf. Shaking her head with disappointment as she observed the behaviour of her countrymen, a waitress called the cops. Joey and I went outside, ready to get the full story once the dashed diners returned – *if* they returned. (My head was full of schemes where you run off from a restaurant without paying by pretending that your bike's been stolen, so I wasn't even sure that they would come back.) They did – one on foot and one on his retrieved bicycle, the one that the male thief had nabbed but relinquished because it was slowing him down. The thieves had used industrial wire cutters to snap the locks. The gone bike – a thousand-guilder mountain bike – had been owned for less than two hours and the ex-owner looked absolutely devastated. I bought him a whisky (single malt; ƒ8.50) which he drank in a semi-grateful trance. The cops arrived and after hearing the whole story, particularly the part about how the mountain bike guy had all the insurance forms at home, *unsent*, suggested that he post the insurance forms and report the theft the next day. I liked that. As Sally later said, the Dutch live by the rules but they love a loophole.

While the whole thing was pretty horrible, I did like the way everybody rallied round – the waitress on the phone immediately; Joey telling the guy, '*Hou je borst vooruit en je kin omhoog!*' (Keep your chin up) every ten seconds (he knew how the victim felt – in his ten years living here Joey has had forty-two bikes stolen, although he's evened things out a little by stealing around ninety himself); me buying the guy a drink; the cops suggesting insurance fraud. There was a real sense of community. Lucky for Sally and I, our bikes are real pieces of second-hand junk. In fact I wouldn't be surprised to come home one day and find that our bikes are still there, but our locks are gone.

10.30 a.m. March 31st, 1999

A telephone call.

LARRY FREY, 180 creative director: Sean?

SEAN CONDON, almost penniless, unemployed: Yes.

LF: Sean, it's Larry Frey.

SC (nervous): Oh, hi Larry. How are you?

LF: I'm doin' okay. Listen Sean, I was impressed with your folio the other day . . . (SIGHS) Actually, no, I gotta be honest with you. I thought your advertising work was pretty awful.

SC (disappointed but not surprised): Oh . . . Well, I –

LF: But there was a lot of other stuff in there – your books and articles and so forth that I was impressed with. There's some inneresting stuff there.

SC (surprised): Really?

LF: Sure. Why not – you don't think it's inneresting?

SC: No, I think it's interesting. But it's interesting that *you* think it's interesting.

LF: Well, whatever. Anyway, we have a project, it's an inneresting project, and we'd really like you to work on it. Can you come in and meet with us?

SC: Of course, but I have to ask – are you absolutely *sure* you're talking to the right person? I'm the one who wrote the line: 'If you intendo to buy Nintendo come in here and spendo'.*

---

*Actual line actually written by me that appeared in an actual newspaper ad.

Bertie and Mrs X

Did you know that the English words *brandy, poppycock, bundle, drill, freight, landscape, coleslaw, snack, spook, cookie* and *yacht* are of Dutch origin? Now that you know, do you care? Before I came to live in the Netherlands, I neither knew nor cared. But now that I live here I both know *and* care: they're excellent words, every one, and English would be a much poorer language without them. Especially *bundle* and *poppycock* (although I realise certain readers will prefer *yacht*).

However, the fact that those words share a history is not really such a big mystery (even though nobody said it was) because Dutch and English belong to the same language group – the Low German branch of the West Germanic group of Indo-European languages. And despite how Dutch may sound to certain ears, Dutch and English are more closely related than Dutch and German. Nonetheless, Dutch and English only *look* the same; they don't sound the same. Other semi-interesting Dutch language discoveries I have made include the following:

- Hollandaise, although both a Dutch word and sauce, sounds and tastes better if somebody French is in charge.
- Dutch is almost identical to Flemish; however, a Belgian will deny this when pressed.
- Just about everybody in the Netherlands speaks better English than I speak Dutch. So when I attempt a conversation in Dutch, say at the *slagerij* (butcher) and do so with audible trepidation and an unavoidable foreign accent, the Dutch person with whom I am having the meat exchange will very often answer in English, which is both belittling and hypocritical because the next thing you know some local person is berating you for

having lived here for *drie jaren* (three years) and not *spreek* (speaking) fluent Nederlandse. *Klootzaks*! (Assholes!)

- The Dutch don't call the language they speak Dutch. Some call it Nederlandse and some call it Hollandse. But really one or the other would do perfectly well.
- The Germans call their language *Deutsch*. Nothing else, just *Deutsch*.
- The Dutch call Deutsch *Duits*.
- Many English terms which employ the word *Dutch* do so to express some form of negativity. Consider Dutch courage (for booze-based bravery), Dutch treat (where each diner pays their own way), a Dutch concert (meaning general pandemonium), a Dutch auction (where the bidding works from highest to lowest), speaking double Dutch (an impenetrable language) and Dutch comfort (cold comfort). Most of these rather toothless expressions are thought to have appeared in the seventeenth century, back when the Dutch were the feared commercial and military rivals of nations too lazy and stupid to think of methods other than etymological to avenge themselves.
- The following is about the origin of the word *Yankee* and will be of particular interest to American readers. Readers of other nationalities may wish to skip and search for something relevant to their particular country. (Note to readers from The Gambia – you are not represented. Except just then.)

Although the subject of fierce, yet pointless debate for several centuries (or perhaps only one), the Yankee theory most commonly accepted was put forward by H. L. Mencken, someone whom I believe to be both authoritative and amusing (although sadly, in no way Dutch. Or possibly very Dutch). Mencken maintained that the expression *Jan Kaas* (or *John Cheese*) was a derogatory term levelled at the Dutch by the Germans and the Flemish in the 1600s, a time when cheese was especially horrible. Later the English got in on the act by applying the term to Dutch pirates (how it must have hurt). Later still Dutch settlers in New York got their own back by using the term on English settlers in Connecticut (oh, the pain). Then, during the French and Indian War, the British general James Wolfe took to referring derisively to the native New Englanders in his army as Yankees. The word was then widely popularised during the Revolutionary War thanks to the song 'Yankee Doodle'. By the war's end the colonists had perversely adopted the term as their own, as was their right, since they won. Luckily another war – the American Civil one – came along and gave Southerners the opportunity to use Yankee as a pejorative to describe Northerners; the Southerners lost, however, and were made to apologise individually to everyone they had slighted. Finally a third war – the First World one – happened just in time for *all* Americans to be referred to as Yankees by the Limeys (English), who, once and for all, reclaimed naming rights of the term.

'We're a new agency and we need publicity,' Chris explained bluntly. Chris was a Connecticut Yankee who'd spent a lot of his working life at Wieden + Kennedy busting his hump on the Nike account. He was a little younger and more successful than me but I liked him anyway. 'That's basically your assignment.'

I was sitting in the boardroom with the four founders of 180. As evidence of my prodigious talent and creativity I had brought with me an unpublished short story and a scrap of paper with the word *wow* on it. I was scared and nervous, and completely confused about why I'd written *wow* on a scrap of paper and brought it with me.

'What we're looking for is something that eeehhh . . . that says something about who we are. What we umm . . . what we stand for,' added Alex, a genial and constantly snacking or smoking Scot who was deaf in one ear. (Talking to deaf [or partially deaf] people unnerves me because the whole time I'm with them, and even for around twenty minutes after, I act like every person I'm speaking to is deaf.) Like Chris, Alex had spent a lot of his time at Wieden + Kennedy working as a planner on Nike before leaving to run his own agency. 'What . . . eehhh . . . what . . . *do* we . . . actually . . . umm . . . stand for?' he asked of nobody in particular.

I quickly looked away. How the hell would *I* know? What does any ad agency stand for? Making tons of dough was pretty much it in my experience. How would this place be any different? Profit-sharing? Nudity? No back-stabbing and dark politics?

'Exactly what we stand for, apart from being a brand-new part of the advertising landscape and winning a huge piece of the adidas business, is somewhat negotiable.' This was Guy, an Englishman with reddish hair who was younger than me, but looked and dressed a lot older. Like Chris and Alex, Guy too had, until very recently, worked at W+K on Nike in account management. I was detecting a pattern. 'The anti-Wieden, perhaps,' he added.

What did that mean? I hoped that I wasn't getting myself into some sort of Mafia-style advertising war. Wieden's principal client was Nike, the world's number one sportswear company, while 180's only client was adidas, the world's number two sportswear company.

'See what you can come up with, Sean. We'd like you to start after Easter. We're open to pretty much anything, so long as it's good,' Larry advised me. He too had spent a long time at Wieden, but most recently in Tokyo rather than the Amsterdam office which was less than a kilometre away, on the same side of the same canal. 'But try to go for great. Wanna cookie?'

I declined the biscuit Larry offered while the other three partners all enthusiastically agreed that whatever I did had to be good, but preferably great. Speaking as though everyone in the room was deaf, I loudly and confidently assured them that I would come up with something GOOD OR PERHAPS *REALLY* GOOD, POSSIBLY EVEN GREAT! I liked each of these guys – they seemed friendly, honest and smart – and I wanted to please them, but the truth was I wasn't very confident at all. Exactly how would I promote an agency with such a ridiculous name?

And as a result of those few reckless words, I became Michael Corleone in *The Godfather III*. 'Just when I thought I was out, they pull me back in.' It was not an inappropriate feeling: advertising really is like the mob – once you're in, baby, you're in for life.

One morning soon after that meeting, Sally and I took a long bike ride because it was sunny and because I thought I might find ad inspiration whilst pedalling. After riding around the Oosterdok we ended up at the top of the newMetropolis science museum, a huge building designed by either Ennio Morricone or Renzo Piano, which looks like the sea green prow of a ship looming over the Amstel River. At the top we turned for an easterly view of the city, the highest point either of us had reached since we arrived. I have to say that it wasn't too impressive; from up there, Amsterdam just looked like any old city with a low, jagged skyline; from up there you'd never know how beautiful it was down on the ground. Not that that should stop anyone else from visiting – in fact the museum needs all the visitors it can get as it is in imminent danger of closure due to being highly unpopular. On the other hand, if you visit the newMetropolis in search of ideas to promote an advertising agency, you will probably be disappointed.

April had been unusually hot and so, because we're Australian whether we like it or not, Sally and I bought a barbecue from a chain store called the Kijkshop. The Kijkshop is so named because everything is on display in glass cases so you can only *kijk* (look) at it. Once you've had a good *kijk* round and decided on something, you have to find a sales clerk, point at the product through the glass, go to the cash register, pay for it, get issued a ticket for it, then go to another window where you hand over the ticket and they give you the item. Somehow this needlessly attenuated retail process allows for lower prices at the Kijkshop. And you don't get much cheaper than a *f*40 barbecue – it was a real piece of crap.

From our back balcony we could see about twenty other back balconies and I knew there wasn't a barbecue on a single one of them, so I made sure to ask the young fellow at the Kijkshop whether it was actually legal to barbecue on your apartment balcony. 'It's legal. Just don't do it inside. Your house will stink,' he told us, somewhat obviously. Then he asked if we were English or American. I told him that we were somewhere in between, that we were Australian.

'Oh!' he exclaimed, apparently happily. 'Crocodile Dundee, yeah? Harrison Ford!'

'Yes, that's right.' The kid was wrong, of course – *very wrong* – but I much prefer Harrison Ford to Paul Hogan. The thing is, even though we're from Australia, Sally and I never had a barbecue back home. We *went* to plenty of barbecues, but we'd never actually owned one. Living in the Netherlands seemed to be making us more and more Australian. As I assembled the thing in the sun out on the balcony, working up a light sweat, Sally kept calling me Dad and offering me beer.

The next morning Sally and I had an interview with the Foreign Police, another element of the lengthy process of attempting to become official Dutch residents. This required a 7.45 a.m. wake-up followed by a long bike ride to Amstel Station through the pouring rain, which very nearly put us off the idea completely. (Quarter to eight for us was like regular people getting up for work at 3.30 a.m.) But I was glad it didn't because the subsequent passport sticker explaining that we were now in the Dutch system made me feel very European.*

It was tiresome (there were about two hundred forms to be completed), but not particularly difficult for Sally and I to attempt residency. Disappointingly, the fact that her father was born and raised here was 'of no consequence', our interviewer Victor told us firmly. This was because by the time Sally was born, her father Josephus had been fully naturalised and become known as 'Joe'. Australia's petty, nationalistic immigration laws of the early 1960s, I curse you!

We hadn't really considered the ramifications of being refused beyond the dismal idea of having to pack up and go home in a hurry. However, the idea was introduced to us in dramatic fashion as we sat sleepily in the waiting room and saw an African woman leaving an interview office in tears, her boyfriend placing a comforting arm across her shoulders, and a sheepish fellow clutching a briefcase trailing behind them whom, judging by the palely defeated look on his face, we took to be the woman's payment-on-success-based lawyer. At this pitiable sight vague feelings of horror descended upon us. What if we *were* refused resident status? Would we stay and live secretly like Keith? Or would we merely accept the decision and return home just in time for the Australian winter? Or should I start weeping in the interview, hoping to reverse the judgement? Or should we angrily point out to the public servant who held our destinies in his paper-shuffling hands that

---

*Especially when I later travelled to the United Kingdom where I was made to feel continentally European and quite unwelcome because of it.

this damp, flat, grey place wasn't exactly the Bahamas and he should perhaps even feel a little flattered that we were actually bothering to try and make our presence here legal? If I was a gambling man, I'd probably have put my money on the weeping option. But thank God I didn't have to: after a ten-minute interview during which he ascertained that we were not criminals or revolutionaries, Victor told us that he would recommend that we be given official residency status. The decision would come through in a few weeks. Meanwhile I had to start working semi-legally at 180.

I am always nervous starting a job, and while people who have worked with me will doubtless find this hard to believe, I am, in those initial moments at a new office (or building site, scientific laboratory or seat of higher learning), very quiet and shy. On my first quiet and shy day in the office at 180, I was given a desk right next to Larry (who greeted me thusly: 'Hey Sean, I'm goin' out for some crack. You want me to bring you back some?'*) and a blue iMac which crashed on me seven times, either due to its being a Macintosh or its blueness. I was near a window and could see Keizersgracht from where I sat. I felt so lucky and privileged and happy that I was almost sick when I thought about how much my fortunes had changed.

I met some very nice people there, from all parts of the world, although I was the only Australian. It was difficult keeping track of everyone's names, especially with the Dutch employees. Telling the difference between all the Romkes and Femkes and Schamkes and Marijskas and Hiskas and Anikas and Innekes and Ingeborgs and Ingemars was made doubly difficult because of the fact that, due to some peculiarity of the Dutch education system, the students who learn English (and that's almost all of them) come away sounding as though they were born and bred in either Hackney or Los Angeles, such is the strength of their English or American accent. ''Allo. Pleased to meetcha. Orright?' a pretty woman named Rosmarijn might say, looking me up and down, clearly disappointed that I was not the Australian surfer cultural

*He was kidding.

archetype she's been led to believe so many of my countrymen are (and, in fact, are). 'Hey dude, how's it hangin'?' a handsome young Boudewijn would say, pumping my hand, clearly disappointed that I was not a pretty woman.

The aspect of being in the office that I was most uncomfortable and uncertain about was the actual job – I still hadn't the faintest idea of how to go about drumming up publicity for an international start-up in Amsterdam with only one client. Larry suggested I work with Hendrik, the in-house director, fresh out of film school. Working with him, however, meant that I would have to overcome my natural and intense dislike for the film-school graduate, a type of person I had long wanted to be, but which, since it never came to pass, I usually cannot stand. Hendrik was a sharp-faced, squirrelly young fellow with a doleful, paranoid manner, and a voice like Peter Lorre. He was immature, sloppy, defensive and arrogant; in many ways Hendrik reminded me of me – or the me I might have been had I not been refused entry to film school five times in five years.

'Hi Hendrik. I'm really looking forward to working with you on this thing,' I said, not meaning a word of it.

'Yeah, me too,' he replied in exactly the same tone.

For the next few weeks we gingerly circled around one another like two big cats (or small, cowardly dogs), snarling but unwilling to pounce.

It was the day before the day before Queen's Day and all over the country the subjects of the House of Orange were getting 'orange fever'. Cafés, restaurants and bars were festooned with orange crepe paper, orange-framed pictures of Queen Beatrix and flashing orange lights. Multi-Vlaai, the Limburg-based cake manufacturers, had proclaimed this 'Oranje Week' and were selling special orange *vlaais* with apricot, carrot, peach and scallop toppings. Billboards featuring women wearing orange underwear were everywhere. Sales of orange juice soared. Oranjeboom beer was *the* alcohol of the moment. Orangina was liquid gold. My favourite knock-knock joke enjoyed a new lease of life. (*Knock Knock. Who's there? Orange. Orange who? Orange you glad you're in Amsterdam and it's nearly Queen's Day?*)

The main reason for all this was that orange is the national colour of the Netherlands, and that's fine by me – it's a nice colour. Not very serious or threatening, and fashion-wise it doesn't really go with anything but itself, but a very pleasant colour it is all the same. The secondary reason was that Beatrix is the Queen of the Netherlands and widespread orangeness is the way her birthday is celebrated. Another inescapable element of the lead up to Queen's Day were the chalk marks proclaiming *Bezet!* (busy or taken) covering every bit of sidewalk. Everywhere you went there were big squares from building front to curbside with something like '*Let op!! Anapol and Jan komen!!*' written on them. The more enthusiastically territorial *bezeters* added a skull and crossbones to their squares. The lazier just wrote 'B'. But beware interlopers of either space, because this is how people reserve places for their stalls. They have stalls because, apart from wearing, drinking, eating and thinking orange, the Dutch celebrate Queen's Day by selling stuff. The whole city turns into a giant flea market. Why a city which already has flea markets all over the place wants to become one giant one is almost beyond my simple powers of understanding, but my guess would be that it has something to do with the way the people of this country like to celebrate just about every other day of the year – by making some dough.

I was a little hung over on Queen's *Dag* and my condition was not at all helped by the fact that the colour orange was, as I've mentioned, everywhere, including on my actual self in the form of a very garish (but beautifully tailored) tangerine shirt. Add to this oompah bands strutting up and down the street bashing big bass drums and honking big brass *neder*phones, and you have a hangover cure that is swift and brutally effective.

In accordance with tradition, every bit of sidewalk was taken up by some sort of stall selling everything from shirts to Shinola to shoelaces. ('For all your shoelace needs,' I advised the two youngsters to put on a sign, since I was once again becoming an adman. 'C'mon, that's gold!!' They ignored me.) Everywhere Sally and I turned there were groups of kid choirs screaming out the national anthem, old people trying to shift the contents of their attics, bars and cafés with karaoke machines and beer taps set up out front, and above it all a very strong sense of conviviality that sometimes seemed to approach a sheer mass joy that was impossible not to be swept up in. The first time round, anyway.

A few days later we left for the south of France. I had never been there before and was very excited – after all, that was why we came to Europe. Because of its proximity to Europe.

When we returned, Sally and I were presented with a multitude of small horrors – the most pernicious and alarming being that a Woningdienst (housing authority) representative was coming around in a few weeks' time to 'inspect' the flat, whatever the hell that meant. Perhaps it was to ensure that we'd decorated it in an appropriately Dutch manner which would necessitate Sally and I rushing out and buying large quantities of chintz and moquette as well as dark, heavy wooden furniture and far too many indoor plants. We were quite worried as we'd virtually built our place from the ground up and finding another joint like it would be next to impossible. Or next to Venlo.

All this had come about as a result of having gone 'legit' and registered as temporary Dutch residents, giving the authorities the opportunity to pester the hell out of us with their beloved rules, regulations, laws, bylaws, recommendations, insistences etc. With her approval, we decided to embark on the deception that our landlady, Mrs X, still lived in the apartment because her relationship with her husband, Bertie X, had become very rocky. This involved getting a new nameplate made and stuck on the door, setting up the spare room to look as though Mrs X slept in there, putting photos of Mrs X on the walls, posting Post-it Notes saying 'Hi Mrs X!' all over the place, setting the dinner table for three and casually scattering mail addressed to her everywhere. Although cunning, I was sure this plan would fail and we'd, once again, be on the streets.

The next week Joey took me to a kind of boat graveyard out on the Ij River to work on his seven-metre sloop, an ugly piece of steel and rubber that could hold about six people if everybody stood up and didn't try to raise their drinks all at once. He was putting in a floor and, apparently, a few nights previously at Fockink, I'd eagerly agreed to help. It was a grey, overcast Monday, a public holiday, and there was a light drizzle, perhaps the same light drizzle that seemed to have been falling endlessly for weeks. We were working right on the Amsterdam–Rhine canal, a wide waterway that connects Amsterdam with Utrecht and which was consequently heavy with water traffic – enormous boats lumbering up and down the seaway hauling oil, coal, sand and corn. For some reason, every time a ship slowly floated by I found myself almost unbearably sad.

I'm not much good with my hands and I hate rust, the way it flakes and stains, and I'm not that keen on water and floating, so overall I wasn't much help. The Dutch male, however, loves being a handyman, both as an expression of his masculinity and as a way to save money on boat repairs. I asked Joey why his people were so crazy about nauticality.

'Because our history is on the water, I suppose,' he said. 'And we have all these canals around the city, maybe you've seen them?' He's quite sarcastic, old Joey. Then, somehow making it sound sarcastic, he asked me to please pass him a hammer.

Advice from Joey regarding the Woningdienst situation included, 'You are in great trouble. You are finished, forget it. I have been kicked out of a place with my kneecaps threatened. Everybody I know has been kicked out of a place.' He was smiling the whole time, enjoying my torment and horror. He does have a pretty nice smile though.

'But where do they kick you out *to*?'

He said two words which chilled me to the core. 'The suburbs.' Then he started laughing.

'Do you have any friends in the Woningdienst who might be able to help us?' I asked.

Joey howled with laughter. '*Nobody* has friends in the Woningdienst,' he said, his blue eyes filled with tears. 'And the Woningdienst *have* no friends!'

I became sure that the Woningdienst were the same mob that fingered Anne Frank.

It was a windy day and nearby a long stand of tall birch trees was bending like a chorus line warming up. There was no one else around, just concrete and boat husks and hulls, lumps of rusted engines and tractors and welding equipment, drills and cables, and far away I could hear the buzzing of an electric saw carried over by the wind which had changed direction and was now urging the trees to bend the other way. It struck me that I knew this sort of weather; it was something I'd seen somewhere but not actually experienced until that very moment.

Around five o'clock, Joey thanked me for handing him that hammer a few hours earlier and we headed back to his car as light fell away. I looked up at the low, dark clouds rolling toward us like crushing terrors and realised where I'd seen them before. It was in a painting from the late 1650s by Jacob van Ruisdael called *Dunes in Stormy Weather* and the sky was precisely as it appears in that painting: heavy, dark, portentous. My connection with the Dutch landscape of 350 years ago temporarily overwhelmed me and I began to walk a little faster toward Joey's Saab, eager to get back home.

NEWS ITEM, MAY 16TH, 1999: An escapee from a psychiatric clinic in Utrecht has lacerated a painting by Picasso valued at between US\$5 and 7.5 million. The 1956 oil, *Naked Woman in Front of a Garden*, housed in Amsterdam's Stedelijk Museum, had a large hole cut out of it by the 41-year-old man, who used a knife. The man has been under the supervision of the clinic since 1978, when he tried to hijack a KLM Royal Dutch Airlines jet from Amsterdam to Madrid using a toy gun. He is also suspected of throwing a bottle of acid at Rembrandt's *The Night Watch* at the Rijksmuseum in 1990.

One day late in May it suddenly occurred to me that there weren't as many Dutch doors in Amsterdam as I thought there would be. I think I'd only seen about six. 'Is this a good thing or a bad thing?' I wondered. 'Is it even a thing?'

It also occurred to me that after almost two months, Hendrik and I were still coming up with close to what I call nothing on the 180 promotional front. His prickliness and my oversensitivity when it came to criticism of my ideas ensured that this was a far from fecund partnership. Every time I walked into the building, I felt sick. I was sure I'd be discovered and fired; it would be the

unceremonious humiliation I deserved. 'Advertising,' I used to
cry every time I arrived at 180. 'Why are you so shallow and yet
so very difficult?'

The house deception reached crisis point. Mrs X had called the
Woningdienst inspector a couple of times and attempted to dissuade
him from coming to the flat, but he would not be put off and, on June
1st, he told her that he would be there at noon the next day. Mrs X
agreed to show up half an hour earlier and we planned to go over the
cover story once more: that she was having marital problems with
Bertie, her very quiet, nice, innocuous, likable, harmless, small, nonviolent husband, and, as a result, was forced to spend several nights
a week at the apartment. I suggested that we never mention that he
was called Bertie as nobody would believe that anybody so-named
could be anything other than cuddly. Meanwhile, Sally and I had
already been down to the used-furniture store and staggered home
with a second-hand single wooden bed and mattress to dress the
room more authentically as a place where somebody would sleep.
We also put a wardrobe in there, then took out my computer and
other dead giveaways such as the numerous pictures of Sally and
myself, and the sign that said 'Mrs X does not live here'. We also
removed our nameplate from the front entrance downstairs and
replaced it with one that says 'Mrs. X lives here'. We placed a third
toothbrush in the glass in the bathroom and watched *Green Card*
fourteen times for extra hints, ensuring that we knew only too well
what brand of face cream Mrs X favoured. How could it fail?

It could fail in a number of ways: Mrs X cracking under
Woningdienst pressure and tearfully blabbing; Mr Condon doing
same; the inspector asking some trick question such as 'What did
you have for dinner last night?' and Mrs X saying 'fish fingers' at
precisely the same moment I blurt out 'a lovely beef Wellington!'
Another dismal scenario that sprang to mind was the inspector
taking a quick look round the quite obviously phoney bedroom
and saying, 'Oh come off it, how dumb do you think I am? You've
got two weeks, then you're out.'

10 a.m. June 2nd, 1999

It's D-day. The inspector is due in two hours. Sally has a shift at
Boom Chicago, leaving me and Mrs X to be interrogated by the

man on our own. I imagine him looking like an Eastern European Cold War spy – a stocky gentleman in a heavy camel's hair coat and a homburg. He has a grim, tight-lipped, officious manner as he takes note of odd things and writes them down on a pad with a pencil he occasionally licks with the end of his sharp, darting tongue. After half an hour of ice-cold questioning, during which he nods slowly, we think we've successfully duped Inspector Von Liebensraum and offer him a glass of schnapps. He takes it and drinks it in a single gulp, goes to leave and just as he's out the door, he turns, narrows his eyes to all-seeing slits and says, 'Oh, zere is just vuhn more zhing . . .' And the game's up.

But vhat is the vuhn more zhing he might want to know? That tiny, critical fact of cohabitational domestic verisimilitude which has eluded us?

The inspector turns out to be a tubby, dough-faced man who chews gum loudly and introduces himself simply as 'Abels', which I presume is his surname. He wears cargo pants and a 'sporty' striped yachting shirt and speaks very broken English. After a guttural and, to my ears at least, hostile chat with Mrs X about who exactly lives here, who the hell these other *mensen* (people, meaning me and Sally) were and what we had for dinner last night (Mrs X and I had earlier agreed on *stampot*), Abels asks for our passports and copies down the details, pausing to suspiciously look from my passport photo and up at me several times, as though I have somehow transmogrified into Errol Flynn or someone since the picture was taken. Satisfied that me and the fool in the passport are indeed the same person, he then asks where Sally works. And here things become a little complicated . . . Mrs X proffers that Sally works in an advertising agency at the very same time as I say that she works for a magazine (which Mrs X does not know has evaporated, as we felt it would be prudent not to tell her). But where Mrs X got the idea that Sally was some sort of huckster, I don't know. For a moment the three of us sit there giving each other confused looks, creating a delicate, almost precoital air of expectation and faint hostility, until, brilliantly, I ejaculate, 'They have advertisements *in* the magazine, you see.' Abels makes some notes and asks for the address of the magazine's office. I am almost sick. 'Well, actually, I don't know,' I say, and it is then that I realise Master Criminal is never going to be an employment option for me: the slightest bit of pressure, one unprepared-for question, and I fall apart, singing like some pathetic stoolie offered a five-spot and a cigarette. This all comes as a bit of a surprise to me as I quite like lying and used to think myself pretty good at it, but if I can't stand up to a pudgy public servant armed with a pad and pen, how much hope would I have in a holding cell with a bunch of cops and some phone books? None, that's how much.

I hand over Sally's old work diary (which has the former address of the magazine in it) and babble some lame story about how the office is moving into a space occupied by a theatre company so that might explain any confusion if he ever happens to call the place and ask for her. The inspector nods slowly and I mentally wave goodbye to our flat.

Abels takes out a folding ruler and begins measuring the hell out of the apartment – every doorway and window frame, all the rooms and various features of the hallway such as the hall and its way – and writing down the measurements for reasons that I cannot fathom. This completed, he asks a few more questions in Dutch to Mrs X, concluding with, 'Wat is ere de telefoon nummer?' Thank God my broken Dutch picks this up because Mrs X, not living here, of course has no idea what the new phone number is.

'*Fiersisdreenegeneendreeacht!*' I shoot out. Abels looks at me, rather startled. 'It's the only Dutch I know and I really like saying it,' I explain. He nods and asks me to repeat it, in English.

Then he rises to leave, telling us that the Woningdienst will make up its mind about the flat and its occupants in due course. Mrs X goes to 'her' room to lie on 'her' bed and enjoy 'her' posters, while I accompany Abels to the front door, practically pushing him out and down the stairs. After he's put on his coat, he stops, turns and looks me dead in the eye. 'Dere's just vuhn udder ding I need . . .' I feel faint and nauseous. 'Have you a . . .' It is just like how they caught that guy at the end of *The Great Escape*. I am sure he is about to ask for my papers or my ration book or something. '. . . *glasje vater*? I'm very dirsty.'

After I quench Abels' evil thirst, I go downstairs and take Mrs X's nameplate off the wall and reattach ours.

That night an emotionally exhausted Mrs X rang to say that she'd discussed the situation with her nonabusive, nonviolent (but apparently quite decisive) husband, Bertie X, and decided she could no longer continue with the ruse, and that if Abels or one of his henchmen contacted her, she'd fess up. We were on our own. I went downstairs and took our nameplate off the wall, leaving the space blank.

The song 'New York, New York' is wrong – the truth is if you can make it in Amsterdam, you can make it anywhere. (Interestingly though, New York used to be called New Amsterdam. I guess they changed the name when all the song-writers were born.)

'I feel so depressed,' I told Sally as I felt an unhappily familiar throbbing behind my right eye. 'This moving to another country thing is much harder than I thought it would be.'

'You're probably just hungry, baby,' she said. 'Have something to eat.'

I jammed the heel of my hand into my right eyesocket. 'This would never happen to proper people.'

'What are proper people?'

'You know, people with the security of a large corporation behind them. Dual-income husband and wife who are goal-oriented team players who sell like hell and have watertight employment contracts and plenty of money in the bank because they're too damned tight to spend any. US dollars, probably. Their company – Sony or Arthur Andersen or whatever – pays for their large house on Prinsengracht and they fly business class everywhere. They drink infrequently and sensibly because she's thinking about having their first child – which they're gonna name after her mother who passed away last year – and he works long hours, including most weekends. They're super-expats.'

'Yuk. They sound fiendishly dull. I bet she's a good golfer, too.'

'She is, and they are. But they have very stable lives. Dullness is the price you pay for stability.'

Sally made a face. 'And she dresses absolutely terribly – I can just see it. A wardrobe full of Liz Claiborne. The square!'

'Actually, I quite like her taste in clothing. He, on the other hand . . .'

My annual six to eight week period of debilitating, twice-daily cluster headaches was upon me, and they were the worst in the twelve years I'd been getting them. These powerful headaches were awful – like the slow progress of a cockroach burrowing into my brain – but at the same time I could never escape the feeling that I somehow deserved them, that they were due punishment for all the bad things I'd said and thought and done in my life. Even though CAT scans I'd had long ago revealed no tumours, I still often wondered whether what was wrong with me might be something fatal. And, were it not for Sally, I really wouldn't have been all that upset if it was. I wouldn't be thrilled of course, but compared to a couple of years ago, when I was even more too young to die, I seemed now to be reacting with relative equanimity to thoughts of my possible demise. Did this mean I'd grown up? That my calm, agony-induced meditations on mortality had placed me on a different spiritual plane than the one I'd existed on before? I very much doubted it.

I began dreaming of air accidents: in-flight fire leading to a fatal ditch into a swamp; microburst-induced wind shear causing a stall on takeoff; failure to set wing panels that would help slow down a landing on a slick runway; complete loss of hydraulics due to rear bulkhead pressure failure; midair collision; uncommanded deployment of thrust-reverser; clear ice conditions during holding pattern; failure of airspeed indicators; undetermined mechanical fault.

Inspired by these dreams, I took my potentially fatal bike to a repair guy – my light gyro having come loose a few days earlier and jamming itself in my front wheel, causing me to fly over the handlebars and lose two spokes and almost a life. The guy didn't speak too much English and I haltingly explained my problem in bicycle-based Dutch. He spun the wheel, peered at it through one half-closed eye and seemed to indicate that it'd be fine. I asked what he could do about the busted gyro. He reached down with a rough hand and just pulled it off, handing it over smiling. While I was certain that I was now riding the streets on a deathtrap, at least the consultancy hadn't cost me a cent. I needed my bike in good working order because I was spending a lot of time riding to doctors' offices.

Since three visits to three different 'normal' doctors who prac-tised 'western' medicine in typically doctorial fashion (i.e. com-pletely disinterestedly) had proved useless (inasmuch as they did not know what was causing the headaches and did not prescribe morphine or euthanasia for the pain), I decided to try acupuncture. Even if it didn't cure the problem, the treatment would prove once and for all whether or not I was inflatable and I did *not* want to be seen walking the streets with needles poking out of my face. I planned to ride the back streets, swiftly and unnoticed.

My acupuncturist was a very small woman named Dr Roberta de Haas and her 'practice' was located in a room in her third floor apartment, a ten-minute cycle from our place. A tinny radio I couldn't see was squeaking out that Prince song as I explained what was wrong with me (or part thereof, anyway). It was a strange feeling sitting on a chair a few moments later with four-teen tiny needles poking out of me, looking like the cover of a Clive Barker novel and chatting with a diminutive doc about this and that – local restaurants here in the east, the free broadcast that evening in the Oosterpark of Dick Wagner's Ring Cycle, whether she'd mind switching the radio off – while every twenty minutes or so she gave the needle a bit of stimulation by urgently twiddling the end of it. All of this with my pants off. It was a situation I would normally find extremely disconcerting and uncomfortable – and did. I wasn't sure if the acupuncture would actually do any-thing about the headaches – I doubted it since nothing over the previous twelve years had worked – but ever the cheerful optimist, I remained hopeful. And full of small holes. When it was time for me to go, Dr de Haas told me, as I feared she would, to leave five small needles (two in each ear, one under my lower lip) in for the following ten days.

'Can I take them out when I'm in public?' I asked.

'Keep your dignity or lose the headaches – it's your choice,' she said.

'Okay. D'you know where I might buy a mask that looks like my own face?'

That night Sally and I checked out the concert in the park, a large-screen broadcast of a performance by the Nederlandse Opera

Company of the first part of *Der Ring des Nibelungen*. Because I was sitting way up in the back row and covering half my face I found it difficult to know what the hell was going on – the singing was in German and the surtitles were in Dutch – and to me the whole thing sounded like a very loud argument about what to have for dinner in the underworld. The highlight was a drunken madman in the audience who kept shouting out 'Naaaazzziiiis!' during lulls in the singing, and making a throat-cutting motion with his finger across his neck. Exactly what his point was, I'm not sure, but he was no opera-lover, that's for damn sure.

It was six months since Christmas and I decided that it was time to remove our extremely dead Christmas tree from the balcony, drag it through the bedroom and down three flights of stairs then dump the dried-up brown bastard out on the street. Waiting half a year to get rid of the festive tree was a very bad idea. I wanted to just throw it over the edge of the balcony into the weird between-building wasteland down below but feared that a child might suddenly rush into the bomb line and I'd be charged with manslaughter. (And with my luck it'd probably be a Jewish or Muslim kid, so on top of being charged with manslaughter, because a Christmas tree was my 'weapon', I'd be stitched up for religious persecution as well.) Anyway, the entire building was coated in several billion dried-up pine needles after I'd moved the thing to the outside world and it took me two hours to get rid of them all with a combination of sweeping, dust-panning, vacuuming and individual picking up. I couldn't help feeling very sad that my life had come to the point that it had at that moment.

Or I could embrace the fact that my life was what it was at that moment. I was young (well, under thirty-five) and alive in Europe's most beautiful city on a delightful, warm day and even though I had a headache coming on and knew that I'd be in agony for the next two hours or so I could at least try to forget how physically pathetic and intellectually enfeebled I was by being very domestic, very Dutch. I defrosted the fridge, swept the stairs, scrubbed bird shit off the balcony, beat the crap out of some rugs, vacuumed the floors then mopped them, washed the toothbrush-holding glass in the bathroom and cleaned my fine-tooth comb with a finer-tooth comb. It was difficult, draining work (especially because I had to keep rushing into the bedroom to faint for short periods) but it did get things marvellously clean.

'What's wrong with the flat?' Sally asked when she got home from a Boom shift.

'I cleaned it.'

'Oh you did *not*.'

'I did.'

'Really?'

'Yes . . . I think I did it wrong, though. Sorry.'

I believed that I had finally cracked the 180 promotional idea but did not want to actually say what it was, or run it by Hendrik because I couldn't help suspecting that I might have been very wrong and get very embarrassed. Nevertheless I wrote it up and planned to present it (along with a few backups) as soon as I could. Then be chased out of the building. My ten acupuncture days had passed by then so I gratefully removed the needles that had been inserted into me and called Dr de Haas to ask if she wanted them back. She told me that she did not.

'What should I do with them?'

'Don't you know how to dispose of needles!?' she asked a little scornfully.

Well, as a matter of fact . . .

Following a successful meeting with Larry and Chris at 180, in which I presented various ideas for a promotional film – including one that was simply two guys driving across America talking a whole load of crap, an idea which appealed to me greatly – it appeared that I might be going to San Francisco to interview (or attempt to interview) Francis Ford Coppola, director of, among other things, *Finian's Rainbow* and the short film *Life Without Zoe*. Why? All because of the agency's wacky name, that's why. Oh, the irony!

The agency was named after an obscure quote of Mr Coppola's and one of my ideas was to see if we could get him to comment on this fact. But, since we probably wouldn't be able to – him being a Hollywood type and all – I thought it would be interesting to make a brief documentary about my attempts to extract such a comment from him. It couldn't fail! Either that or it could fail very dismally. Larry and Chris thought it was a fine idea and suggested that Hendrik and I get to work on it right away and try to produce something good BUT PREFERABLY GREAT. I tried not to get too excited about going overseas to chase a famous film director, but already I felt fantastically giddy. 'San Francisco here I come!' I thought to myself. Then added, 'Possibly.'

My excitement about the Coppola film (mine, not any of his) was quickly tempered by a phone call from Sally that afternoon. We'd received a letter from the Woningdienst which, she said, seemed to be telling us that the jig was up and that we had to get out. Clearly, nobody had bought the old spare single bed and pretty poster of a cartoon bear as a believable bedroom. I put down the phone and laid my head on my desk, swiftly taking myself through the five Kübler-Ross stages of grief – denial, anger, bargaining, depression, acceptance – then straight back to stage two.

But the day's emotional roller-coaster (or perhaps Dodgem car) ride was not over. A few hours later Sally took the letter to work and had it *properly* translated by a Dutch colleague who told her that what it in fact said was that, barring any objection from the owner, the Queen or the mayor, we were now actually the apartment's official and legal head renters. We had circumvented a five-year waiting list and slipped through the bureaucratic net because they'd decided that it would be more trouble than it was worth to get rid of us, especially since we were reliable rent-payers and quite nice people to boot. We were overjoyed – our lovely, expansive, suddenly much cheaper sunlit apartment with a balcony and trees was finally truly ours.

That evening, as a symbolic first step, we put our nameplate back up out the front. 'We're here,' we were telling our fellow tenants. 'We belong.' But just a week later we would learn that, while symbolically it was a fine thing to do, in reality the nameplate gambit was somewhat premature.

Six days of Coppola-related hassles passed. Recording everything we did on either video or audio tape, I tried to set up an interview with him through his New York City PR office ('Impossible!'). I called Zoetrope, his production office in San

Francisco, in the hope that he would answer the phone (he did not). I tried to reach his film director son Roman (I failed) and his film director daughter Sofia (I failed). I couriered a crate of excellent French wine and some very fine Cuban cigars to his home at his vineyard in the Napa Valley with a note imploring him to meet with me. He did not respond.

On the seventh day, a day on which I usually prefer to rest, I was torn out of bed by the telephone (not literally, but close. *Very* close). It was the apartment's *makelaar* (real estate agent) telling me that we had two weeks to get out of the flat. That this was absolutely final, complete and non-negotiable. That the owner had decided that he expressly did *not* give his approval for our living there which therefore constituted our being there illegally so we'd better hoof it quick smart or have our furniture broken and our kneecaps thrown out on the street.

'Well, can we talk to the owner and seek his permission to live here?' I asked Johnny Real Estate.

'No,' he said.

'Why not?' I said.

'It is not possible.'

'Why is it not possible?'

'Because you are there illegally.'

'We have a letter from the Woningdienst telling us that we do have a right to be here.'

'Only with the permission of the owner.'

'So can we talk to the owner and get his permission?'

'I am the contact between the leasee and the owner. And he say that he don't want you there.'

'When did he say this?'

'This week.'

'When?'

'This week.'

'*When* this week!?' I shouted.

'Ahhh . . .' A long pause ensued in which I could hear his tiny little cogs turning. 'Aaaahhh . . . yesterday.'

'I don't believe you,' I said boldly. There was more silence. 'Do you understand? I *do not* believe that you've spoken to the owner.'

'He also say that he want to renovate the property. And that he has some other tenants for it.'

'So you're telling me three different stories now.' I couldn't believe my bravado. But there I was, bravading all over the place.

'You have two weeks.'

'You sonofa –'

Sally grabbed the phone from my white-knuckled grip and, in order to deal more effectively with the guy, put on her 'good cop' hat and matching voice (a combination of heiress and widow).

'Hello, this is Sally Van Es,' she purred, leaning hard on the Dutchness of her name. 'I understand that we need to leave the apartment but it's simply inconceivable that we vacate in two weeks' time. Might it be possible for us to have until the end of next month?' She nodded and nodded and made mmm-hmmm-ing sounds. 'I see. And if we haven't found anything by then, I presume that we can stay until the end of the following month.' More nodding. 'Good,' she concluded. 'Thank you very much.'

Employing the crafty tactic of not shouting or calling the guy a 'sonofa –', Sally had managed to secure us a bit of room to breathe.

'That sonofabitch better not stand outside with butter on his head any time soon,' I said, then went downstairs and once again took our nameplate off the front wall. Just for the hell of it.

Sally and I went to a legal aid lawyer, a tall, blond, handsome guy – the usual Dutch type. Unusually though, he didn't speak English too well – which is rare for a Dutch person under seventy. It seemed especially odd for a university law graduate. (Sure, my Dutch is *niets* to *schriven thuis* about but I don't have a law degree and I didn't go to university. In fact, in the light of these short-comings, it's a wonder I can even speak English.) Anyway, our free lawyer's less than fluid bilingualism aside, we explained our situation – with complete honesty – and he told us that the *make-laar* could not toss us out; that in the absence of Mrs X, a contract automatically existed between us and the landlord. Further, that if the landlord wanted to get rid of us, he'd have to go through the courts to do it.

'So what should we do?' I asked.

'Not a one thing!' he said with a Dutch, legal smile.

'And you're sure the *makelaar* can't send around some burly men to throw us and my TV out on the streets?'

'Not with the legal right!' he said.

'What about without the legal right?'

'With not the legal right they can do as they wish.'

Later that evening, after a small celebratory dinner, Sally and I once more put the nameplate back up. But who knew for how long . . .

Francis, Monica, Amopolo and Me

Hendrik and I had done everything we could from this part of the world, so one afternoon early in August, I sat down with my creative leader Larry Frey and convinced him to bite the promotional bullet and send Hendrik the Director, Esther the Producer and Sean the Untitled off to San Francisco in the vain, unlikely and desperate hope that we might be able to get Francis Ford Coppola to appear in our film. (I left out the 'vain, unlikely and desperate' part and practically assured him that by the time we returned, Francis and I would be great pals.) Larry bit that bullet, chewed on it for twenty-four hours, swallowed it, and three days later, Hendrik, Esther and I were on a plane headed for the Windy City. No, I mean Frisco.

Upon arrival in the Big Easy – I mean San Francisco – the first person we spoke to, a US-resident Australian cab driver whose glance kept flicking to the rear-view mirror so he could eye off Esther, asked us what we were doing there. I explained that we were hoping to talk with Francis Coppola about this quotation of his that was inscribed on a brass plaque and usually screwed into the wall at the front of our building, but which was now in the trunk of his cab. 'Ha! Good *luck*!' he said, with typically Aussie dismissiveness. Esther and Hendrik looked horrified. I felt homesick for Aussie dismissiveness.

'You mind turning the radio off?' I asked the cabbie.

'Don'tcha like Prince, mate?'

We checked into the Convention Center Holiday Inn, an old, flimsy building that looked as if it had been constructed entirely from drywall, and spent the next few days talking with, and filming, cab drivers, couriers, hotel clerks, PR flacks and other people deeply connected with Francis C. Happily, practically everyone in SF had a Coppola-related story to tell.

'I sat next to him once at the Hunan Palace. He was eating crab claws.' (A cab driver.)

'I found his business card in the street about five years ago and I was hoping to maybe parlay that into something. But I guess I never did . . .' (A Mason Street cigar retailer.)

'I delivered some film cans of *The Godfather* back in . . . oh I guess this was around '72. He told me, "Don't lose these or you'll be working for me for free the rest of your life." Ha ha ha . . . cough!' (An enormously fat and cancer-smelling courier we'd hired to deliver still more expensive wine and cigars to Coppola's home in the Napa Valley in yet another attempt to bribe him into speaking with us.)

'*The Godfather* . . . that wasn't a, that wasn't a, that wasn't a war movie, that was a, that was a, that was a *Mafia* movie, right?' (Another cab driver.)

'Right.' (Me.)

'Who? Who is Copla? Is it you?' (A dry-cleaner whom we thought might do Copla's clothes.)

We also placed many more calls to Coppola's PR agency in the Big Apple (New York City) hoping to set up fall-back interviews with his son Roman, his daughter Sofia, his wife Eleanor or his podiatrist, whomever he or she might be. When we weren't making calls or having arguments (Hendrik and I did not exactly share the same vision: I thought that the occasional establishing shot might be a good idea; he thought I should leave the 'directing' to him), Hendrik, Esther and I visited Nicolas Cage's house, Robin Williams's house, Danny Glover's house and Danielle Steele's palace/house. The weather was great and we were all feeling depressed: we were getting nowhere.

On the Saturday we hired a car and drove up to the Napa Valley, having been told that Coppola often showed up at his vineyard there, greeting people and signing bottles of wine if he was feeling generous and expansive. We had, however, been warned repeatedly by Coppola's PR agency that he was 'very busy' and 'unequivocal about not being disturbed', so we didn't hold out much hope that he'd be strolling about christening children and patting women on the ass, and even if he was, that he'd be happy about being filmed doing so. About five seconds after we arrived

– Esther draped in sound equipment, Hendrik with a large camera on his shoulder, me in a suit, sunglasses and large microphone ensemble – we were pounced on by security people and Niebaum-Coppola Winery PR staff and told that under no circumstances could we film or sound record anything at the winery without specific approval from the proper channels and to turn off everything immediately. We made a big show of turning off the camera but, using a special code of winks and twitches, told Esther to keep the sound gear rolling, which she did, capturing some terrific audio of a truly nasty woman telling us to get lost. We spent the next four hours in the sun on the very beautiful property drinking the outrageously overpriced and not particularly good wines produced on the estate, being visited every fifteen minutes by some flunkey sent to ensure that we weren't recording any of the great secrets of the winery, such as the ideal overcharge on a mediocre glass of shiraz. It was very pleasant and highly annoying. Then Esther, on her return from a brief walk, caught a glimpse of our quarry, behind the wheel of a large automobile. She told us that she'd smiled and that he'd waved back at her with what she described as 'creepy hands'. We waited around for another hour, hoping that, lured by Esther, Mr Coppola might deign to come talk to us, however, alas and alack, he did not. But at least we now knew that he was in the country. Then it was closing time and we had to get lost for real. So we drove back to Motown – no, San Francisco – and that night overcame our depression by dining at Rubicon, the restaurant we thought Coppola owned with fellow famous food fans Robin Williams and Robert De Niro, in the vain, unlikely and desperate hope that FFC might be rostered on as celebrity waiter for the evening. Which he was not.*

Sunday we hung around the North Beach gelato outlets because we'd heard that Coppola sometimes liked to buy himself and his family ice-treats. It may be true, but it's no weekly ritual.

On Monday we at last visited American Zoetrope, Coppola's postproduction facility/genius HQ located in the Sentinel Building, a lovely old flatiron style building in North Beach. We

*Our information on this was bad – he'd in fact sold his shares in Rubicon some time earlier.

had decided to leave this place for last because we didn't want to establish a solid reputation as a trio of stalkers and thereby completely ruin what we felt would be our last chance at finally pinning down FFC. In several calls I'd made to American Zoetrope, I'd been told that nobody could speak to anybody about anything, especially any things related to Mr Coppola.

'But is it all right if we come there and shoot the front – I mean *film* – the front of the building?'

'Well, it's a free country,' I was told. 'We can't have you arrested.'

But I suspected that if they felt like it they could do precisely that.

On the ground floor of the building is Café Niebaum-Coppola, a relatively new venture for the very entrepreneurial Francis, where he sells his own wine as well as Italian food. It's a very pleasant place, all red banquettes and plenty of mirrors so you can see who else is there from almost every angle. We chose a table on the sidewalk and prepared to park ourselves there for the entire day. The weather was excellent; we felt sick. How could we face 180 after spending almost a week in San Fran, only to return with footage of cab drivers, dry-cleaners and various merchants? We couldn't. So what if Coppola hadn't made a decent film since *Tucker* in 1988? Without him we might just as well have stayed in Amsterdam and interviewed any fat man with a beard.

A few hours after our seventh round of coffees the staff began to get suspicious and I was more or less obliged to explain to Alfonso the restaurant manager exactly what we were up to. Alfonso said that it was a great shame that we'd come all the way from Amsterdam because Francis was sitting at his usual table every single day last week, practically *waiting* for impromptu interview opportunities, right up until around noon Saturday. 'He loves meeting people. Just loves it!' Alfonso told us. 'He's leaving for Italy tomorrow. You shoulda been here last week. Oh this is such a shame.' I agreed that it was indeed a shame. Alfonso pointed to the interior of the cafe. 'Sean Penn's inside.' I peered in and saw Sean Penn lunching with a cellphone and a glass of red. He looked handsome and yet ordinary, even vaguely dirty.

The next day we arrived at the café early, planning to spend another whole day there in the vain, unlikely and desperate hope

that we might corner Coppola. Sean Penn was there again, looking far less handsome than he had the previous day, perhaps
hung over. A short while later I suggested to Hendrik that, since
we were spending so much time there, he ought to get a covering shot of the Sentinel Building. Hendrik suggested to me that
I hadn't gone to film school whereas he had, so why didn't I
mind my own business? Esther rolled her eyes a lot. It was our
last full day in San Fran; time was running short and we were all
getting a little tense.

Around noon a small man with straw-like blond hair and such
bad breath it would show up on radar sat down at our table and
introduced himself. He was Lester Bernbaum, CEO and *con-
sigliore* of the Coppola Group of Companies. 'Alfonso tells me
that you guys are here from some place in Europe hoping to do
some sort of interview with Mr Coppola, is that right?' I nodded,
as likably as possible. Mr Bernbaum then started the spiel I'd
heard many, many times before: that we should have called ahead;
that we should have spoken to Coppola's PR agency in New York;
that Mr Coppola was a very private person; that *The Godfather*
wasn't a war movie, it was a Mafia movie; that Mr Coppola
doesn't really give interviews anyway; that he was forced into
making dreadful films like *Jack* and *The Rainmaker* by the studios. 'And I'm real sorry to tell you this guys, since you've come
all the way from somewhere in Europe, but I just drove Mr
Coppola to the airport. Dropped him off less than an hour ago.
He's gone to Italy.' Our disappointment was almost physical, and
mingled with the bad breath that delivered the terrible news, I
thought I was going to hurl. 'But hey look, Sean Penn's over
there.' We looked. Sean Penn was over there.

'So how long is Mr Coppola gone for?' I asked.

'I have no idea,' Bernbaum said. 'All I know is that he's gone.
I took him to the airport this morning myself and he is gone.'

'Right . . .' I said, trying not to sound too suspicious. Bernbaum
shook hands with each of us and left. There was nothing to do
except eat lunch and maybe drink quite a lot of booze. None of us
were hungry but we ordered anyway, especially wine.

Ten minutes passed before Bernbaum returned and, without
even a hint of shame or embarrassment, said, 'I'm sorry. I had the

wrong information. Mr Coppola is still here. He's coming down to wait for his limo to the airport. He'll be along any minute.' *Had the wrong information*. What a liar! I *knew* my clogs were tingling . . .

BRUSHOFF WITH FAME NO. 1:
THE PIZZA ENTHUSIAST

Moments later Francis Ford Coppola stands ten feet away from me. Taking deep breaths, I walk over to him, introduce myself and, trying not to hyperventilate, tell him why we are here. 'It's our agency's one year anniversary in October and we'd really like to have you say something for this film we're making.* The agency is named after a very inspiring quote of yours which is on a plaque outside the building. On the building. Actually, strictly speaking the plaque in question is just over there on our table. It's not for broadcasting†, or anything, the film, I mean, it's just for our own use‡ and it'd really mean a lot to us if you could just say something, anything, for the camera.§ We've come all the way from Amsterdam. Somewhere in Europe.'

Up close, Coppola is an imposing figure. Not for the last time, he looks me up and down then takes a deep breath. 'Well, I'm sorry that you've come so far,' he says. 'But I've been ambushed like this before and it's come back to haunt me, so I'm afraid I really can't agree to it. You should have gone through the proper channels.'

'We did. The channels told us you were too busy. If I could just show you the plaque . . .'

I run back to our table – literally run – grab the plaque, run back and thrust it into Coppola's hands. As he reads it a smile creeps across his face. '*I* said this?'

'You did.'

'These exact words?'

'Those exact words.'

'Well, you're kinda hoisting me with my own petard, aren't you? Using my own sentiments against me.'

'Yes,' I agree. 'It's a sweet irony isn't it?'

---

*This small lie is our cover story. †True. ‡Sort of true. § Very true.

'Possibly.' Coppola takes another look at the plaque and nods. 'I may have said something like that.' Then he pauses, his huge stomach rising and falling beneath the ill-fitting linen suit he's wearing. Through his glasses he looks me up and down once more, trying to decide whether I am trustworthy. I smile wanly, trying to seem likable, desperate and honest. Then he looks past me, over to Esther, and his face seems to open and almost glow with pleasure. 'Okay, go ahead. You got sixty seconds.'

Mr Coppola and I sit side by side in a banquette and I kick things off by asking him to read the quote, which, very very kindly he very very badly does – placing a nonexistent break in the middle of a sentence and thereby completely obscuring its meaning. My head swims. Coppola hands me a glass of wine and a slice of pizza with a general command: 'Here.' I eat while he babbles down at Esther, who's kneeling at his feet with a boom, about how he's going to Italy. 'Right down to the *boot* of Italy. You know the boot of Italy? That's where I'm headed. I love Italy, love the people. You been to Italy? You musta been to Italy, you being in Europe. I'd like to live my life in Italy.' I chew away, wondering whether or not I have the courage to ask the director of *The Conversation* and *Apocalypse Now* to reread the quotation. We have come too far to screw things up now – especially for *him* to be the reason for the screw up. I make myself think hard about the movie *Jack*.

'Ummm . . . excuse me, Mr Coppola. I wonder if I could get you to, uhhh, to read the quote one more time. Just for coverage, y'know.'

'Ha!' he says, to the gathered staff. 'Get this – the guy wants me to do take two!'

The guy who wants take two from Coppola turns a shade of red that matches the leather he's sitting on. 'Please?' he adds.

Mr Coppola rereads the quote perfectly, then puts a slice of pizza into his mouth.

'So what's your opinion of advertising, generally speaking?' I ask, not wanting to get back to Italy. The boot of Italy.

He looks at me for a moment, swallows, then screams, 'Who made the pizza?' A lengthy discussion between Coppola, a chef and, to a lesser extent, myself ensues and somehow manages to seamlessly incorporate pizza dough, wheat and advertising. Then all of a sudden he leaves, just gets up and walks away, without a word, a nod or a wave goodbye.

Esther and Hendrik and I were absolutely overjoyed: against all the odds, we'd got the shot. It was a miracle. In celebration, we drank several bottles of rosé and it all would have been perfect, if only Niebaum-Coppola produced better wine.*

At 6.05 p.m., as I lay dozing on my bed at the Holiday Inn, thinking vague and pleasant thoughts, I felt a series of dull thuds coming from the wall behind me. Then my room started swaying. Then the walls creaked and plaster began raining from the stucco ceiling. My first thought was that there must be an enormous party going on all around me, until with a sick feeling I remembered where I was – San fucking Francisco. I leaped off the bed, staggered around the still swaying room and ran to the balcony, deciding not to jump because I was way the hell up on the tenth floor. Then everything stopped.

It was the biggest quake (a 5.1) in San Fran since that number in 1989 which wrecked part of the Bay Bridge. It was also one of the scariest things that's ever happened to me – the fact that no one was injured and apparently not a single pane of glass in the whole city so much as cracked notwithstanding. I didn't sleep that night and am convinced that at around 4.30 a.m. I was thrown from the bed during an aftershock. Esther and Hendrik thought the whole caper great fun, but they laugh at the fact that I wear my seatbelt in cabs, the Dutch evidently being under the impression that no one has ever been killed in a car accident. Or an earthquake.

*And, I was to realise when I saw the footage a short time later, if only that halfwit Hendrik had gotten a two-shot of Coppola and I; as it was I appear only vaguely and distendedly reflected in a side mirror above our banquette. But for my off-camera voice and charm, I may as well have not been there at all.

The next day we hired a convertible and began the drive down to LA, from where our plane back to Amsterdam was flying out the following Monday. It was my first time in a roofless car and although quite terrified a lot of the time, I made myself enjoy the spectacular scenery and superb SoCal weather.

BRUSHOFF WITH FAME NO. 2:
'THAT WOMAN'

Some years ago, my friend Dr Chris Burns, PhD, met a bubbly, big-haired woman in a New Jersey hotel lobby with whom he'd remained friends ever since. They were, in fact, such good buddies that they sent each other Christmas gifts annually, and it was through Chris's fine taste in gifts that his American friend had received a copy of my book *Sean & David's Long Drive* in 1997. And it was because of her professed enjoyment of that book that she expressed an interest in meeting me while I was in Los Angeles. So on Friday afternoon I telephone 'that woman': I pull out a scrap of paper with her number on it and call up Monica Lewinsky.

My dinner with Monica the following evening at an Italian restaurant with a view of the Pacific Ocean is, unsurprisingly, a very strange experience – not so much the dining or her company (which is perky, witty, self-mocking in a smart, astute manner and generally very enjoyable) but the simple fact of being with *her*. The American public is completely unashamed about pointing, staring, stopping in their tracks, turning around and actually following her.

'This is my first time out in public in almost a year, Sean. It feels weird.'

'You're telling me.'

Standing at the restaurant bar and feeling the eyes of every person in the joint staring at her, and by association me, is extremely odd. And, I have to admit, pretty enjoyable. Plus I have on a rather flashy shirt and kid myself that it is my outfit that is getting all the attention.

'So, Monica,' I say, handing back her fork after tasting the ravioli she insists I try, 'Chris tells me that you enjoyed my book.'

'Yeah, I was really enjoying it. I got about halfway through –'

'Only halfway?' I moan, disappointed that I'd lost a reader. 'Why?'

'I got a call from Kenneth Starr.'

'Oh. Fair enough.'

I take no photos and ask her for no autographs, so you'll just have to take my word for it that it actually happened. But just to be on the safe side, I kept the dress I was wearing that night.

Back in Amsterdam. The next day

As soon as Esther, Hendrik and I got back, we went to sleep because we had to get up at 4.15 the next morning to catch a plane to Seville where, as a team-building/alcohol-drinking exercise, the whole agency was being airlifted to learn bullfighting at a *finca* in southern Spain (or, as I now know it, the middle of fucking nowhere). This day also had its fair share of drama . . .

My ordeal with a phantom burst appendix begins by the hotel pool in the early afternoon. I worry that I may have flown all the way from LA to Spain via Amsterdam and prepared myself to get all liquored up with my colleagues for *nada* if that useless organ explodes, so as research, just for my own peace of mind, I ask at reception if there's a hospital with some scalpels in it nearby. I am clutching my side rather dramatically and sweating (but only from the heat). We are staying in a small town called Carmona, about forty-five minutes from Seville, because all the hotels there are full of athletes participating in the world athletic championships.

'Are jou sick?' the receptionist asks.

'Well, not right now,' I tell her. 'But I might be soon.'

'Jou want me to call an ambulance?'

'No.'

'A doctor?'

'No . . . Oh, all right, go ahead.'

A few moments later our tour guide, Jose, appears and, acting as a go-between for me and the hotel staff, tells me that he's spoken to a doctor and that the doctor has told him that he won't be able to diagnose very much just by poking and prodding my stomach (and this guy hadn't even seen the thing) and that he, the tour guide, should call an ambulance. 'Jou want me to call an ambulance?'

'No,' I say firmly. Things are getting out of hand.

'They can take a picture of your appendix and see if you need to go to the hospital. They park right outside.'

'Really? Right outside?' I am intrigued by this. It seems . . . seemly.

'You go wait in your room. I call them. They be here in ten minutes.'

'I'd rather wait by the pool.' I wait by the pool.

A while later Jose the tour guide comes to the pool and tells me to go upstairs and wait in my room. 'I told them you in a lotta pain or they won't come so you be in pain. They be here in ten minutes.'

I go upstairs and wait for half an hour whilst my phantom pain phantomly recedes, and finally I decide to tell Jose to cancel the ambulance. So I go back downstairs and find him. 'No, is okay,' he says insistently. 'They went to the wrong hotel. They thought jou was an athlete. They on they way. They be here in ten minutes. Go back upstairs and be in pain.'

I head back to my room and, in between receiving concerned visitors who have no idea that this whole thing is a snowballing charade, I practise faking the symptoms of nausea, cramps, stomach ache, dread and touristic stupidity. Thirty minutes later there's a knock at the door and three white-suited SAMU (some Spanish medical acronym) people enter: two women and a silent guy who sweats a lot. Behind them is Jose, who looks like a cross between John Waters and Freddie Mercury – lots of big teeth and a long, thin black moustache. One of the women is a doctor and the other is a nurse. Seconds later I'm lying on the bed with my belly exposed and they're poking and prodding me and sticking thermometers in me wherever they can. They're very nice, and sexy too, in that fast-talking, lisping manner of the Latin *chica*. I explain to the doctor, rather sheepishly, that although I am not in much pain at this precise, exact moment (no matter how hard she is jamming her hand into my groin), an hour ago I was in virtual agony. This of course is a lie, but one that is met with *mucho* approval by Jose who, whenever he catches my eye, nods furtively. The doctor asks me if I want to go to Seville for an x-ray, this whole business about the mobile laboratory that can park outside being pretty much bull-shit. Wanting to say *si*, so that this whole transparent fiasco won't be a complete waste of everybody's time, I nonetheless tell her thanks but no thanks, that I'd really rather stay here and work on my acting . . . I mean my rest. So they leave – but not before I am forced by my fun-loving colleagues to come downstairs and pose with the medical team in front of the ambulance clutching my side in mock agony . . .

Later, on the bus taking us to the *finca*, I carefully avoid eye contact with Jose in case he asks me a question about my clothes and I give the wrong answer, causing him to fly in an emergency tailor from Madrid. *He be here in ten minutes . . .*

When we arrive at the *finca*'s arena to learn bullfighting, just about everyone in the agency has a crack at it, except me because I am afraid of upsetting the phantom appendix, which by now I am convinced is some sort of hernia which might develop into a heart attack if strained. Even though the six-month-old bull has no horns and is named Amopolo (which means 'butterfly'), it is still pretty scary and makes a hell of a lot of noise when it head-butts the iron hide I am crouched behind.

Looking back, I regret not facing the beef but I figure sooner or later they'll release a matador game on PlayStation – then I'm in. In the meantime, employing Coppola's words of wisdom, I console myself that I did the right thing under the difficult circumstances. Or maybe not – when you look at it closely, that 180 quote of his really doesn't make a whole lot of sense.

> Whenever you find yourself in difficulty just keep going. Turn the situation halfway around. Do a 180-degree turn and don't pull back from the passion. Turn it on full force.
>
> – Francis Ford Coppola

Four Hundred Years
Too Late

By early September, summer was on the way out; the weather
cooled and the sky clouded up and lowered down. Rain began to
fall more steadily and the chilly mornings were coated in light fog.
Most of the tourists had left and there were fewer people drinking
on the terraces of Rembrandtplein and Leidseplein. The arrival of
September in 1999 also meant that Sally and I had lived in
Amsterdam for one year. In those twelve months, some quite
incredible things – both awful and wonderful – had happened to
us. I was grateful for all of them, I really was. And I planned to be
grateful for whatever else was to come.

First my bike was stolen. I had come downstairs, planning to go
to de Bijenkorf and buy a new coffeepot, when I discovered my
bicycle to be unthere. All that *was* there was my trusty lock, still
attached to a lamppost. This quickly led to deep confusion – how
could my lock be all perfect and my bike be all gone? Surely they
should have cut through the lock, rather than the bike, otherwise
the bike would be mangled. Unless I slipped up and merely
attached the lock to the post and just *leaned* the bike there. But
surely I wasn't that stupid. Surely. Then there was the fact that my
lock was worth more than my bike . . .

I didn't worry too much about my stolen bike, though, because
according to newspaper reports the famous white bicycles (*witfiets*)
of yore were once again to be found at various locations around
Amsterdam. The program was the revival of a concept that was
first tested here in the mid-1960s (the aforementioned *yore*) when
a city councillor, environmentalist and former hippie-agitator with
too many double letters in his name, Luud Schimmelpennink,
dreamed up a plan to put free bicycles on the streets. Semi-correctly,
Mr Schimmelpennink figured that if there were enough bicycles

lying around, people could just grab one wherever they were, ride around a bit and then leave it at their destination for someone else to use. Predictably, only the first part of his grand altruistic plan came true: people did take the bikes, but tended not to leave them lying around for other people to use. In short order all the bikes were lifted, the program was cancelled, thieves went back to stealing regular bicycles and everything returned to what passed for normal in the 1960s.

In 1986, once again under the auspices of the indomitable Mr Schimmelpennink, a similar program was attempted in the city, this time involving a free battery-powered vehicle called the WitKar ('White Car', which was actually mostly orange). Problems with this particular harebrained scheme included, but were not limited to: absurdly limited range of car due to minutes-long battery life; extreme smallness of car; poor electronics of car; too few depots for deposit/pick-up of car; complete impossibility of impressing chicks whilst driving car; car could not compete with fairground Dodgems for either speed or fun. After less than five months this experiment was abandoned and, like an orgy, rarely spoken of afterwards except in terms of shame and regret by all parties involved.

So I was surprised (but relieved as well, due to my sudden bike-lessness) to read that the admirably idealistic yet sadly deluded vision of transportational Utopia was once again being revived by the irrepressible (and possibly insane) Luud Schimmelpennink. With the help of new technology and corporate sponsorship, the white bikes were, apparently, back. However, the sixties were a long while ago, so this time the bikes were to be equipped with electronic locks and hidden microchips to track users and help ensure they didn't get stolen. Or that if they were stolen, they were stolen by the likes of Ethan Hunt from *Mission: Impossible*.

The way it worked was that after a participant inserted a card with an embedded microchip into the console, they selected a destination and booked the use of a bicycle for thirty minutes. The central computer logged the passenger's identity and made a reservation for them at another parking lot near their final destination (by which I do not mean heaven, hell or a cemetery). The cyclist then had half an hour to get to where they were going and deposit the bike. If they missed the deposit time there was a penalty, which, if it was over *f*10, was more than they'd pay for a stolen non-white bicycle. (Then again it need only be five cents a day for the Dutch to get all panicky about it.) It was apparently possible to keep your bike out longer (perhaps even forever), but if you kept it out too long (like forever), you risked being denied the use of the bicycle next time (which, if you planned on keeping the bike forever, you wouldn't care about anyway).

All this is predicated on the fact that these bikes exist at all; I have my doubts because in the whole time I've lived in Amsterdam, I've never seen one. I've seen photographs of them though and they are truly hideous-looking things, all thick and white and functional like they've been made out of industrial piping, with solid blue plastic where the spokes should be. I presume they are constructed thusly so they can't be stripped for parts, as well as to ensure that no one would want to own one.

I have a theory about why I've never seen a '98 model white bicycle and this is it: about ten minutes after its most recent revival the scheme was probably once again abandoned in preparation for Mr Schimmelpennink's latest free transport idea – white elephants.

So rather than counting on the white bikes, I called Joey to see if he could put me in touch with someone who might have a bike to sell. 'You can have my bike, Sean,' he told me. 'I won't be needing it in Poland.'

'No, I guess you won't,' I said. 'But what exactly do you mean by that?'

'I've quit Heineken. I'm moving to Warsaw in a few weeks to work at an IT consultancy some friends of mine have started.'

My emotions about this were very mixed: I was torn between losing my friend and gaining his bike – he had a really excellent bike.

'That's very sad, Joey. When can I pick it up?'

On September 10th, we received a letter from the Justice Department telling us that our long-delayed application for residency in the Netherlands had been denied. We were shocked, stunned, depressed, outraged, saddened, horrified and generally aghast. How could they? We weren't criminals or even bad people. How could they not want us here? Sure, it was no America*, but we loved the place and wanted to live here happily ever after. The thought of returning to our former lives in Melbourne was simply inconceivable. What would we do there? It was the same with the idea of leaving 180 – I just couldn't stand it. Nevertheless, the letter told us that we had to leave the Netherlands in four weeks, or appeal. We planned to appeal – loudly and with lawyers of the paid-for variety.

What especially outraged me about this decision was that back at the end of the sixteenth century, Amsterdam vigorously pursued an immigration policy whereby the city actually *paid* people with certain skills to settle here. Of course, these were skills such as glass-blowing, silk weaving, lace making and the manufacture of gilded leather wall hangings, without which, apparently, the city simply could not function. Things would have been so much better for Sally and I if we'd arrived four hundred years earlier – except for getting the plague, which would've been very unpleasant. Meanwhile, at the close of the twentieth century, my lack of glass-, silk-, lace- and leather-based skills ensured that I was not an attractive commodity to the city so we had to get legal representation fast.

We chose our immigration lawyer because we'd seen him on TV one night, and if television has taught me anything, it's that lawyers who show up on television are the best lawyers. His name was Jan Koopman and he was a sarcastic, funny fellow with long greasy grey hair and large yellow teeth jutting out at what I'd previously thought were dentally impossible angles.

Mr Koopman, Sally and I discussed our lamentable situation, the main problem of which was that neither my wife nor myself was

*But it's closer than most people know: apart from the previously mentioned purchase of Manhattan by the Dutch, two elements closely link Amsterdam with the United States and its fundamental ideal. In the last quarter of the sixteenth century, Amsterdam was, more or less, the first city to develop without a monarchy and had at its foundation the pursuit of wealth in conjunction with what was then the very new idea of liberty. Two hundred years later, when the American colonists drafted their Declaration of Independence, with freedom and equality at its heart, they borrowed phrases straight from a 1581 document in which Dutch rebels refused to recognise the power of King Philip II of Spain. The copyright case is still pending.

born in the EU. (Frankly, I don't see what's so great about the whole EU idea anyway, especially now that it means you can't buy duty-free booze if you're flying within it. Except for being able to live in different parts of Europe, what's the point? Keen isolationist readers from England will no doubt sympathise with me.) Koopman & Co. were charging ƒ420 an hour so Sally and I tried to keep the conversation going at a pretty rapid clip. Jan put together a plan, centred around my writing a book about my life in Amsterdam, which he said would virtually guarantee us an extra eighteen months to two years in the country, relying on the sluggish machinations of the Dutch civil service. This inspired some confidence in us, despite the green tie and shabby blue suit our lawyer wore. And despite the fact that I had no intention of writing any books about my life in Amsterdam. I mean, what the hell would I say?* Peter Mayle didn't go through anything like this in *A Year in Provence*; indeed it seemed to me that by virtue of being English and wealthy (he'd struck it rich in both advertising and the sale of saucy, novelty calendars) he was welcomed with *les bras ouvert* by the French. Just showed up, bought somewhere fancy and renovatable to live, ate stuff and had an easy time of it – as though this were truly a free world. Which, I suppose for those with plenty of dough, it is.

I asked Mr Koopman if the path to residency might be smoothened if I were a multi-thousandaire.

'Not so much,' he told me. 'If you had some millions in US currency perhaps. But not from the thousands. Anybody can have the thousands.'

---

*Critics and reviewers: here is an ideal opportunity for those of you so inclined to take what I've written and use it to make snide, yet obvious remarks about how I needn't have bothered writing this book and didn't end up saying much, if anything at all. Try this on for size: *At one point Condon disingenuously writes that he had no intention of writing a book about his life in Amsterdam. 'What the hell would I say?' he asks. Unfortunately, the answer is very little.* Or: *Condon makes much of his dislike for Peter Mayle's* Provence *books but the Australian's endless whining about his difficulties with the Dutch authorities have none of the charm of Mayle's keen cultural insights or storytelling verve. I'll take a year in Provence with Peter Mayle over a week in Amsterdam with Sean Condon anytime.* Or how about: *At one point Mr Condon even has the temerity to suggest fatuous criticisms of his book, as though this po-mo (yawn) reflexivity will somehow absolve him of the literary crime of being self-obsessed and dull.*

'Plenty of people don't have the thousands.'

'Then they should not think about moving to Amsterdam.'

One day at work I passed two Dutch women talking on the stairs. Their conversation was taking place in Dutch, as is customary with the Dutch when talking to other Dutch. The thing was, without even thinking about it, I understood what they were saying. '*Ik ga zondag naar Madurodam – leuk, hè?*' The meaning of the lumpen, strangulated sounds arrived into my head, seemingly without going through my own somewhat lumpen and strangulated process of translation. It was a strange but deeply gratifying experience. What Anika (1960s Carnaby Street accent) was saying to Angela (Valley Girl accent: possibly an actual Valley Girl) was that on Sunday she would be visiting an attraction in The Hague called Madurodam, a kind of miniaturised Holland (although in a country this small it's not much of an achievement), and that she would enjoy it ('*Leuk, hè?*'). Sure it's uncomplicated and rather banal but I understood it immediately. And I began to wonder if perhaps that was what I had going on in my head, a kind of miniature Dutchness, whereby I could understand the smaller, less important things; the bite-size morsels of information about custom, country, language and people. Easily digested and simple, I slowly consumed my new home, mouthful by mouthful.

My linguistic diet to that point had been mere baby food. I'd managed to absorb some simple words and phrases by getting up early and watching children's TV programs such as 'Sesaamstraat' and 'Tweenies', where the language is basic and repeated to the point of brainwash. (I tried 'Het Teletubbies' but that gurgling sun-baby thing gave me *nachtmerries* [nightmares].) I took notes in crayon or with chalk on a small blackboard provided by my tutor, Sally, and in just a few months I was able, when the necessity arose, to discuss numbers, flowers, farmyard animals, the alphabet, rainbows and the difficulties of life as a garbage tin-dwelling puppet. (I was also familiar with developments in the second series of 'Beverly Hills negen nil twee een nil', which was on at 9.30 a.m.) The fact that few of my colleagues were interested in my observations – 'Have a *kijk* at that *lekker regenboog*!' – did not dissuade me from making them loudly and frequently. Also, I kept pushing for an agency day trip to the nearest farm or preschool.

In celebration of something or other – Larry's latest wisecrack or the hiring of a new writer from New York named Simeon A. Roane II – 180 threw a party. It was a costume party held in a deconsecrated chapel at the edge of the Vondelpark and I wore my tuxedo, passing myself off as James Bond or a member of a wedding. I liked Simeon – a big fellow in his early thirties who could be both gregarious and guarded at the same time – within fifteen minutes of meeting him. I liked him partly because he'd grown a beard and was wearing a *guyabera*, claiming to be a 'lower order Guatemalan gangster', but mostly because of the story he told me early in the night.

'When I was around eleven years old we lived in Palos Verdes, California, right on the edge of a golf course and a few doors down from Ray Milland's place. I'm talking about Ray Milland the actor.'

'As opposed to?' I asked.

'I dunno. Ray Milland the unknown retiree, I guess. Anyway Ray Milland the actor, he's around a hundred by this time, gets around with a walker, and he's got this fantastic steep sweeping driveway in front of his house, perfect for skateboarding, BMX-ing or whatever. One morning I see him coming out front to pick up his newspaper and he looks a little worse for wear so I bunny-hop up to him on my bike, do a quick tabletop, come to a skidding stop and say, "*Another* lost weekend, Ray?" He's kinda stunned for a moment then says to me, "I won an Academy Award for that picture, you little prick!"' Simeon laughed archly. 'I guess I was a little prick,' he said. 'I kinda like to remember that Ray was waving a cane over his head at me as I rode off, but I don't think it really happened that way. Rest is all 100 per cent, though. C'mon let's get a beer.'

Later, everybody got very drunk and said things they meant or didn't mean. *I need a payrise. The work is very fulfilling. My ideas are completely original.* And very late, on the edge of the spinning, coloured dance floor where people were partying to (and like it was) '1999', one of the partners leaned in to me and said that I was the spiritual heart of the agency, that I represented everything they wanted to stand for – originality, daring, creativity. He said that my presence in the office was uplifting, joyous.

That I was good for the morale of the place. 'And what you did with the Coppola film was wonderful. Just perfect,' he said. 'We're very pleased to have you with us, Sean.' I was being bathed in warmth and gratitude and it felt great.

'I've never been happier in a job,' I told him. 'By the way, your waistcoat looks terrific,' I added, which was a lie. The rest was all 100 per cent, though.

No book set in Amsterdam would be complete without some mention of the tulip speculation that swept Holland and reached its frenzied peak in 1637. So consider it mentioned.*

October is my favourite time in Amsterdam, especially for watching the city on television because it's warmer that way and there's less chance of being rained on. The Amsterdam marathon is held on a Sunday around this time, giving me the chance to sit on the couch and look at other people panting through the streets. Marathon Day 1999 was a very beautiful autumn day – sharp, crisp, clear, all the colours dazzlingly accentuated by the rare sunlight – and on television, the city looked stunning. The aerial shots helped to give me a greater sense of the layout of this extremely confusing, horseshoe-shaped city. I could see now that Sally and I lived in a completely different part of the city than I'd previously thought. In fact, we lived in Rotterdam.

Not that it mattered where we lived at that moment because our free lawyer had failed in his attempt to keep us in our flat and we'd finally accepted that we could no longer stay there. So we'd spent a week looking at tiny overpriced dumps around various non-canal parts of town – an attic with a toilet over in the Old South; a bland corporate executive box way the hell out by the Amsterdamse Bos (forest) – and felt that familiar can't-find-any-where-to-live queasiness all over again until our realtor took a chance and showed us a very expensive apartment in a Berlage building in the west. It was an absolutely enormous place with polished floorboards, a large balcony, a study/second bedroom, a

---

*If you would like to know more about this widely covered phenomenon, Simon Schama's book *The Embarrassment of Riches* probably contains something about it.

huge living room, a bathroom with a bath, a kitchen, a dining room, a storage room, an elevator, a bike garage and a great big master bedroom. After we'd taken it all in and fallen in love with the place, a hushed conversation followed.

Sally was understandably concerned about the massive jump in rent but I assured her that my job at 180 – albeit highly freelance and only semi-legal in nature – would easily take care of the matter. 'Don't we deserve something like this for the first time in our lives?' I beseeched. 'We're adults – we should live in an adult environment.'

'But *are* we adults?' Sally asked. 'Really?'

I insisted that we were and, at the end of October with the assistance of Ray, Terry and a hired truck, we moved from east to west. It's true what they say about moving house being the second most traumatic thing after the death of a loved one (and they *do* say it). But in Amsterdam, with its tiny, steep stairs and anorexic hallways, you can't help wondering if people would rather receive news of Grandma's passing than an eviction notice. Luckily all my grandparents are already dead so it's not a moral question I'll ever have to face.

The neighbourhood we moved to was one of large dark brown brick buildings with white windows and dim doorways littered with paper scraps and plastic bags; plain, squat mosques and monolithic Marinatha churches; dank and greasy grillrooms; long streets permanently bathed in shadow. It was not beautiful by any stretch but it was worth living amongst the ugliness for the increased size, security and sanctuary of our apartment within it. My only real complaint was this: in a city that names its streets so inventively and interestingly (we were right near Vasco da Gamastraat, Balboastraat and Shackletonstraat – the explorer neighbourhood), I couldn't help but feel somewhat disappointed with landing Gerardus Mercator, Flemish mastermind of the meridien straightening Mercator projection map, as our postal namesake/identity. Sure it's better than back in Australia where almost everything is named after bits of England – in an attempt to conjure up the idea of another green and pleasant land rather than accept the hot and orange one it actually is – however, on the other side of town is a small area consisting of Charlie Parkerstraat,

Chet Bakerstraat and Count Basiestraat. Now *that* would make one cool address. Man.

Once a year the city tested out its public emergency sirens. In the days leading up to these eardrum-rupturing occasions there were announcements warning everyone not to panic when they heard the sirens, that the series of great long lowings which built to piercing shrieks were merely practice runs. What sort of country was I living in where tests of this nature were even deemed necessary?* Nothing like this had ever happened in Australia. And what about the day that the sirens would begin to wail suddenly, without warning? What would that mean? What would I do then?

Unlike in the rest of the world, or at least Australia, the position of human resources boss in Holland is one of great power. Power, mystery and immense intimidation. Among other mysterious, powerful and intimidating qualities, the new HR guy at 180 was tall and thin and muscular and bald and confident and Dutch and named Simco; the last point I found especially scary, the name more aptly belonging to a chemical manufacturer than a human being. As soon as he arrived he made it his business to approach every member of the agency and have a chat with them in a room with the door closed. I find these sorts of conversations, even if I'm not actually involved in them, extremely distressing because once the 'chat' is over, I always expect to see the door creak open and one party leave the room in tears – usually not the HR party.

Inevitably, one icy morning, my turn came for the dreaded conversation, and with his hand gently pressed into the small of my back, Simco ushered me into the dimly lit boardroom then closed the heavy door behind us, creating what seemed like a kind of time/space vacuum, then, with his big tanned head just inches from mine and looking me right in the eye and speaking in a disconcertingly soft voice that suggested intimacy and confession, he said, 'So, tell me a little bit about yourself, Sean.'

I hate that ridiculous question so much I want to vomit every time I hear it. What exactly do people think they mean by it? Do

*One that was invaded by the country next door sixty years earlier, I know.

they want a Playboy Playmate type of response, to hear about your turn-ons and turn-offs and star sign? Or a Miss World answer about your devotion to charity work? Or do they just want vital stats – height, weight, date of birth? How about, *I think that drug companies should be more closely monitored by independent bodies and held more accountable for their pricing and distribution policies?* Or, *I'm a 36-28-34, thanks for asking, Simco.* Then I totter a little on my high heels. *Tell me a little bit about yourself . . . I'll tell you a little bit – I think that is the stupidest question on earth. I'd rather tell you a little bit about Fermat's last theorem.*

'Sean?' Simco urged.

And so I began babbling. 'Oh, y'know, there's really not that much I can think of, to tell you the truth, Simco. Truthfully. I'm just . . . I just work here, sort of. I'm married. And I used to live in Australia. That's about it. But I really like working here. And being married. And I love Holland. Or, if you prefer, the Netherlands. Thank you very much for your time.'

Then he asked about my 'plans' for the next year, whether I wanted to work at 180 or was I considering leaving the Netherlands in the near future. My immediate thoughts were: *Plans? Who has plans? Plans rarely work out* so why bother having them?* Of course, what I told scary Simco was that all my plans were inextricably bound up in working at 180 because I loved the company so much. Other than that, I really had no plans. Except, hopefully, to be employed in a full-time capacity (and therefore sponsored for residency) by the agency.

Simco nodded slowly and, in the near darkness, I could not help being reminded of Colonel Kurtz's huge bald head bathed in moonlight as he grilled Captain Willard. 'So Sean, what service or function can you provide that a Dutch person could not?' Simco asked, and I began to suspect that he was a keen nationalist, one who believed in the principle of Holland for the Dutch. The subtext being pretty clear: will you please leave my small, over-crowded country?

This was a tough question to answer without insulting Simco's country or his countrymen, and although I'm fairly sure it's what

*See Operation Market Garden if you need proof.

143

he wanted to hear, on a purely personal level I felt the wrong answer would be, *Why none!* So I thought for a moment before saying, 'Let me tell you a little bit about myself . . .'

All too predictably, a few weeks after our little chat I was fired in a blunt, brutal fashion by Simco. 'I have to tell you that after the end of the day your services will no longer be required.' He actually used the phrase 'your services will no longer be required', which made me hate him all the more for his English-by-the-book unoriginality.

'So you won't be offering me permanent work and sponsorship?'

'I don't think so,' Simco said coldly. 'Why would we?'

I thought about mentioning that some saw me as the spiritual heart of the company, that I was fun to have around and good for morale, that I'd been there a lot longer than he had . . . But the fact was he was Dutch and I was only Australian. He had a right to be there.

'Well,' I said. 'I guess that's . . . that then.'

It was shortly before Christmas and I couldn't help feeling like some pitiable character out of Dickens. In the absence of readers, however, I did most of the pitying myself. I hated that I felt so great a sense of loss over a mere job but I couldn't escape the fact that I'd enjoyed working at 180 more than I cared to admit, that I'd met some terrific people while I was there and that I would miss them, that I'd miss the sense of purpose that working there had afforded me.

'Oh come *on*, Seanie,' Chris said, when I blurted these feelings out to him one day when I'd returned to collect some of my things. 'You'll be back.' Chris put his arm over my shoulders and I tried very hard to believe him, but when Simco called a week later and told me that I would not be paid my remaining salary until I returned my front door key and electronic security pass, I decided never to invest any real commitment or trust in the corporate world again.*

*Just a few months after I was let go, Larry Frey, a big part of why I so enjoyed 180, left the company to live in Manhattan where he devoted himself more fully to directing commercials and writing Christmas specials for sports broadcasters. His departure belatedly softened the blow of my dismissal, and his subsequent regular returns to Amsterdam to freelance for the agency he co-founded were always a happy reminder that advertising, while evil, is not an *absolute* evil.

'So how are we going to afford this fiendish flat?' Sally asked on Christmas Eve.

'That's a very good question, baby.' I nodded to add to the question's legitimacy. 'Very good, indeed. Why don't you audition for an acting job at Boom Chicago? That'd surely pay better than the box office.'

'They couldn't pay me *enough* to get up there. Why don't *you* – you love showing off.'

'I dunno, it's pretty hard what they do – being funny all over the place. And remaining so fucking happy all the time. I don't think I could pull it off. I can see myself alienating audiences pretty quickly.'

'We'll have to move.'

'We're not moving. Another move would kill me. Besides, look at all this space and light.' I made a kingly sweep with my arms, indicating space. 'I'll sell some blood or a kidney or something.'

'I hope you haven't bought me a Christmas present.'

'I haven't.'

'Because I know your capacity for financial self-denial. It's sweet, but right now I think you should act more like how other people act when things go wrong.'

'I really haven't got you anything.'

The next morning I gave Sally the diamond earrings I'd bought prior to my little chat with Simco. She cried.

The day after the day after Boxing Day, Melbourne was flooded and I felt both very far away from home and glad not to be there. But *was* I not home? Wasn't I home here in Amsterdam? It was hard to tell; without a job I suddenly felt set adrift all over again. About the only thing I took pleasure in was the fact that I probably wouldn't be hearing that Prince song every ten minutes next year. (On the other hand I knew I was going to come face to face with a lot of misspellings of *millennium*.)

2000: A New Millennium?

Amsterdam's weather early in the new century was pretty crappy. For some reason I'd expected a new millennium to usher in all-new weather along with it. I realised this was very naive – and scientifically untenable – but held out a secret hope for the same time the following year, when the other new millennium showed up.

Apart from the pre-millennium flooding, Melbourne was haunting me in small, unexpected ways:

- A kind young woman in a bank on Kinkerstraat forgave me the *f*10 'touching your money' fee they like to charge for even the simplest transaction (such as thinking about money), merely because she was from Adelaide and I am from Melbourne. Had she known my true feelings for Adelaide (see *Sean & David's Long Drive* pp. 33–37), however, I am sure she would have charged me double.

- I began watching 'Neighbours' in order to remain in touch with what was happening back in Melbourne, and somehow convinced myself that, because they were so tedious, repetitive and unremarkable, the goings-on in Ramsay Street were real.

- My friend Eric, a former Melbourne resident turned NYC resident, came to Amsterdam for an advertising party and stayed with Sally and I for a few nights.

- Ray, whom I first met in Melbourne, got a job as special projects editor on KLM's in-flight magazine the *Holland Herald* and promised that he would give me as many writing assignments and Sally as much editing work as he could.

- Terry held a farewell party before he left to go back to Melbourne (at the party I told him that, despite my abominable credit rating, my bank had given me a Gold MasterCard.

'There's a bank born every minute,' he said, which caused me to literally* fall on the ground laughing).

- Boom Chicago sponsored Sally as a resident which meant that we didn't have to face the question of our own return to Melbourne.

- In celebration we spent a February long weekend in Bologna (as a break from being in Amsterdam and thinking about Melbourne).

NEWS ITEM, FEBRUARY 4TH, 2000: Amsterdam's streets are littered with dog droppings – and city leaders have come up with a way to solve the problem. The city's pedestrians are being offered ƒ5 per hour to pick up dog dirt from the city's pavements. There is little danger of the work running out as Holland is home to nearly 1.4 million dogs. Anyone volunteering to clean the streets while strolling will be paid.

My new career . . .

Some time in February

I am not the only person around here who spends their days cooped up inside, looking out. On the other side of the street from the room in which I work – a small, former child's bedroom with coloured wallpaper and curtains with ice-cream print on them and memories of wailing and gurgling – there is a four-storey apartment block, built in the classic Amsterdam School architectural style of long institutional rows of reddish brown brick and windows with white wooden trim. On the second floor, right above the *huisdieren poli* (veterinarian), there is a young Turkish girl of sixteen or seventeen who appears late in the morning every day, always wearing the same outfit – jeans and a striped jumper – and who does very little all day, every single day, but stare out the window. Occasionally she is joined by another young woman who may be her sister or a friend, and the two of them will stare out the window together or turn and watch the large television which sits

*Not *literally* literally.

147

in the far corner of the room. Occasionally they dance, with their arms raised and twisting their wrists in the popular Turkish style. Recently the girl's eye has begun catching mine, fleetingly, before she redirects her gaze back down to the street where very little ever happens.

I want to know the things this girl says to her brother who sometimes sits with a guitar propped on his knee, and to the other woman who sometimes joins her in her mission to stare; I want to know if she speaks in Dutch or Turkish; I want to know what she thinks I am doing sitting here all day, every day, staring in front of me at my computer screen or occasionally to my left, glancing at her, wondering about her.

From our living room window we also had a perfect view across the courtyard into our opposite neighbours' living room, thirty feet away. The guy was about my age but, judging by the fact that he kept surfboards and mountain bikes on his balcony and spent a lot of time walking around his apartment with his top off in order to display his fine collection of tanned abs and other hard bumps, he was quite a different person from me. The thing was, he too worked from home, sitting bare-chested at a computer for long stretches, and I desperately wanted to know what he did for a living. Was he a writer as well? A Web designer? The lazy scion of a wealthy family? His girlfriend, the very definition of a tall, willowy blonde, appeared to be some sort of painter, perhaps an amateur, perhaps a professional. Either way, she had very specific tastes in subject matter.

'Sally!' I said one afternoon, whilst partially concealing myself behind a curtain. 'Quick! Come here!' Sally joined me at the window. 'Try not to stare, but see that big painting in the opposite flat? Look closely at the two sienna lumps in the middle. I'm not sure it's what I think it is, but if it is, we're living in kink city, baby.'

Sally took up a position behind another curtain and peered opposite. 'Oh my God. How disgusting. Is that . . . ?'

'Yes – a hyper-realistic representation in oil of our neighbour's giant testicles.'

'Oh, I can't wait to meet these two.'

As it happens . . . some time in March

As it happens, all I want is to make sure the three of us are back at the hotel in time for the live broadcast of the Academy Awards, due to begin around midnight Antwerp time. Our friend Chris Potter, a nurse in the Royal Australian Air Force, finished a long and harrowing six-month peacekeeping operation in East Timor just a few days ago and is on his first visit to Europe. He has returned from his tour of duty more sarcastic and bitterly blithe about life than ever; but somehow he retains his humour. 'Oh you've got to love the Timorese, Sal,' he said earlier. 'It's a standing order – love them or shoot them.' Sally and I have shown him Amsterdam and now we are introducing him to Antwerp. Paris is next. It is our last night in the city and after dinner the three of us are headed back toward the hotel. I keep a close eye on the time, ensuring that we'll be back in time to watch every one of Hollywood's stars come out to shine. Antwerp is a small city but it contains lots of antique stores and our route hotel-ward takes us along Lange Nieuwstraat, the centre of antique Antwerp. There are too many beautiful, unaffordable things to stop and stare at.

'Come on,' I keep having to urge the others. 'We've only got twenty minutes 'til Oscar time.'

'Shut up, you fool,' Sally says, then turns to Chris. 'Look at the grain on this Eames chair.'

'Is Sean serious about this?' Chris asks Sally. 'Does he really care about all those Hollywood people?'

As it happens, I am serious and I do care so I set the pace, quite happy for the others to lag as they window-shop in fantasy land. Sally and Chris are some distance behind me when I turn a corner and the great, dark cobbled expanse of Vogelenmarkt opens up before me: to my left is the Stadsschouwburg, its looming height home to *The Phantom of the Opera*; diagonally opposite is our hotel; and about twelve feet ahead of me there is a person lying face up on the concrete. From the corner of my eye I notice a bi-cycle leaning against a wall nearby. Had I been alone I would have skirted around this person – drunk or on drugs or whatever – late on a cold night as a light, misty rain begins to fall; not because I didn't want to miss celebrities climbing out of limousines and pos-ing on red carpets, but because this is just the way I am. I see people slumped or sleeping on the streets all the time and most often I ignore them, confident that they are all right or that if they are not all right, somebody else, somebody more inclined toward simple kindness, somebody more qualified, will be along shortly to take care of them. This, I believe, is the way the world works. And it works because of people like Chris Potter, who, as soon as he sees the girl, walks quickly over to where she lies, bends down and, almost as though he is trying to seduce her, says, 'Are you all right, darling? What's wrong? Have you been drinking? Taken any drugs?' *Darling*. That really gets me, the way he can just do that, call a person in trouble 'darling'. She tells him, in English, that she hasn't so he asks her again what is wrong.

She says, 'I love you.'

I mutter some crack to Sally about being young and stupid and taking ecstasy. The girl's right shoe is not on her foot; it's a few feet above and to the right of her head. She must've fallen off her bike and gotten a bit dazed. *But how does your shoe come off in a bike accident? And if she fell off her bike*, I wonder, *why is it leaning against the side of the theatre?* As Chris gently asks her more questions, Sally and I move a little closer and Sally points to her club kid style tracksuit saying, 'She's got something stuck on her pants.' I see now the girl is strikingly pretty, maybe twenty-three years old with long curly hair and big, nice teeth. A bit like Hilary Swank, it occurs to me.

'I'll get it,' I say, and I reach down to get whatever it is off her pants, to give the kid a little dignity while she's lying on the concrete freezing, but what I get between my thumb and forefinger is a stubby, hard, wet bit of bone sticking through her skin and track pants. 'Oh Jesus,' I say, feeling unbelievably sick, and very scared for the poor girl. 'Chris, her leg's busted.' I run across the square to call an ambulance from the hotel, hearing her say 'I love you' once more just before I take off. 'I love you,' she says to Chris, plain and clear. I turn to look back as I'm running and can see that Chris has moved her onto her side and is sticking his fingers into her neck, busy and looking very worried. As I pound across the pavement I keep wondering if I should run up to the room and grab my camera to document what is happening back there. Even as I have the thoughts I'm disgusted with myself; nevertheless the internal debate continues until I reach the hotel lobby and tell them to call an ambulance because there's a girl with a horribly broken leg outside, in the rain, being attended to by a stranger.

When I come back, panting and kind of in a wild shock myself, the girl has stopped breathing. Chris gives her chest a thump and begins cardiopulmonary resuscitation. After a moment she takes two short breaths then vomits into his mouth which makes him gag and swear a lot. Chris tells us that her temperature is way down, that she's clammy, breathing shallowly, that she's in shock and that I have to take off my leather coat and put it on her right away.

After I've laid my coat on the girl, who is very, very pale now, I look at Sally and cannot think of one thing to say – not a word, not a sound – that will be appropriate, that accords with what is going on: a young girl apparently dying at our feet. Sally looks frightened; there is, quite literally, fear in her blue eyes and that fear seems to make her eyes bigger, lighter. It's dark but I can see her eyes clearly.

When the ambulance crew arrives, Chris has put the girl back on her side and is trying to clear her airway. She vomits on the concrete and onto my jacket. The ambulance crew are two extremely idiotic-looking men, like a couple of goofs from a bad comedy; a short, fat older fellow and a doleful, tall, thin younger guy. And they don't have a clue what to do, this classic comedy duo. Chris is in charge while the ambulance men simply assist him, while Sally and I take small steps back and forth, deep breaths in and out. Chris secures a clear airway with an endotracheal tube, orders one of the ambulance guys to put a needle into the girl's arm, then continues CPR. Chris is now convinced that her lung has collapsed so he takes a cannula from their medical kit and sticks it into her chest, waits to hear an audible hiss and then starts blowing into it after the blood has stopped shooting out.

Two doctors arrive a little while later and in moments the beautiful young girl who was dressed for a night at a club or a party is covered in tubes and needles, most of her clothes are cut off, Sally is standing by holding an IV drip of some sort and I am shining a torch onto her delicate, pale, vomit-flecked face and trying not to cry while these five men are doing all sorts of unbelievable things to get her heart started and make her breathe again.

But all too soon, maybe forty-five minutes after we found her, she is dead. She dies right in front of us all, with the light from the torch I am holding shining into her face, and I can tell, from one moment to the next, precisely when she dies. It is in her eyes, then it isn't.

I love you, she had said, and these were the last words she ever spoke.

Much later, in the hotel bar where we have been drinking for several hours, a pair of Belgian policemen arrive and tell us that the girl had jumped from the outside stairway of the Stadsschouwburg. She had written on her arm in Flemish, 'I don't care about myself'. I asked the policemen what her name was and they told me I could call the station the next day to find out who she was and anything else I wished. Which, needless to say, I did not do. What I did do was see *American Beauty* and have trouble breathing all the way through it. I hated that film so much – its shallow depiction of unhappiness and alienation, its moral hollowness – I cannot even begin to say.

For a long time afterward, I planned with great and sincere intent to go back to Antwerp and find out who this girl was. I wanted to find out who her parents and friends were and tell them what had happened that night. I wanted to tell them what she had said. *I love you.* That these were her last words and that they were not meant for Chris or Sally or me, that they were meant for them – her mother and father, her sisters and brothers, her friends.

When we returned from our short trip there were three important letters waiting for us. One was from our immigration lawyers telling us that the Department of Immigration was considering whether to let us stay but that in the meantime we were not allowed to remain in the Netherlands. Unless we appealed by Monday. Then we were allowed. There was also a letter from the police telling Sally to come and pick up her residency permit, valid for one year. The third letter was a big fat bill from Koopman & Co. Oh, the thrice-baked irony.

April 21st, 2000

I got my first flat tyre ever this morning. It happened right opposite a bicycle repair store – coincidence or not? Probably. While I was in there getting a new inner tube I asked for a bell to be fitted. 'Nothing too feminine,' I requested, thinking myself hilarious. Come to think of it, I *was* hilarious: the guy laughed his head off. I do what little I can to entertain the Dutch.

There is a funeral procession right outside our apartment. The staring girl opposite isn't even at her window – if only she knew; this'd be viewing gold for her. They're removing the coffin from the hearse to take it into a house for the wake. It seems a little early for a wake – it's only 11 a.m. Sally wonders if the apartment's on a higher floor and whether they'll use a hook and pulley to hoist the casket into the room. Ooh, she's a sinful one. There are a bunch of black people below our dining room window, milling in the sunshine, dressed in semi-black (checks, greys, items with a *bit* of dark in them, but nothing actually black), smoking and chatting and laughing. The street is all unpaved down there, giving the whole thing a kind of 'funeral in a South African township' feel. Nobody's crying though. I find that odd.

There is a corpse just a few feet away from me. I really don't like it. I'd have thought that after Antwerp it would be easier but it's not. It's worse.

About 9 a.m. April 23rd, 2000

The telephone rings. I answer it.

VOICE ON THE TELEPHONE: 'Allo darlin'.

ME: Keith?

KEITH: Yeah, lissen, you got any bread an' unny I can borra?

ME (mentally recalling my last bank statement): Well . . . I guess. Not thousands, but I have a couple of hundred.

KEITH: Where you livin' now?

ME: In the west. On the Mercatorplein. Do you know it?

KEITH: Yeah. I'll see you in a little while.

ME: Is everything all right, Keith?

KEITH: Nuffink I can't 'andle.

An hour later Keith has left our place with ƒ300, explaining (if that's the right word, which it isn't) that he 'got into a situation in a parking lot in den Helder a few hours ago' and that he needs to disappear for a while. Which he promptly does – we do not hear from him again for another seven months.

NEWS ITEM, APRIL 28TH, 2000: KLM Royal Dutch Airlines is to be prosecuted for putting 440 live Chinese squirrels through a meat grinder. KLM decided to slaughter the rodents, similar to the North American ground squirrel, after they arrived at Amsterdam's Schiphol Airport from China without import documents or proper cages. They were en route to a collector in Athens. Once discovered, KLM said it had little choice but to destroy the animals; however, the cruel manner of their disposal shocked the nation and prompted a debate in parliament. After accusations that it had similarly killed turtles and birds, KLM stopped all exotic cargo shipments and closed its 'animal hotel' which cared for illegally imported animals before they were returned home.

Boy, will I be making sure I bring my passport, visas, insurance and other proof that I am not a squirrel next time I'm at Schiphol.

I kidded myself that I was coping without a job but I knew the illusion couldn't last. In May, various things started getting to me. I became aware of a more or less constant tightness in my chest, a general shortness of breath, of an acute, suffocating despair. I saw a doctor who told me that I had a more or less constant tightness in my chest, a general shortness of breath and a feeling of despair. He asked me why I might be suffering from these things. I told him that the Lockerbie trial had begun at Camp Zeist near Utrecht the previous day, that all 259 passengers and crew as well as eleven residents of Lockerbie died when the Boeing 747 had disintegrated in midair and crashed on December 21st, 1988, thirty-eight minutes after leaving Heathrow Airport bound for New York. 'The trial is expected to last for at least a year,' I said.

'Did you know people aboard this flight?' the doctor asked me.

'No, but it's still a very horrible thing to have happened. It still upsets me.'

'I see. I think you have a general hyperventilation panic reaction and that's why you have pain and breathing trouble.'

'So do I go on Paxil now?'

He shook his head and told me to see a physiotherapist, then wrote the name and number of a psychiatrist on a piece of paper, telling me to call him if I wished to. And I probably would have done so if I'd been able to decipher either the name or the number.

I did however see the physiotherapist, a nice young woman named Misja, who outlined a series of breathing and relaxation exercises I was to perform before I went to sleep and whenever I felt nervous. One Friday I asked her what she was doing that night (because I'm a polite and friendly person). 'Call my friend, see what she's doing. If nothing, I'll go on ICQ,' Misja told me.

I thought that ICQ might be some sort of volunteer program where people in urgent need of physiotherapy are given emergency treatment by women such as Misja. 'What's ICQ?' I asked admiringly.

'It's an Internet chatline. I seek you.'

'Oh.' After that I decided that I could no longer leave my mental health in her healing hands and stopped seeing her. She needed more help than I did.

In May the Dutch clog industry came under threat because there was not enough poplar wood to make the shoes. According to *de Volskrant* newspaper, the price of the wood had been the same for the past thirty years, which was discouraging people from growing it. Just 100,000 poplar trees were planted in the previous year, far below the 700,000 needed to keep up with demand. This came as a surprise to me: I had figured the greater clog threat would be that nobody in their right mind wanted to wear heavy, uncomfortable, impractical, silly-looking footwear. Made of wood.

Trouble

In June, we Amsterdammers all got caught up in the orangeness of Euro 2000, which I enjoyed very much, particularly because it wasn't called 'Euro the *year* 2000'. (Very few people seemed to be able to refer to 2000 as simply *2000*. It was always *the year 2000*. Yet nobody used to strut around saying, *Well, this is the year 1998*, back in 1998.) Anyway, back to the football: the Netherlands got knocked out in the semifinals which was unfortunate. Still, as an Australian, I was used to this kind of disappointment (but it usually came in green and gold).

In July the Turkish girl who stared from the window disappeared. All of a sudden she was no longer there every day pretending not to see me. Her whole flat was dark, empty, abandoned. Had she moved suddenly? Been taken away? Was she dead?

Curious as I was about it, I had little time to consider my neighbour's fate because Ray, now well established at the *Holland Herald*, was sending me on my first international assignment . . .

Dateline: Monaco. August 1st, 2000

From a distance he looks pretty good, trim and tan, especially his ankles which I have a good view of since he is wearing deck shoes with no socks. He isn't the only one – there are a lot of sockless older gents in blue blazers and white slacks hanging around. The place is like a floating country club. It isn't until some time later, when I get close enough to smell his aftershave (Hai Karate, I think), that I get the sense that he is actually quite frail and much, much older than he was in *Live and Let Die*. He still maintains a nice tan though.

The strange thing is that it is Roger Moore that keeps trying to get near *me* and not the other way around. I step out of the head –

which is what they call the can* on ships – and there he is, on his way in, nodding at me and smiling with teeth that look like they're cleaned by people from NASA. Or I might be up on deck three, climbing through one of those round metal doors, in search of a daiquiri, and Moore is there lurking on the other side, alone and ready with more nods and familiar smiles. I am wearing a name tag that says 'Sean Condon' and figure maybe he's hard of seeing and thinks it says 'Sean Connery' and is looking to play me a little chin music when no one is around. I begin to get a bit scared. Sure he was a second-class 007, but he made pretty short work of old Jaws in *The Spy Who Loved Me*, didn't he? The only time I feel safe from Moore's stalking is when he is squiring tiny (and possibly valium-assisted) Queen Sylvia of Sweden around the ship, a task he pursues with licensed-to-kill attention and aplomb.

The ship is the *Royal Clipper* and it is (Roger) moored in Monte Carlo, the capital of what is always referred to as *the tiny principality of Monaco*. Roger, Sylvia and I are there on official business: the ship's naming ceremony, a ceremony during which a ship is named with the assistance of an oversized bottle of champagne, some celebrities and the queen of some country you never knew even had royalty. And, of course, idiots like me to document the proceedings and help at the bar.

At over 133 metres from nose to tail, the *Royal Clipper* is the biggest sailing ship in the world. It has a lot of sails. It also has some engines in case the world's supply of wind ever runs out. What it seems to lack, to my eyes at least, are lifeboats, life jackets, flares, iceberg/reef detection equipment and some plucky youngster willing to give up his life as he sits in the radio room tapping out SOS in Morse code.

Following a long and pointless conversation about Princess Grace with a German television producer, I put on someone's abandoned name tag and pretend to be a Mr Carlos Juno (whoever he is) of Latutid 4 (whatever that is). Interestingly, my life remains largely the same while I assume Mr Juno's identity. He must be a rather dull fellow. Nevertheless, he enjoys drinking free booze just as much as I do.

*Toilet.

BRUSHOFF WITH FAME NO. 3:
THE SPY WHO TOLERATED ME

Spying Roger Moore and his approximately tenth wife at the bar, I decide to drop by for a brief chat, my life being somewhat deficient in the area of encounters with James Bonds. Thinking it prudent not to introduce myself in some hilarious fashion that he had very probably heard a thousand times before – *Condon, Sean Condon* – I launch straight into what I believe at that moment to be a rather interesting anecdote. (But which, upon reflection, I realise is actually not.)

'Hello Mr Moore,' I begin superbly. 'I was at a museum the other weekend and I saw an exhibition of TV and film memorabilia and they had on display an old favourite of yours – the gun from *The Man With the Golden Gun.* How about that?'

Mr Moore slips off the bar stool, smiles, shakes my hand and, in a rich, well-modulated voice, says, 'Thank you, my pleasure.' Which, the dullness of my story notwithstanding, doesn't really make sense.

I say nothing, however, because I have two more requests to make of the Dodger. The first is to ask for an autograph, and while he is happy to oblige, the result seems to indicate that Roger Moore is under the impression that he is someone called Pam Larth. Or that he is drunk. Or that I am. My last request is for a photograph. Again, he is happy to oblige, although he has no choice but to appear in it as himself, something which works better at a distance than it does up close. We pose like heads of state, double-handed handshakes, smiles straight into the lens. Once a couple of snaps have been taken I feel I have nothing to lose and finally ask the question the world wants to hear. 'Whom do you prefer, Mr Moore: Ian Ogilvie or you?' (Ian Ogilvie played the Saint on television, a role which had been earlier – and much better – played by Roger Moore.)

'Ian Ogilvie,' he answers tawnily. 'They were all better than me.' Then he walks away, leaving me feeling small and a little sad in the wake of his unexpectedly wry self-deprecation.

Later that evening the *Royal Clipper* pulled out of the tiny principality of Monaco and set sail (or engine) for Cannes, in the large country of France. It was a beautiful, balmy night and as I stood on deck watching the lights of Monte Carlo twinkle and disappear, I thought how lovely the black sea looked and started to wonder how long it would take to turn the ship around and pick me up if I leaped into it. Suspecting that I was actually drunk enough to try and find out, I headed straight below to my cabin.

The next day everybody aboard was roused at 7 a.m. for an enormous buffet breakfast featuring bacon slices so hefty I'm sure they were from boars. By holding back on the fruit, I could only eat five. I searched the three-tiered dining area for Roger Moore, hoping to apologise for my smart aleck remark about Ian Ogilvie, but he was nowhere to be found. He may have been hiding under a piece of bacon – or Queen Sylvia of Sweden.

After breakfast it was, sadly, time for us to disembark and join the sunshine and beautiful people of Cannes, a small, sunny city which is an ideal place to quench a hangover. I returned to my cabin, packed and was taken back to land in a small boat. Once there I realised that I'd left my camera on the *Royal Clipper* and took a small boat back to the ship, where I failed to find the camera. Then, once again, I took a small boat back to land, feeling thoroughly nauseated by both the choppy ride and the knowledge that I had no proof of my encounters with Roger Moore. People would just have to believe that I really *did* meet him and all of this really *did* happen, because it did. Much as I wish certain things didn't . . .

Early September

Following a bowel movement I discover a large amount of bright red blood in the can. My reaction is this: 'Oh' (gasped in an extremely worried voice). I immediately head to Dr de Bruijn's office around the corner which is open but completely unmanned for the ten minutes I stand listening to Dutch voices in other rooms behind closed doors. I see a note explaining that the place is on holidays from tomorrow until the 25th and to call another doctor for an appointment at a different office. I go home and do so and am told by the woman on the phone, 'But Dr de Bruijn is still there today.'

'Yeah, I know but it's the last day. They're full and busy.'

'Well I cannot make an appointment for this doctor while your doctor is still working.'

I explain that she isn't so much *my* doctor as *a* doctor that I go to.

'I cannot do it.'

'Until tomorrow, when de Bruijn's gone, right?'

'Monday. We are not open tomorrow.'

So I call back the first doctor – 'my' doctor – and am told that this is their last day before *vakantie* and that they are very busy and that unless my complaint is urgent I cannot see anyone. I claim, not untruthfully, urgency, and am booked in that afternoon.

Meanwhile I search the Internet for clues, typing in unhappy combinations of words such as bleeding+rectum and blood+bowel and cancer (plus nothing). This is a really terrible way to start a day, and I become very scared. The thing is, I've eaten an awful lot of crap in my (too short so far) life and am pretty much a prime candidate for bowel cancer or colon cancer or stomach cancer. Plus it's probably hereditary. But why can't this happen to someone who deserves it, like Saddam Hussein or Marco Borsato? I don't deserve to die – not yet, anyway. Perhaps not ever.

It becomes impossible to concentrate on anything following a revelation like this. I look out the window at the flat opposite and wonder where that girl has gone. Is she on – *bowel cancer*. Do I have bowel cancer? I see the low, heavy clouds of late summer, wondering if it will – *diverticulitis*. Is it *that*? Why does blood have to be red? Why could it not be a calming blue? (Although, if it was light blue, would we then associate everything so tinted with mortality and terror? Would we look at the sky and shriek in fear? Would the colour for stop on traffic lights be azure?) It's never off my mind, and won't be until I endure the indignity of a Dutch endoscopy (which'll cost a bomb, no doubt – a bum bomb, I cannot help thinking) then the agony of waiting for test results.

I decide to try and save time by collecting a . . . sample. This is not as easy as I first think it will be, certainly not as simple a process as I'm accustomed to. I feel that the toilet would be the most appropriate venue for this operation and bring along the following materials: white paper (for spillage), aluminium foil (as a landing pad) and a plastic, sealable container (for collection of result). I squat and strain, spattering blood on the paper and the foil, pick up the foil then roll and urge the small stool into the container. Now I'm worried that they'll detect high levels of aluminium in my sample and think I'm radioactive or something. So, should I tell them of my unusual method of collection and delivery? It's kind of embarrassing. The whole thing's embarrassing, if you want to know the truth. Embarrassing and possibly fatal . . .

'Do you want me to put it in, or will you do it?' She is holding up a glass thermometer. The question can only mean one thing.

'Umm . . . I'll do it,' I say. The doctor is around fifty, a handsome woman with shoulder-length grey hair and a light brown mole in the hollow of her left cheek, dressed in baggy yellow jeans and a matching yellow denim vest – a horrible outfit. I pull down my pants and reach around behind to my behind.

'You can't do it that way,' she says. 'You must lie down.'

I tell her that if I lie down I will be unable to reach my ass, or more specifically, my anus (but I leave out that particular specific). She takes the thermometer from me and points to the paper-covered bed thing. I lie down on my side with my underpants (shame-inducing white briefs riddled with holes) at my ankles. She parts my cheeks (I seem to recall now that she did it without gloves, which shows a certain amount of bravery and foolhardiness on both our parts – but mainly hers) and slips the thin end of the thermometer into my – I have to say it – anus. I say 'thin end' but it may as well be a marrow. I grunt solidly. 'It must remain there for three minutes,' she tells me. Meanwhile she does some typing, takes a few phone calls (from her travel agent, probably), asks me a few more questions and, in what seems like no more than an hour or two, the three minutes have passed. The doctor looks at the mercifully removed thermometer and pronounces my ass temperature as normal. After pressing my abdomen for a short while, she concludes that what I have is probably a bacterial infection of the colon or gastrointestinal tract. 'Not bowel cancer?' I ask.

'I had not thought of it until you mention it now,' she says. 'You're too young for that, I think.'

'I'm older than I look,' I tell her. (I am.)

'Is there a history of this cancer in your family?'

'No, not that I know of,' I lie.

'Do you *know* your family?'

'Most of them.'

'It's not impossible, but not very likely. It should . . . how do you say in English, heal itself? If not after two weeks, come back again to here.'

'Two *weeks*?'

'You think that is a long time?'

'One day of passing blood is a long time, ma'am,' I say. 'Isn't there any medicine I can take?'

'Is best not to take anything for this.'

'Two weeks, huh?'

'That's right.'

'Which is just about when you'll be back from your *vakantie*.'

'That's right.'

'I have a . . . sample with me. Shouldn't you send it out for tests or something?'

'They cannot tell anything from a stool! If there is blood, there is blood. What more do you need to know?'

'*Why* there's blood. That's my main area of interest,' I explain. 'Also, whether I'm going to die.'

'You're not going to die. *Daag!*' It is brutal, typically Dutch in its stony bluntness, but quite reassuring nevertheless. And I decide as I leave the doctor I am grateful for that. But there remains one last problem – how best to dispose of my plastic container.*

That evening we met our absurdly tall and handsome neighbours Arnout Groen (owner of the testicles) and Diana 'Dee-Dee' Heemskerk (painter of the testicles). They're in computers in some way. Or software. I was too drunk to remember anything for more than five minutes. God, I hope we didn't disgrace ourselves or our country. Although I do remember angrily demanding of Arnout, 'What sort of economy can afford to charge *f*4 for a sponge?' Even though I was serious, he laughed a lot – this very

---

*Two weeks later blood tests reveal nothing deadly but there is an accompanying note from the doctor and countersigned by a pathologist suggesting I invest in new underwear.

deep, subterranean laughter full of joy and good humour. He also showed some very nice teeth and high, pronounced cheekbones whilst doing so. And now that I think about it, his blue eyes seemed to sparkle as well. Diana was very attractive close up, and tall, too. It's nice to be friends with your neighbours – at the very least you can borrow cutlery from them and they can look after your pets when you're away. We really should buy a dog to get the most out of our neighbours.

The reason we won't – apart from the fact that I'd be too upset when it eventually died – is the Dog Tax. Originally, the Dog Tax was implemented for companies who used dogs to pull carts (this was before horses were invented) but is now part of a more general environmental tax which is used to create places (commonly known as *parks*) for dogs to run and play and yap, as well as to clean up after them, although I see no evidence of this. It also covers the cost of what they call a 'dog badge', another thing I have never seen. Everyone who owns a dog must pay the tax. This is why we will not have a dog.

But Sally and I are not entirely without fauna: for ten months of the year we have to sleep beneath a mosquito net. I had never associated Amsterdam with problems like large, pestering mosquitoes, but they're here in tropical abundance. They're different from Australian mozzies in ways other than plenitude and size – here they shoot you full of some sort of insect caffeine. Every time one sneaks through the net and bites me, I am jolted awake, scratching for about forty-five minutes after each attack, dimly reviewing the dream I have just been removed from.

I dreamed about Katharine Hepburn one night. She was young and freckle-faced and we were kissing a lot. 'God, you're so good-looking,' I told her.

'Yeah, I've heard that before. Shut up about it,' she said, in that braying Yankee tone of hers before we began kissing again. She was sitting in my lap on the porch of a large Connecticut home and boy was she good-looking. A real knockout. When I woke up I was pretty surprised to hear that she hadn't died during the night. Other celebrities whom I have kissed in dreams include, but are not limited to, Jodie Foster, Reese Witherspoon, Kylie Minogue, Renée Zellweger, Parker Posey and Burt Reynolds. I think I have a thing about celebrities. The thing I think I have about celebrities is this: I resent them, I am deeply jealous of them in all sorts of appropriately fantastic ways and yearn to be one, principally because I would be better at it than many of them; Elle MacPherson, Gwyneth Paltrow and Guy Ritchie to name just three.

The young staring girl from the window opposite is suddenly back after two months. I have a theory about what may have happened to her – she and her family went on holiday. But on holiday from what exactly – lying on the couch and watching television, alternating with long bouts of dewy-eyed staring out the window? You don't deserve a break from that. Well, actually you do, but you don't deserve a break *for* that.

The first time she caught my eye since she returned, the girl gave me a look of such vivid contempt that I was the first to pull away – and damned quickly. I was shocked, but also relieved in a certain way; after all, the last thing I wanted to get into was some sort of cross-window waving and smiling relationship. Every day we'd feel obliged to grin or nod or waggle our fingers at one another. And then there'd be the dreaded meeting on the street during the one hour a week she's allowed out of the flat. She'd have no idea that I wasn't Dutch and would probably be all embarrassed that I didn't speak the language properly and we'd conversationally shuffle about before an uncomfortable parting; the whole tenor of the waving and smiling relationship we'd established would be ruined, replaced by embarrassment, nervousness and suspicion. It's better this way, it really is.

Sally and I *have* become properly friendly with our opposite balcony neighbours. Arnout grew up in Holland and Washington DC because his father worked for the World Bank. Diana's dad was in flowers, meaning she had to grow up here. They're both very nice people but they make me a bit sick with their Dutch perfection of height, health and pulchritude. We went to Diana's birthday celebs in the Vondelpark on Saturday and met many of their friends and family, all of whom also seemed very pleasant and attractive as well. God, it must be gratifying to be Dutch.

It was on my way back from the park that I had one of my rare encounters with the Dutch *politie* (police). Because my bicycle was heavily laden with leftover beer, I was cycling along the road, adjacent to the *fiets pad* (bicycle path), waiting for a less spine-crushing, beer-spilling opportunity to enter the bike lane. But before I found one a police car cruised up beside me, one of the cops leaning out the window and saying (in Dutch), 'Hey mister, there's a very nice bicycle path just there on your right. Why don't you give it a try?' How friendly and reasonable, I thought. God, it must be gratifying to be a Dutch criminal.

NEWS ITEM, OCTOBER 12TH, 2000: **Three Dutch citizens who spent three months in prison in Yugoslavia accused of plotting to kidnap Slobodan Milosevic face a *f*100,000 bill for the rental car they left in Belgrade. Following the collapse of the Milosevic regime the three men were released. Upon their arrival home they were charged for the new Citroën Evasion they left behind. Ronald Diks, owner of Diks Car Rental, said, 'I don't know what they are going to do, but we have to get the car back.' He added that they would be charged an additional *f*200 for each day the car was not returned.**

Just one of the many hidden costs when you play soldier of fortune for real.

BRUSHOFF WITH FAME NO. 4:
BIG DADDY

The most enduring and perhaps satisfying relationship of my life has not been with my wife or my family or any of my friends – it has been with television. It's been that way because, in the words of Homer Simpson (the TV character, not the Nathanael West character), television asks so little and gives so much. So when, as a representative of the *Holland Herald*, I get the chance to ask John de Mol, co-creator of the TV phenomenon 'Big Brother', which television programs he most enjoys and he tells me that apart from football matches there is really nothing in particular, I am shocked. Football matches aren't even programs; they are, at the risk of stating the obvious, football matches. His answer seems somehow disrespectful of the medium to which de Mol has contributed so little of worth yet which has given him so much.

'Big Brother' is produced in over twenty countries; it is probably the most popular and successful program of its odious type (so-called 'reality TV', although de Mol prefers the term 'real people television') produced in the last twenty years. 'Big Brother', the germ of which came to de Mol during a conversation about the American experiment in isolation and deprivation Biosphere II, has made him and his company very, very rich.

Nestled in the heart of a forest just outside Holland's media capital, Hilversum, is the headquarters of Endemol Entertainment. Inside as well as outside the sleek, striking Richard Meier building are dozens of televisions – it's not so much a case of Big Brother is watching you everywhere you go, as everywhere you go you are watching 'Big Brother'.

John, or as I come to know him, Mr de Mol, is a dry, humourless fellow, rarely smiling or laughing, despite my (admittedly feeble) attempts at levity. However, his personal energy is strong and palpable. He is a buzzy, busy, vibrant presence, always moving quickly, drinking coffee and smoking cigarettes almost incessantly – at least half a dozen during the hour we talk. The only time he appears to slow down is when he answers questions, which he does with a very focussed – or practised – attention.

I ask Mr de Mol whether he thinks that television is power. There is a long pause before he speaks. 'The medium is power . . . but the power is controlled by the [television] station, so I don't consider myself to be extremely powerful.' Coming from a man whose company produced more than fourteen thousand hours of television in 1999, which, by his own reckoning, reached around twenty billion people, I find this absence of hubris rather odd, if not wilfully naive. When I remind him that 'Big Brother' has created quite a bit of international cultural chaos – an attempt by the German government to have the program banned; hysterical reports from the UK that the show would spawn 'fatal copycats'; numerous lawsuits; the instant creation of instant fifteen-minute media stars, some of whom went on to pose for

Playboy; dozens of internet sites; *and* a board game – de Mol remains demure: 'I'm just a television producer who tries to make the best programs. That's it.'

'Because if it was me responsible for all that,' I tell him, 'I'd feel fantastic!'

'Oh, I feel fantastic,' he responds mildly.

In an attempt to elicit something more . . . fantastic, I try another tack and ask how the 'Big Brother' board game is doing. 'I don't know. I really don't know.' I can understand that the guy would have far more important things on his mind than a mere game, but personally I remain intrigued by it and ask how it actually works. 'Well, I should know but . . .'

I give up the board game angle and ask whether he thinks the success of 'Big Brother' might have an adverse effect on the Big Brother charity program (wherein brotherless and sisterless children are assigned 'big brothers' for afternoons and weekends of fun and entertainment).

'Never heard of it,' he says.

It is time to break out the big guns. 'Do you own any records by Janis Joplin's former band Big Brother and the Holding Company?'

He does not.

'Do you have a big brother?'

He does not.

'Do you wish you did?'

'Sometimes yes, mostly when I was younger.'

Fascinating. I wonder how much the success of 'Big Brother' has changed his life.

'Well, "Big Brother" is just a very, very small part of the business we do; it just gave us huge attention. We've succeeded before in creating formats like "All You Need is Love", "Love Letters" and "Forgive Me" that were seen in nineteen, twenty countries.'

I am struck by de Mol's use of the word *formats*; I realise that it is appropriate production parlance but it still seems a rather cold, joyless word to describe the things that one creates and, presumably, takes pride in. Especially all the ones with 'love' in the title. But that, I suppose, is the result of being in the business, rather than the pleasure, of television.

'I ended up in television by accident,' Mr de Mol tells me. 'Radio was my big love. In the beginning I hated television, but after three or four months I thought, well, let's try it.' I presume that his feelings have changed quite a bit since then – not about what he *sees* on TV necessarily, but what he derives from television.

And the future of the medium?

'I think that the ["reality TV"] genre will see a lot of new formats which will see a lot of failures because a lot of producers think all they need to do is just put a number of people in whatever room in whatever configuration and put cameras on them and you have interesting television. And I don't think that's the case.'

Indeed. I ask my final question: 'What do you think George Orwell would have to say about "Big Brother"?'

There is another pause before Mr de Mol says, somewhat despairingly, 'I can imagine anything from "terrible" to "exactly as I thought it would turn out".'

I have to agree – with both possibilities. As I pack up my things I ask de Mol whether his company is still producing feature films. He tells me that they no longer are. 'What a shame,' I say. 'I've got this really terrific script . . .' Mr de Mol and his press secretary laugh politely. My last request is a photo and I ask de Mol if he minds having his photo taken with his arm draped across my shoulder in a big brotherly fashion. He sighs, grinds out his cigarette then dutifully stands up and poses as requested – even smiles.

I leave knowing less about John de Mol than when I arrived. All I really know is what he isn't; he isn't fascinating, insightful, fun, funny or particularly charming. He seems too ordinary, regular – someone you'd choose for a third cousin rather than a big brother. I mean, I *liked* him well enough, I just wouldn't want to *be* him. Which, considering how very successful he is and how very unsuccessful I am, surprises me. Actually, it completely shocks me. But then I wonder, exactly what *did* I expect of a triumphant TV executive? A combination of newsreader authority and tonight show host warmth? Someone with a smooth, velvety charm who kept cracking gags and winking at me every so often? Perhaps I wanted more of what he'd derived from the medium. But then I realise he's just a television producer who tries to make the best programs, while I'm just a viewer who tries to watch the best programs – that's it. And with that thought I suddenly know which of the two of us has truly gotten the most from television . . .

For my entire life I have been what is generally known as a trouble-maker. I got into a great deal of it while I was in high school – hundreds of hours of detention, a couple of suspensions, several near-expulsions, and many imploring calls to my parents from the headmaster urging my transfer to another 'more suitable' (by which he meant 'any other') school – and when I left high school I got into quite a lot of trouble in my working life. I was fired from my first thirty-six jobs (including a termination after just three days at the Department of Foreign Affairs, a truly miraculous achievement considering the fact that it is all but impossible to be fired *ever* from the public service, let alone after seventy-two hours), and at every advertising agency I joined subsequent to these three dozen test runs, I was warned most sternly by creative directors and managing directors about various questionable behavioural and performance matters. I was placed on probation; told to take time off; removed from accounts at a client's request; hauled out of meetings when it was feared I might attack/be attacked; upbraided for making a (quite accidental and entirely oblique) Nazi reference* during a presentation to some German clients; and fired. I have also courted trouble (perhaps even married it) in various forms as a television script writer, travel writer and even as a novelist (mostly with other novelists, who are a prickly bunch of kittens if ever there was one).

Obviously, leaving trouble behind in Australia (or behind in various careers, the bridges back to which I had very much

*Back at 180 I had named a character in a TV commercial script Sarah Von Runstedt, and while I was aware that there was a prominent Second World War General Karl von Rundstedt, it was news to me that he was a Nazi. Plus, Sarah's surname was spelled differently.

burned) was an unlikely scenario, and now it was my time to get into trouble as a journalist. One week after my trip to Hilversum, Ray received an email from John de Mol's press secretary. Apparently Mr de Mol was 'very irritated' by the fact that the interviewer (me) started 'talking about' and trying to 'pitch' a film scenario. He was also annoyed at being 'forced' to be photographed with 'his arms around' the interviewer (me).

RAY: *Did* you try to sell him a film script?
ME: Of course not. I made a rather wry joke about one, that's all. It was the only time he laughed, for God's sake.
RAY: What about the photo?
ME: Well that happened. But I asked first. And as we both know, Ray, there is most certainly a word for 'no' in Dutch. He could've used it if he was that uncomfortable.
RAY (laughs): Well, be gentle with him when you're writing it up.
ME: You know I will be.

Oddly enough, considering the fact that I wasn't particularly gentle with him when I wrote it up, following the article's appearance, Ray received another email from de Mol's press man saying how pleased he and the subject were with it. The Dutch, they're so . . . tolerant.

One day in November there was an unmarked envelope in our mailbox. Inside the envelope were three one-hundred guilder bills clipped to a piece of paper on which was written the word 'Ta' in green pencil. And that was the last we heard of Keith Finney for another year. But I still thought of him often, bound up as he was with so much of my very first impressions of Amsterdam. His ghost, fleeting and furtive, was everywhere.

NEWS ITEM, DECEMBER 17TH, 2000: The FBI has ruled out foul play and mechanical malfunction in the death of a San Francisco resident's 2000-foot fall from a company jet. In what is considered a suicide, the Dutch woman fell from the aircraft after apparently opening an emergency exit. Friends claimed that she was unhappy following a recent move to San Francisco from Europe. Her family had urged the woman to seek counselling. An FBI spokesman said that two passengers who saw her fall from the plane, flying between Sacramento and San Jose, were so distraught they could not tell the pilots what had happened and therefore authorities were not notified until forty-five minutes after the plane had landed. Police discovered the woman's body in a community vegetable garden in Sacramento on Friday afternoon.

2001: Another New Millennium?

My crazy life in the early months of 2001 was wild, dynamic, unpredictable and rich with incident:

- My bank account plumbed an embarrassment of poverty (under ƒ1000) which caused extreme fear and the immediate cancellation of the Bentley full of caviar and saffron threads I'd ordered the previous week.

- Days later I received a *deus ex machina* telephone call from Chris at 180 asking whether I was interested in working on a 'top secret project' for a client whose identity he could not reveal but who would pay cash (being a penurious lover of 'black ops', how could I refuse?).

- I began reading a biography of Howard Hughes which caused me to keenly lament my own life of sanity, poverty and non-plane crashing.

- To Sally's voluble objection and dismay I became very fond of the disgusting but delicious Dutch dinner of *rookworst* (smoked sausage), mashed potatoes, peas and sauerkraut, the last included because it was available for just thirty-five cents a bag and I had begun shopping like an old man – an old Dutch man, it seemed.

- I grew addicted to 'Soldier of Fortune' (the computer game, rather than the magazine or the calling).

- I did some dj-ing at Boom Chicago for a lousy ƒ75 for four hours' work (being a penurious lover of my own taste in music, how could I refuse?).

- I met with Chris and the secret client and agreed to be paid a lot of money by him.

- One Friday I had a drink with Joey, back for the weekend from Poland, and became a little blue when it hit me that he really did live in Warsaw now, not just around the corner in de Pijp where he belonged. ('When are you coming to visit me in Poland?' he asked. 'Soon,' I told him, by which I meant 'never'.)

• Sally and I had dinner at a restaurant called Bofinger in Paris one night. Befitting a famous Parisian dining institution, the place was packed. I slimed through the crowd of Gallic smoke and chatter, trying to sound extremely French as I asked the maitre'd how long a table might be. I was told forty minutes and given a glossy purple business card with the name Alban Berg printed on it and informed that that was my *nom pour ce soir*. While I'd never been exactly thrilled about my actual name, this strange turn of events did confuse me somewhat; however, I did my level best to appear Alban Berg-ish, having had some experience in assuming the identity of other men such as Carlos Juno of Latitud 4 back in the tiny principality of Monaco one afternoon some months before. Sally, Alban and I stepped outside and wondered what to do for forty minutes, stepped back in and found that Mr Berg had missed his table despite the fact that only twenty minutes had passed. Clearly it was a vexing world that man lived in. Close to midnight we sat down in the large dining area where Sally vomited up her onion soup as soon as she finished it. Despite this hiccup, it was a pleasant evening, but, apart from the regurgitation, not as memorable as I'd have liked – perhaps Alban Berg had a better time pretending to be me back in Amsterdam.

• Back in Amsterdam the actual me was still having enormous trouble deciding what he wanted to do with his life (the rest of it – the past – was, sadly, pretty much taken care of), and, in a move of startling weirdness and desperation, applied for a job as a TV programmer with UPC thusly:

Dear Ms B,

I am writing to express my interest in the job of scheduler at UPC. A copy of my curriculum vitae is attached. My experience in television is principally in the area of watching it; however, I have created it – both as a writer and script editor on various television series in Australia and as creator of TV advertising in Australia and in the Netherlands. I am a great admirer of the form and would respond to the challenge of being a programmer with great enthusiasm and excitement. Further, I am in possession of a photograph of John de Mol in a mildly compromising position. Should you give me the opportunity of an interview, I have no doubt that you will find the right man for the job.

Regards, Sean Condon

- I read that twenty-six-year-old Peter Keller from Tilburg, Holland, finished third in the Pokémon World Championship in New York, placing him among the world's elite Pokémon players.
- I felt that compared with that of twenty-six-year-old Peter Keller from Tilburg, my life wasn't actually as sad and pointless as I'd previously thought.
- Nevertheless my liver hurt and my soul ached and one morning I woke up drily sobbing over a short film screened in my dream about a semiretarded death-row prisoner whose brother despises him until three seconds after he gets fried in the chair.
- I was turned down as a UPC TV programmer because of 'over qualification' (they wanted someone just starting out in any career and preferably – seriously – with 'no higher education' because the job was programming the extreme sports channel).
- One day there were no English pork sausages at Marks & Spencer (while I loathed appearing like some dreary, pathetic expat in search of that tea-and-crumpety touch of home by shopping at M&S, the truth was that those sausages were things of pink, porcine beauty, easily the best of their type available in Holland), due to those infernal BSE and foot and mouth crises that were blighting meat across Europe. With people like me around, being a pig is not a good thing to be, but being a pig in England in 2001 especially sucked.
- Ray was approached by some book publishers in Leiden, a city about an hour south of Amsterdam, who were looking into starting a magazine about contemporary Japanese culture. He told them that he would consider editing the magazine only if Sally was his deputy editor. Ray's unfailing decency and loyalty – the Henry Blake in him – threw a most welcome lifeline to my wife's editing career (which is not to say that Sally isn't a first-

class editor, she is. But also, she had, as I mentioned, spent some time as a showgirl in a Japanese hotel back in the mid-eighties, so she was more than qualified for the position).

• I met yet again with Chris, an ex-Wieden producer called Peter Cline and the secret client in order to present some ideas for the secret project. It went well and two days later I was . . .

On the way to London with Peter Cline

'Are you really Patsy Cline's cousin?'

'Yes.'

'Really? You're really her cousin?'

'I really am. Why is that so difficult to believe?'

'It's not difficult to believe, it's just odd. You don't expect things like that. Plus, shouldn't you be a lot older?'

'I'm not a direct cousin. I'm forty-three.'

'Can you sing?'

'We don't have much in common apart from the name.'

'Thank God for that.'

'Why?'

'I'm sitting next to you on a plane, Peter. With your family history, it's kind of unnerving.'

For good reason, I don't enjoy getting semi-naked in front of other people of any sex or nationality, but a couple of hours later I was standing in the Spy Shop in Mayfair shirtless, my arms held up over my head, surrounded by men and women of various sexes and nationalities. An English man with superb halitosis bent and circled me, his fingers fiddling with my lower back, while Peter, an American with regular breath and a dry sense of humour, stood back and took photographs. A Scottish woman kept averting her eyes and trying to stifle either giggles or vomit. Mr Halitosis warned me never to give away details of what was taking place at that moment 'to anyone, *evah*!' A few minutes later I had about eight pounds of high-tech recording equipment strapped to my back, held in place by a thick white Velcro belt, a series of wires running up my spine and connecting to a huge pair of black spectacles with a tiny camera in the bridge. In my pants pocket was a switch that set the bulky, uncomfortable operation in motion. I looked like a nerd with several hernias.

'How d'you feel, then?' Halitosis asked, then winked at me through a cloud of brown.

'Surprised,' I said. 'I never imagined my life would reach the point where I'd be wearing undercover film gear. It's quite a shock.' Having said that, there was in fact an odd and jarring element of *déjà vu* about what was happening – being sent to another country on behalf of an advertising/marketing company to film something or somebody who did not wish to be filmed and dealing with a person who had shocking breath in order to do it. 'It's unique.'

'Go stand outside in the street,' Peter told me. 'I want a shot of you looking stupid in public.'

Just before we climbed out of the cab Peter lifted my shirt and made sure the recording device was on. 'The light is on,' he said, putting NASA control room style pauses between each word. 'And we are good to go.'

As I tucked my shirt back in over the lumps, I saw the cabbie peering at us through the rear-view mirror. 'What are you geezers up to, then?' he asked. 'Are you from the telly?'

'Not yet,' I told him.

I took a deep breath and marched straight into the reception area of a large ad agency and, barely stopping to even think about it, spewed out what would become my frequently repeated cover story for the next few days. 'Good morning, ma'am. My name's Sean. I'm from a very small agency called Bing! Bam! Boom! in Melbourne, Australia – we advertise the Dunlop Volley tennis shoe, mainly. And I'm over here in England on a kind of cultural tour because I'm a really big fan of English advertising. I think it's the best in the world. And I particularly like your work – you people are the best of the best and I was wondering if I could possibly get a photograph of myself in your reception for my scrapbook as a kind of souvenir of my trip. You don't have to take the picture, my friend Benny will take the picture.' I would then point to Peter Cline who would be standing several feet away, generally pretending he wasn't standing there with me, reduced to this. 'That's Benny over there.'

Usually the receptionist – polite, friendly and charming – would say something along the lines of, 'I don't see why not,' before she suddenly thought of several reasons why not and made a phone call to seek the permission of a higher authority. During these waiting periods I'd make idle chatter with the receptionist who would treat me with an uneasy combination of fear and pity (as though dealing with a semi-retarded jaguar), both elements a direct result of the big black spectacles that loomed back down at her, my eyes rolling about behind the lenses, my loud Australian voice bringing a harsh, yet naive quality to the proceedings.

'Gosh, London's very BIG isn't it?' I might say.

'Mmm hmm. You're a long way from home, aren't you dear?'

'Yes, I AM! It's my first TIME IN LONDON. Gosh, it's a BIG PLACE!'

'Okay, you can take your photograph now dear.'

At which point I'd go and sit down on a couch so that Benny/Peter/Patsy's cousin could snap my ludicrously grinning mug while the receptionist eyed me carefully, no doubt wishing there was a secret security buzzer hidden under her desk.

Sometimes, however, we encountered problems:

'It's company policy not to allow pictures of our reception area.'

'Is that because you don't want people STEALING your INTERIOR DESIGN IDEAS?'

'We have to protect copyright, you see, on all of our ads.'

'But won't they be ON TV or IN MAGAZINES soon anyway?'

'I can't allow you past this point without an appointment.'

'But I don't HAVE anyone to see. I just want to look at the RECEPTION AREA. Please!'

'Oh come on, you must be 'avin' a larf. What's this *really* all about then?'

What it was *really* all about was simple: to make little movies out of each of these encounters which would show what various agencies' receptions (and receptionists) were really like. The plan was that we would then put them on the secret client's website* to create instant hype and buzz in the London ad world. Of course, we couldn't let anyone know *that* . . .

*See www.advanceparty.com.

BRUSHOFF WITH FAME NO. 5:
THE LESSER MINOGUE

On day two, whilst trying not to worry about the plunging world economy and being hit by a stray bit of the MIR Space Station as it re-enters earth's atmosphere, I bump into Dannii Minogue in a Soho Starbucks.

'You're DANNII Minogue, aren't you?' I say loudly, holding out my hand for her to reluctantly shake. From her face, two things are clear: that she most definitely is Dannii Minogue and that at that moment she very much wishes she isn't. She takes a moment to consider denying her identity, but, while being extremely surgically altered, she simply can't. Plus, she's a celebrity and addicted to fame, even when the price is enduring a conversation with a yelling nutjob wearing glasses with thick ribbon attached to the ends. She nods and gives me a smile which, had she greater control over her mouth, would have been wan, but cannot help being dazzling. 'I'm Australian *too*!' I say overenthusi-astically. 'How do you like LONDON?'

'Well, after eleven years you get pretty used to it. Heh heh.' Another wrinkle-free smile.

I point to her Starbucks coffee mug. 'And you like STARBUCKS *too*!'

'I'm addicted to it,' she says quickly.

'What's your sister up to these –'

'Bye.'

Sadly, my recorder runs out of film and fails to capture the whole uncomfortable – and deeply actual – occurrence, but I'll bet old Dannii thinks about it often and remembers every last moment of our encounter with great clarity and fondness. Perhaps even a niggling sliver of regret. Had she only known what I was packing that day . . .

Over the three days we spent in London, Peter and I filmed and/or photographed the interiors of about thirty advertising agencies, most of which were pretty glamourous, clean and friendly. And in between – in the backs of cabs, at restaurants, as we wandered Soho – we talked about the things people do for money.

'What did you do at Wieden?' I asked Peter, imagining him in a glassed corner office, several assistants outside his door.

'Well, I guess the biggest thing was producing the Good versus Evil spot.'

'The one where Cantona kicks a hole in the Devil's stomach?'

'Uh huh.'

'Good lord, you did that? That was a huge commercial. Huge! And now you're doing this crap here with me?' I gasped. 'What *happened* to you, Peter?'

'Yeah, I've come a long way,' he said drily. 'Mostly down.'

'God, the things we have to do to make dough, huh?'

'Well, we're having fun, aren't we? We're seeing some nice-looking broads. We got some laughs going on.'

'Sure, but, y'know, you're from New York.'

'Woodstock,' he reminded me.

'Yeah, but you lived in Manhattan for a long time. You had the high life in the king of cities, man. Now what've you got – me.'

'Why are you trying to make me feel bad about my life, Sean? What've I done to annoy you?'

'I'm not, I'm just . . . Wouldn't you rather be producing a feature?'

'We all do what we have to do, Sean. And we never know what we're gonna have to do next.'

I knew what I had to do next – buy Sally a scarf from Hermès in Regent Street. After that, I had no idea. Write something to pay for the scarf, I supposed.

What I did next, when I returned to Amsterdam, was watch *Every Which Way But Loose*. And even though I was enduring it (for the second time in my life) in order to write a piece about it, I could not help but feel that my life was really hitting a new low if it had come to the point where I was watching monkey movies in the middle of the day.

'You're thirty-five,' I said to myself. 'You shouldn't be doing this. You should be . . . Oh, I don't know. Maybe this is *exactly* what you should be doing. How do I know?' So we left it at that and I watched the movie. And this is the result of my televisual labours:

The great apes

There are lamentably few orang-utan-based movies. Of the handful that exist, *Every Which Way But Loose* (1978) and *Dunston Checks In* (1996) stand out. (The missing link between the two is the 1981 Tony Danza + orang-utan outing *Goin' Ape*, an all-too-rare find at a video store or cinematheque screening.) And they stand out because of one thing – the o'tan actors.

Of the two, Manis, who plays Clyde in *Loose*, gives the more carefully nuanced performance and, despite the film being an essentially comic vehicle, director James Fargo has wisely provided great latitude for Manis to show his impressive range, from sympathetically pensive when a heartbroken Clint Eastwood laments his loss of love, to sheer desolation after Clint loses the big fight with Tank Murdock. Manis rawly reveals his pain and invites – *dares* us – to feel every ounce of it along with him. And we do, for *Every Which Way But Loose* is a movie steeped in pain.

However, this is not to say that relative newcomer Sam, as the orang-utan Dunston who checks in, does not show every indication of soon becoming a first-rate actor. His rich conveyance of a range of emotions, from coyness to dolefulness to a kind of dewy wistfulness (which, admittedly, is more or less the permanent natural expression of the orang-utan and perhaps therefore not so much of a stretch) and back to coyness all in a single, brief scene, is remarkable. He also cowers convincingly at the hands of his evil master Lord Rutledge (Rupert Everett).

Both orang-utan actors are skilled in *Pongo pygmaeus* comic stand-bys such as blowing raspberries to fusty blue-bloods, flipping the bird to nasty bikers, making the (usually sarcastic) 'kissy face' to pretty much anybody, general burping and the clapping of one distended hand over the eyes in an expression of simian dismay. While these are certainly the tropes demanded by the orang-utan comedy genre, each brings a fresh touch to the old standards.

The chief differences lie in plot. *Loose* is essentially a man/ape road movie while *Dunston* is a lord/ape hotel movie. Clyde's guardian is truck-driving, peanut-eating, non-smoking, Sondra Locke-loving, motorcycle-stealing, cop-beating, denture-into-chowder-of-uptight-USC-sociology-student-slipping, bare-knuckle boxing enthusiast Philo Beddoe. Dunston's master is a jewel thief with a Terry Thomas style gap in his teeth. Sumatran Clyde walks like a big hairy W come to life (hands waving in the air), whereas Balinese Dunston moves more like an M (hands dragging along the ground). This is telling; there is true love and respect between Clyde and Philo, whereas Lord Rutledge is using Dunston as a mere tool for his own nefarious ends. Each orang-utan brilliantly employs his distinct physicality to bring the plight of his characters to the fore: Clyde – happy, waving; Dunston – sad, dragging.

Further, *Loose* is set in 'loose' late-seventies Los Angeles, a time and place when it was possible for a man to win the heart of supporting actress Beverly D'Angelo just by squeezing her melons. *Dunston* takes place in a more contemporary *mise en scène*, a mid-nineties New York City hotel, where emotions are 'checked in' and there is no place for Beverly D'Angelo or her melons.

Ultimately *Loose* loses the battle of the great ape movies for one simple reason – Clyde never shows up in any humorous outfits, like a nappy or the old Hawaiian-shirt-and-Ray-Bans combo such as the one Dunston wears when we first see him. Both are passable entertainments but I look forward to superior vehicles, truly worthy of talents like Manis and Sam. And I *don't* mean 'BJ and the Bear'.

A Friday in February

One Friday Sally returns from a meeting in Leiden with the news that she has been offered the position of deputy editor on a brand-new magazine called *Japan*. She is thrilled and hands in her notice at Boom Chicago immediately. By way of celebration I insist that we watch the Mel Gibson ponytail show *The Patriot*. This is not quite what Sally had in mind and before the long, rather stupid film is finished, she has invited Arnout and Diana over to drink champagne. '*Gefiliciteerd!*' both of them grin, enveloping Sally in congratulatory Dutch hugs. Just as we're popping the cork on the third or tenth bottle our long lost pal Dr Chris Burns, PhD, arrives, up here from Australia for a chemistry conference. It's great to see him because, like so many of my friends, he is much smarter and in many senses better than me. On top of that, Chris is very funny, morally decent and reliable, and healthy (he swims). These are qualities I like in friends – being surrounded by people like him gives me something tangible to aspire to. On the other hand, some of my friends insist on dragging me ever downward: soon after midnight Arnout rolls some joints and at around three, after several hours of coherent but pointless babbling (much of it concerning the length of Mel Gibson's ponytail and how my own hair could use a trim), I have to throw him out and soon weave bedward.

'You heard from Monica lately?' I ask Chris as I'm tucking him in.

'Not for months, Seanie. Have you?'

'No . . . It's kinda sad – she's the most famous person I ever met.'

'There's more to people than their fame, y'know.'

'Not to most famous people there's not.'

The next day Sally, Chris and I take a walk through the picturesque Jordaan where Sally takes a hilarious, freakish photo of me and the doctor posing with snowballs on a small bridge. In the background of the photograph there are masted ships lined up along Prinsengracht; the houses are all at least two hundred years old and even the joyously deranged expressions on our faces belong to some bygone era when there were more insane people wandering the streets. We look like two French lounge musicians posing for the cover of an EP entitled 'Les Deux Idiotes'. We are the *idiotes*.

The sun is high but may as well be a painting for all the heat it gives off; it's as crisp as a slap on the cheek as we trudge through the snow and folksy beauty of the city's prettiest neighbourhood. When people conjure the clichéd quintessence of olde Amsterdam, the Jordaan is what they see: tall, skinny buildings lining canals.

We discuss Sally's idea for a designer digital watch which tells you the time with phrases such as 'almost midnight: get to bed', 'high noon' and 'Chinese dentist' (for 2.30), which we all agree could make millions – especially of yen. Chris, who knows about such things because he is a scientist, tells us that the guy who patented the intermittent function on car windscreen wipers is now a multimillionaire. 'But since my own work involves prostate cancer research I don't expect to make a fortune from it,' Chris says. 'Nor do I really want to. It's just good work to do. That said, I do have half a million shares in the company.'

Having a friend visit always makes me behave like a tourist in my home town, so from the Jordaan we head across town to the Rijksmuseum. The Rijksmuseum, an impressive combination of dream and nightmare architecture built in 1885, is one of Amsterdam's few monumental structures, the absence being the result of there never having been a consistent period of monarchical rule over the city, as well as the fact that such grandiosity is not part of the Dutch psychology. This is my first time in the home of Rembrandt's large, dark and popular *Nightwatch*. It's a huge museum brimming with the shimmering evidence of Amsterdam's commercial and artistic golden age but I find it hard to appreciate much of it because as we wander the halls and rooms, I am urgently trying to invent something simple, unthought of and absolutely essential. And looking at works of art takes my mind off the more immediately pressing inspirations such as unusual windscreen wiper functions, dog perfumes, tiny scooters, fatality resistant shoehorns and other existence-enhancing ideas. By the time Chris leaves the next afternoon, I have come up with nothing apart from a device which would allow others to hear our voices as we ourselves hear them, and this Van Gogh/ Rembrandt-inspired thought: being a great artist is hard, but making great amounts of money is harder, especially if you attempt to combine the two.

I don't like the rich – hell, who does? – for one simple reason: they're rich. They're rich, and you and I are not. (Unless, of course, you are a rich person reading this, in which case I suggest you stop immediately for one simple reason: you won't understand the point I am trying to make. Or you will grasp it only too well and therefore pity me, and I don't want your pity. I want your money.) By rich, I mean very, very, very, very, very, very wealthy – the sort of person who doesn't so much bet on winning racehorses, but rather owns them *and* the stud farm *and* the studs *and* the company who invented lucerne and clover, which is what I understand your better class of racing stud prefers to eat. I mean *very* wealthy.

I realised just how much I didn't much care for the descendants of Croesus one afternoon when I was leafing through the residential real-estate section of the *International Herald Tribune*. Usually I just go straight to the comics (which also infuriate me because they're so mind-bendingly unamusing and yet have made many of their creators very wealthy – I mean *very* wealthy) but on that day, on my way to investigating Garfield's latest hilarious remark about how much he enjoys lasagne, I paused when I saw a picture of a castle for sale. I paused because I thought, 'Boy, *I'd* like to have a castle. I wonder if I can afford it.' The gaff in question was the Chateau des Milandes, a fifteenth-century 'stone construction' (a real-estate term meaning 'made of stone') in Perigord, France. As well as containing everything you'd expect from a castle – seven-hectare park setting, spectacular fireplaces, magnificent stained glass, traditional *lauzes* stone roof, moat, dungeon, etc – this particular joint had the added feature of once being owned by exotic fruiterer Josephine Baker, who I can only imagine had to shimmy with a lot of bananas to afford it. There was no price on the advertisement, so, taking a deep breath because I knew what the phone call to France would cost me – let alone the property – I dialled. A woman with a very nice French accent answered the telephone.

'Hi, ma'am,' I said, in my not-very-nice Euro-Australian accent (think George Lazenby with a slight head cold talking about superannuation or the perils of British beef). 'I have a question about Chateau des Milandes.'

'Please, go on.'

'How much is it?'

'Twenty-eight and a half million francs.'

'Goodbye.'

But the Baker pad seemed *un bon marché* (a French term meaning 'an absolute steal') compared to the one next door (next door in the paper, not the place next door in France).

'Once in a lifetime . . .' temptingly began the ad for a 37,000 square feet, God-only-knows-how-many-rooms mansion just outside San Francisco, complete with catering kitchen and 'high-tech media facility'. Fortunately there was a price for the Tobin-Clark estate, saving me both the cost and humiliation of a phone call to a southern Californian 'realtor' (American term meaning 'twenty per cent commission') who I knew would not have nearly as nice an accent as the lady *immobilier* from France. They were asking

45 million (US) dollars, or, to put it in my terms, a little over 106 million Dutch guilders. That's AUD$85,017,948. In francs, the figure cannot even be written down without the assistance of an official from Credit Lyonnaise.

Once I'd absorbed these figures, I had some asking of my own to do. Two questions sprang to mind: would there be any discount for cash, and once in exactly *whose* lifetime are these people talking about? Bill Gates's or Adnan Khashoggi's maybe, but not yours or mine. Not even *twenty* of mine.

When I realised that, I began to feel a little dismal about my life and its time. It depressed me to think that I was not now, nor would I ever likely to be, leading the kind of life where I could afford 37,000 square feet of marble floor and Jacobean oak panelling. That I can't even afford 37,000 feet of seagrass matting and pineboard. I started to feel like a complete *charlatan* (French term meaning 'loser') and turned straight to the comics in search of a laugh. And to my great surprise I got one from Garfield when I realised that even he could never afford the Tobin-Clark estate – and he's got *nine* lifetimes.

I'm no stranger to the international tonsorial experience. From anonymous one-man operations across the United States to the swish, swanky salons of swinging London, I've left piles of spare hair (and, I have to admit, a little dandruff) all over the world.

There was *uno vecchietto* (little old man) in the Campo de Fiori in Rome with whom I chatted, I'm pretty sure, about how you don't see circus elephants very often any more. He transformed me, employing a series of tuft cuts and forward brushings into someone resembling an emperor (probably Tiberius, who I presume was some sort of hairstyle hero of my barber). While the result was not particularly flattering (not without an accompanying toga and laurel leaf crown, anyway), I did assume a somewhat autocratic air up until the first wash. Also, I built a pretty nice coliseum. There's a spectacularly incompetent Russian on Geary Street in San Francisco whose sole reason for staying in business is his awesome collection of skin mags. Over the years he's ruined my hair probably half a dozen times, while I have gratefully stayed in touch with the latest trends in . . . art photography.

Whenever in town I used to visit a Scot in King's Cross (Sydney, not London) named Michael who was a former professional rugby player and who had L-O-V-E and H-A-T-E tattooed on his scissor-flickering fingers. He always told very corny but brief jokes along the lines of, 'I bought my ex-girlfriend some flowers and she told me to piss off but at least now we're talking.' Although, now I think about it, I may be imagining the tattoos and possibly the ex-rugby playerness as well, but he was almost certainly a barber – otherwise why did I always leave with less hair than when I arrived? There was a designer dude from a designer chain called Samson and Delilah or something like that in Soho (London, not New York) who charged me a fortune for the privilege of looking like someone who was trying to look like Robbie Williams but who really looked like k.d. lang pretending to be Billie Jean King. And there was a former pet-groomer named Marko in Astor Place, New York (New York), who had pictures of himself embracing satisfied customers like Bruce Willis, Anthony Edwards, Ted Danson and other balding stars who, for just $5, gave me an entirely electric-clipper-based cut best described as 'Number One – With a Vengeance!'. It was easily the worst haircut I've ever had, but on the plus side it lasted close to a year.

The west of Amsterdam is home to more cutters, dyers, curlers and trimmers of hair than anywhere else on earth. On every block there are at least three 'hair studios', many of them apparently the living rooms of self-taught people who didn't know what else to do with their spare mirrors and scissors.* From our kitchen window, Sally and I can see straight into the Ahmet Hair Studio, always busy with shampoo, comb and scissor-based activity. Around the corner from Ahmet is the Franksay Salon, which specialises in straightening and re-curling.

Interestingly, another thing our neighbourhood is not short of is

---

*During a visit to one of the sitting room salons several months ago, Sally complained about the lopsided line of her fringe after the young woman had made several attempts at evening it. 'You know it's very hard to cut hair straight,' she explained to Sally.

'Sure, if it's something you do as a hobby – but this is supposed to be your job, isn't it?'

'It is a very hard job.'

amateur private investigators (perhaps guys who read that same issue of *Esquire* as I did a few years back). Every week or so in the mail we get a small self-printed card advertising the services of a Mr Salim, a Mr Tassi, a Mr Môro or a Mr Fodeba. All these gentlemen offer similar services: collecting bad debts and tracing loved ones, as well as the general and sinister 'getting rid of difficult problems' (although Mr Tassi can also act as 'a known African medium' for ƒ25 extra). The combination of these two popular local industries ensures that anyone missing or on the lam has excellent hair.

At the *kapsalon* I go to, staffed by two women and a man who dresses like a cowboy, I believe I have stumbled upon some sort of haircuts-for-favours ring. For a start, 'Sexual Healing' is playing in the background every single time I go there, which is often, as I have a very fertile scalp. Plus they always touch me beyond the designated tonsorial 'safe areas' of head, neck and upper shoulders, sometimes straying down as far as my elbow. Once, when she dropped a comb, Lady A's wrist brushed against one of my buttocks, causing me to gasp and become tense, while she giggled and winked at me in the mirror. If they don't have any other 'customers', the cowboy-hairdresser dances around the hair-filled floor with Lady A or B, whispering in her ear the whole time and smirking at me with his cocked eyebrows. All of them wear lots of gold jewellery. None of them are very attractive – not that that would have made a difference to me, as I make it a policy not to get 'involved' with tradespeople such as plumbers, pool cleaners and milkmen because my Geary Street magazine research tells me that it just complicates things. And no one believes you anyway.

My Dutch isn't great and none of them speak English too well, but I know a salacious, suggestive tone when I hear one; it doesn't take a linguist to know that 'Would you like a coffee or tea, *jongen*?' has multiple meanings in any language, especially a European one. Naturally, I always politely refuse, while beneath the plastic cape quickly making sure that my fly is firmly buttoned up. As for whether I'd like any 'wax' or 'gel' after the job's done – absolutely not. Do I look *that* naive?

So why do I keep going? Well, for one thing it's cheap, it's just around the corner and, well, while the whole scene is pretty sordid and disgusting, I'd like once to be at least asked if I'd like to join in. Nevertheless I will soon have to cut them loose as I am becoming tired of the strained conversations which take place there and which consist of the same questions and answers every single time.

'You're not working today?' one of the lady *kappers* will ask.

'No, I work from home,' I will say.

'Going on holiday this year?'

'No, I work from home. I feel too guilty about taking holidays. How about you?'

'To Spain. Later in de year. In summer.'

'Well, that'll be nice.'

'You have a lot of grey hair, you know.'

'I know. I work from home. There are mirrors there.'

NEWS ITEM, FEBRUARY 23RD, 2001: An investigation is pending after a Dutch air-force control tower was fired upon by a German jet fighter pilot who thought the tower was a target. Seven rounds were fired into the tower by the Tornado before its pilot realised his mistake. Three people were in the tower at the time; however, none were injured. The incident occurred during a training mission on the island of Vlieland.

When will this damned war end?

It was a custom or habit (or in some cases – notably my own – perhaps even an addiction) on Sundays for our group of friends to convene in the tiny dimness of our favourite bar, Wynand Fockink, where about an hour after arriving cold and sober in the late afternoon, we would all end up getting rather drunk, rather quickly on various fruit-flavoured *genevers* and beer. Despite how I knew I'd feel on the following morning, I loved these Sundays; they were without exception warm, happy, convivial experiences full of loud laughter and chat which I knew sometimes irritated the regulars but which I also knew provided the establishment's owners with a pretty hefty injection of cash.

One Sunday in March, Sally and I met up with Ray and Sonia, Simeon and Darcy, Canadian Nicole MacKenzie and our friends

Nick and his wife Ami, visiting from Atlanta. Simeon had spent part of his 'growin' years' in Atlanta and it wasn't long before he and Nick began singing (pretty quietly, it should be mentioned) a bunch of Lynrd Skynrd songs (especially 'Sweet Home Alabama', even though Simeon and Nick are, strictly speaking, from Georgia) which caused the usually very calm and affable barman Pieter to shout (extremely loudly, it should be noted), 'I told you before there is NO SINGING ALLOWED!' This was both rude and surprising, especially considering that by 'before' he meant about seven months earlier. My own troublemaking came in the form of getting into a scrape with a moody loner regular called Franz about my elbows digging into his back (accidentally, it should be pointed out – it's a tiny, overcrowded bar). We took off soon after, with Simeon, who has a truly excellent singing voice, sweetly and sarcastically serenading Pieter through a small open window. We left just a twenty-five cent tip, as opposed to the usual ƒ20. 'Just our way of saying "screw you" in the international language of money,' Simeon said as we weaved up Pijlsteeg, in search of margaritas around the corner on Warmoesstraat.

I worry that this behaviour makes me and my friends seem like a bunch of drunken assholes, which we are not. If we were, I am confident that the management at Fockink would not have allowed us to keep coming back to the bar to do the same things all over again week after week, month after month, year after year since we first arrived. Nevertheless, every Monday morning, dry-throated and thick-headed, I would stumble to the bathroom, take an aspirin and vow that I was never going back.

Conversation held with self while out grocery shopping. March 4th, 2001

SC: Looking back over what you've written about the past few months, it's hard not to think that you really drink a lot.

SC: Well, yes . . . what's your point?

SC: Well, it looks bad on a number of levels. You come across as something of an alcoholic.

SC: I stated at the beginning that this book was an account of my life in Amsterdam, nothing more.

SC: But does it have to be this dull and repetitious? And there's very little characterisation. I mean, who is Chris Burns, who's Nicole MacKenzie?

SC: She's Canadian.

SC: Yeah, you mentioned. As though that's enough.

SC: She has blond hair and a mouth that suggests she recently wore braces. She was a very sweet, kind of fragile person who worked as the creative group assistant at 180. I refer to her in the past tense because she's back in Vancouver now, where I last heard she was planning to do a course in landscape gardening. Or florist management.

SC: All right, you've made your point. Very cynically, I might add. Let's get back to the drinking.

SC: Now you're talking.

SC: Very funny. You know that's not what I meant. Your father's an alcoholic, isn't he?

SC: (long pause): Possibly.

SC: In fact, definitely.

SC: Whatever you say. Why do you always bring my father into it?

SC: Because I think it's important.

SC: (no response)

SC: This conversation took place in your head, didn't it?

SC: Yes it did. It says so on the previous page.

SC: It says you were out grocery shopping – what else were you buying, Sean?

SC: I bought two bottles of wine – white wine – and eight cans of Grolsch. But I only paid for six cans. There's a special.

SC: Why did you buy all that booze?

SC: Simeon's away shooting an ad in LA with Larry, so Sally invited Darcy over for dinner and to watch 'Sex in the City'. It's nice to have a drink with your friends.

SC: As long as you don't overdo it.

SC: True. Will you please shut up now – I'm hungry and you're incredibly annoying.

SC: Just one more thing.

SC: What?

SC: It's 'Sex *and* the City'.

March 8th, 2001

Last night was the third in succession during which I awoke from nightmares actually screaming. This disturbs me for many reasons, most of which centre around the central question of what the hell is wrong with me? Monday I was shot in the back of the neck three times by Tony Soprano as I crawled along a wooden floor. I could actually feel the slugs enter me; they didn't hurt but felt thick and warm as they ended my life. Last night, in some sort of decontructivist meta-dream, I *dreamed* that I was having a nightmare and was calling out for Sally to help me. 'Al, Al, Al,' I cried rapidly, like a shallow-breathing, feverish dog. Lying to my right (which never happens in reality), the dream-Sally merely mocked my words. 'This is not my beautiful wife,' I dream-thought. Then she began further torment by saying what she knew would be my next words as I said them: 'Please' then 'Help me!' When the real Sally, coming from the left, woke me from my sleep, I screamed aloud twice. It was awful and exhausting; however, her actual response – rancorous muttering under her breath and sharp bedcover-yanking – depressed me even further. I told her not to be such a bitch, to which she really took exception, angrily telling me that she'd been awake for the last two hours. My thought was, if you're already awake, what's the big deal? I think it's more that she thinks I am weak and unmanly because I wake in fright too often. And perhaps I am.

I know that she's under a lot of pressure with her first weeks of getting up at 7.30 and working all day on the new magazine. I know this. But I can't help this. It sure has changed our lifestyle pretty dramatically though, this proper job business. But with its accompanying early hours and non-drinking, it may yet add several years to our lives.

Sally is very happy to be working full-time again, especially to be working as an editor. She and Ray (who is due to become a daddy in a few months) are putting in the long hours required to establish a quality magazine from scratch. They want it to be a sort of *Harper's* of Japanese culture – first-class writing, classic design, outstanding photographs and illustration – and they seem to be doing well. (As indicated by the fact that I have not been commissioned to do anything.) Happily, the magazine's deep-pocketed financial backers are right behind them. It's strange not having Sally around all the time but I maintain frequent (perhaps too frequent, considering how busy she is) telephone and email contact, pitching ideas for what to have for dinner, what video to rent etc. If I had a PlayStation, life would be just like it was before we left Australia, except with inferior weather.

Email from Sally

Subject: chicken or beef?
my fat colleague is sitting at his desk stuffing in huge amounts of mcdonalds whilst looking at the kfc website!!! oh my god. . . i am so darn busy and yet i note that he is now sneakily looking at the burger king website. i am not kidding. have you had lots of water and fruit yet?

re: the holiday, I have organised our health insurance and dental requirements – i had to guess your weight for the health part; luckily i have experience in this as an ex-carnie.

had a strange *cevapcici* thing in *turkse brood* with roasted capsicum and lettuce and cream cheese weirdo stuff for lunch. ray did too, and got it all over his face, including near his eye and ear. fool. did you have the tuna delight?

i forbid you to eat the ice-cream as your lunch!!!!

x

ps my eyes feel hot. i slept a bit on the train, but *i let op for zakken-rollers.*

THIS IS NOT A NEWS ITEM, MARCH 13TH, 2001: The Frisia Museum in Spanbroek has paid 2.7 million guilders for *Ceci N'est Pas une Pomme* (*This Is Not an Apple*) at auction in London. The painting, by the Belgian artist Rene Magritte, depicts an apple. It is part of a series that includes the famous *Ceci N'est Pas une Pipe* (*This Is Not a Pipe*). This is the most expensive work ever to be bought by the museum.

Prince Willem-Alexander and Máxima Zorreguieta's controversial engagement was announced on March 30th. Man, he is one square-looking dude – blond, centre-parted hair, scrubbed pink skin and sincere if highly goofy smile. A real Ralph Lauren type. He could do better personal-grooming wise – the Dutch royal family are the richest in the world. Argentinean Máxima (how I love that name – she should be a pop star with that name, or a PR company) looks kind of cute, but still dumpy, blandly dressed and heavy-breasted enough to fit comfortably into the personal/visual aesthetic of Euro-royalty. By the time she's forty-five, she'll look and dress exactly like all the rest of them.

My (temporary) queen, Beatrix, gave a rare television address announcing the engagement from the royal studio in The Hague. Because she didn't give it in English I couldn't really make out much apart from the words, 'It gives me great pleasure to announce the engagement,' but I think she was lying because she didn't look too pleased at all. She actually looked more tired and depressed and seemed to keep breaking into German (her controversial husband's controversial language from his controversial birthplace), because it was probably a better tongue in which to express her disappointment that her son was getting married at all – let alone to the daughter of a minister in Argentina's Videla military dictatorship. Ah, mothers – they're the same the world over, aren't they? Royal or not.

Of course, I object to the union too, partly because I enjoy objecting to things, but mostly because the Amsterdam authorities have ripped up every brick in the city since they want Billy and Max to be wed in a completely re-paved country. I haven't been able to cross Amsterdam in a straight line for the past six months.

Royal weddings tend to unite the people of a nation (witness England in 1981 with Charles and Di; or the US in 2000 when Brad Pitt and Jennifer Aniston tied the knot) but nothing in recent years has galvanised the Netherlands like this (vaguely) moral controversy. Ever since Willem and Máxima began stepping out, the Dutch news media has been devoting extensive, semi-anguished coverage to the issue of whether or not the prince should place Máxima in line for the queenship. Basically it came down to this headline: 'Máxima: *Ja*. Papa: *Nee*'. It seems that we, the people, have accepted blond and bubbly Máxima based on two important characteristics – her blondness and her bubbliness. However, Máxima's father, Jorge Zorreguieta, has 'decided' not to attend the wedding, to be held early in 2002, after Prime Minister Wim Kok pointed out to him, rather Godfatherishly, that 'it would be better for his daughter's future'.

I, on the other hand, check the mail every day, hopeful of a misaddressed invitation; my tuxedo is pressed and ready.

Around six-thirty one night early in April, Jessika, Sally's former colleague from Boom Chicago, called to say that Angie Driscoll's boyfriend, Rick, had hung himself.

'You mean hanged,' I told her. 'Who?'

'Angie, from Boom.'

'Angie . . . The black girl who looks sort of like Chaka Khan?'

She told me, yes, the black girl. From Boom. I went on to say that that was awful, sad and everything.

'Anyway,' Jessika said, 'there's a kind of a wake tonight.'

I wished Sally had picked up the phone. She'd know what to say. 'And who was he exactly, this Rick?'

'He worked at Boom, too. The wake's just around the corner from you guys.'

'Out here in the west?'

'That's right. They live nearby. You went to a party at their place last summer. In the back yard.'

'Is it there?'

'No, but it's nearby. I think it'd be good for Angie to have people around her.'

'Does she even know who I am? *I* never worked at Boom.'

'If you don't want to go, Sean, don't go.'

'Does anybody *want* to go to a wake, Jess? Is it the sort of thing people *enjoy*?'

I got off the phone and told Sally that Angie Driscoll's boyfriend, Rick, had hung himself.

'Hanged,' she said. 'Who's Angie Driscoll?'

I explained, 'The black girl from Boom. You used to work with her. And him, I believe. I seem to recall that he was a short guy. He was English, right?'

'Maybe,' Sally said. 'Or American.'

We each drank a beer and debated whether or not to go. I barely knew Angie and didn't really know him at all, although I vaguely recalled standing next to him at that party Jessika mentioned, admiring his twin turntables and collection of vinyl. But Sally said that Angie was a nice kid. 'So we should go . . . shouldn't we?'

'Does she look like Chaka Khan?' I asked

'What does Chaka Khan look like?'

'She's black.'

'I know she's black.'

'Lots of hair. Kind of pretty.'

'Could be. So are we going?'

I looked out the window, hoping I'd see rain, but not the sort that would remind me too much of Antwerp . . .

After the wake Sally and I came home to eat some salad and drink a little wine, because we could; because we were alive. We talked for a while then turned on the television, but even as we watched we forgot what we were seeing, as though in silence and shadow, it was disappearing right before our eyes.

Nothing Satanic

It's a Friday afternoon in April and I have just presented the edited London reception video to Chris, Alex and Neil the Secret Client, at 180. All of them loved the stuff, cackling like hyenas during the screening. I am immensely relieved yet cannot help feeling some-what ashamed – some of the stuff *is* very funny, but at what cost to my dignity?

Chris hugs me. 'Seanie, you've got big balls, my friend. Great big brass balls.'

Neil shakes my hand and smiles. 'I paid you a fucking fortune, mate, but it was worth every cent.'

Alex grins and mutters. 'Yes . . . hmmm . . . very . . . funny. Good stuff . . . Great.'

Once it's over, fed-up-with-work-for-the-week Simeon and I cut out of there and go for a drink at t'Smalle, a nearby bar. After a beer or two, we end up at one of Amsterdam's many 'smart' drug shops and buy a 'wild lettuce' joint ('like opium, but weaker and non-addictive' the information card says) and an 'absinthe joint' (like Paris in the 1920s, I presume). It's my first time with smart drugs and, as a somewhat stupid person, I'm hoping that the effect will be profound. Standing by the 'Homo-monument'* on Keizersgracht, we smoke the wild lettuce and feel nothing more than a very strong desire for cocktails, a desire which cannot be fulfilled because, even though it is after five on a Friday, this is Amsterdam, not Rio de Janeiro.

'They make pretty good cocktails at the bar at Boom Chicago, but I don't think we should go there,' I say. 'It might be kinda

---

Homo is the rather blunt and uncomfortable Dutch word for homosexual. *Monument* means monument. Together they mean homosexual memorial/monument.

depressing. This guy who worked there hanged himself the other day. Are you stoned?'

'I don't think so,' Simeon says. 'Isn't it hung?'

'No, it's hanged,' I tell him. 'It's definitely hanged.' We are wandering slowly up and down Rozengracht, where Rembrandt spent his final penniless years wondering what to do instead of drink cocktails. The air is heavy and the sky seems even lower than usual, as though we might almost be able to literally walk with our heads in the clouds – slowly, having trouble breathing, unable to see our feet or where we're going.

Simeon hands me a corner of his trench coat and says, 'Hey Condon, check the thread count on this mother.'

I play the fabric between my thumb and forefinger. 'Impressive. What is it, about six-eighty per square inch?'

'Seven-twenty.'

'Wow.'

'New York City, man. They've got serious clothing there.'

We stop outside an antiques store. Simeon says, 'Do you sometimes wish you could suddenly produce a conductor's baton out of nowhere?'

'Yes,' I say, for it seems that, without my even being aware of it, I apparently *do* occasionally wish that I could. 'Yes, I do.' I look up at Simeon who is staring in the shop window, nodding and smiling at an old porcelain bedpan that is cracked and spotted with blue and white. 'I think I have to go home now.'

'Oh God, me too. Later.' He immediately takes off down a side street and even though he is already far away I can hear him laughing loudly at something he has seen or thought. I return to my bicycle and all the way home my mind is densely preoccupied by many more incorrect thoughts about wrong things. I arrive extremely tired and confused after what seems like hours of breathless cogitation and pedalling.

Two days later I realise that I've been a little crabby lately and wonder if perhaps I'm having wild lettuce withdrawals.

NEWS ITEM, APRIL 8TH, 2001: A naked man caused the adjournment of a debate in the Second Chamber of the Dutch Parliament in The Hague when he began strutting

back and forth shouting 'You are killers' from the gallery. He is believed to be Iranian and voicing complaint about the treatment of foreign residents of the Netherlands.

Did he mean all foreigners, I wondered, or just those from Iran?

April 12th, 2001

Dear Sean,

My Flower and I will be descending on Van Gogh *stadt* on Thursday, April 19th. You and I will leave for the ancestral seat of Mad King George on Saturday morning by ICE first class. We will set up the stand in the afternoon (there will be some heavy lifting and swearing involved), with nothing to do on Sunday except *drunken bier und essen wurstchen.* If the *shiesse* hits the *luftrader* we'll have to *arbiet* on *Sontag* until we are *frei*. You will accompany me to the show on Monday to see my techno-glory. Then you will leave as, by this stage, you will be bored shitless. Plus, from then on I won't have time to talk (even though I would very much like to) as I will have to do serious business, and try and earn some *gelt* to pay for our *urlaub*. Your Fuhrer,

A

PS Saw Michael Caine in *Get Carter* last night at the Astor and if you think those rat-faced English are fuck ugly now, you should see them in Newcastle in 1971.

'A' is my friend (and, apparently, leader) Anthony Kitchener, an inventor working in the twin – but somehow related – fields of screw compressors and wine cooling/storage. He has a fantastically bent and broken nose and, in hair, height and equine length of face, bears quite a resemblance to Alexander Godunov, the dead actor. Anthony is a voracious yet considered and critical reader, and knows more about everything than anybody I have ever met – and I mean everything, from art and literature and science and history and botany to the history of botanic science in art and literature. And he's only forty-four. He is also generous, witty and extraordinarily charismatic. He is, in short, Jesus. His Flower is Stella Barbiz, a newspaper editor and journalist of Polish descent who knows a lot about comic books. She is also greatly amused by the sight of peeing animals, which, in its own way, is quite a charming quality in a person. Stella and Anthony are perhaps the tallest couple in Melbourne.

Stella and Anthony arrived on an unbelievably cold April day – the kind of cold that gave rise to the idea of 'catching' a cold – and although I realised that I was in no way responsible for it, I apologised for the weather frequently and at great length.

'All problems can be overcome by the application of will, except weather,' Anthony said. 'That's Hitlerian wisdom for you, Seanie boy, from *Mein Kampf*. Apart from the meteorological coda, which I added and learned from my own *kampf* with life in general.'

Sally and I were thrilled to see our friends for the all too brief two days that they were in town, and spent breakfast, lunch and dinner with them.

'Any invention must overcome six hurdles,' Anthony told Sally, in response to her watch idea, over dinner at a French restaurant on Prinsengracht. 'The first is in the mind of the inventor who must, obviously, conceive of something new, which, to a greater or lesser extent, you have. Next is building a prototype – much more difficult. You haven't made one, have you?' Sally showed her thin, girlish wrists and shook her head.

'Move along please,' Stella said. 'Less fogging on.'

'Hurdle three is critical – will people pay for your product? Needless to say –'

'But you'll say it anyway,' Stella said.

'I will indeed, my Flower. Needless to say, any invention should have as a necessary corollary the potential to makes its inventor fucking wealthy. Fourth obstacle is popular use. Five – durability. It better take a licking and keep on ticking. Thanks to the Timex corporation for that pithy phrase.'

'Actually, it'd be more likely thanks to their advertising agency,' I said, helpfully.

Anthony ignored me. 'Finally there is the social challenge – will people allow your idea to become popular? Or is it perhaps too far ahead of its time? Or for that matter behind its time? To state the obvious, your watch, Sally, is *all* about time. Hopefully it'll be a timely timepiece.'

Our food arrived and, as is his way, Anthony hung a napkin from his collar to cover his shirt then toasted the success of Sally's watch. 'Now, as for my own latest creation . . .'

The next morning Anthony and I left for Hannover, where for the next week or so he would be proudly showing off his own latest creation. It was an extremely pleasant four-hour train trip in a private compartment during which Anthony spoke pretty much continuously. He was brilliantly entertaining; that rare kind of conversationalist where you come away from the experience feeling intellectually elevated and improved. I learned about the history of lower Saxony (because we were there), safety procedures in a nuclear power plant (because we passed one), that Nietzsche was 'a cancerous tumour on mankind' (generally German), about methods of fishing tuna (contents of our sandwiches) and Germany generally ('They had a poor twentieth century, I'll admit, and they did begin the last millennium by sacking Rome. And I wouldn't care to live here, but how does a middling sized country with no special resources invade France five times in 100 years? *And* invent Dr Scholl's? All fuelled by pork sausage and a beer for which the recipe hasn't changed since 1514?'). Along the way I tried to think of clever and worthwhile things to add to the conversation but, as ever, my feeble brain let me down. I kept wanting to spout limericks or ask Anthony if he had any idea why the producers of *The Living Daylights* let A-ha do the title song.

Shortly before we pulled into Hannover *Hauptbahnhof*, I asked Anthony where we were going to stay – I looked forward to a shower and a moment of intellectually modest solitude before we began our labours. He pulled out a sheet of paper. 'I am staying at Herrenhauser Kirchweg seventeen while you, my friend, will be enjoying the comforts of Daimlerstrasse forty-one in the Ost Stadt.'

'Why are we staying at different hotels?'

'These aren't hotels.'

'What are they?'

Anthony looked at me levelly, paused, and said, 'They're not hotels.'

Boy were they not hotels. They were small private apartments set up to receive what the Germans call *messe* guests (trade guests). I was to be the *messe* guest of Frau Mittel, a short, round widow in her early- to mid-fifties with awful teeth, short, shiny, baby-fine brown hair and a rolling limp that suggested a botched hip replacement. Frau Mittel kept her third-floor apartment in a state of distressing cleanliness and order that suggested obsessive-compulsive disorder, Teutonic style. She and her apartment depressed and frightened me.

'It's very clean,' I told the frau, not in German. 'Very, *very* clean indeed.' It was clear from the empty, white look on her face that the frau did not speak English, so I repeated myself using grand sweeps of my arms and knee bends that looked like I was about to launch into a soft-shoe shuffle, as well as some prestidigitation-style hand waving and short bursts of smiles. Frau Mittel's face seemed to pale and hollow even further so I got the hell out of there before I erased her.

Befitting the location of the world's largest industrial fair, the Hannover Exhibition Center is like a city all its own, attracting over 7200 exhibitors and more than one million visitors – and ensuring that people who did not book hotels five years in advance ended up staying in mausoleums run by widows. Setting up Anthony's display for his (unusually named) Dri-Screw compressor took more hours of physical work than I had done since that time on the boat with Joey, and left us both exhausted. It was amazingly noisy inside the building – just one of seven separate structures the size of aircraft hangars – and there were tradesmen everywhere (many of them Danish, leading me to conclude that the Danes are the world leaders in screw compression), hammering and banging as they erected hundreds of stalls, some of which were very fancy and glamourous (I could just imagine the bikini-clad spokesmodels) while others, like Anthony's, were markedly less so. Anthony told me that he hoped that the Dri-Screw would change his life by setting the world of screw compression on fire and making him rich. And, as I drank the can of Victoria Bitter that my friend had so thoughtfully brought all the way from Australia for me, I hoped so too.

My evening at Frau Mittel's was everything I expected it to be: a long and fitful night (during which I woke once an hour wondering when Beelzebub would arrive) on nylon sheets under a plastic quilt in a quiet, still 'sitting room' in which I could all too easily imagine old Mittel doing a lot of sitting and staring at her collection of porcelain dolls standing on doilies and at her Al Martino records. It was a room, I became increasingly certain, which occasionally saw some action in the form of exorcisms that were regularly performed there. I lay thinking about how she must have felt about this complete stranger with whom she could not communicate lying nearby, perhaps plotting her murder or defiling the sterile sanctity of her room with an act of self-abuse. The whole thing gave me the heartbreaking creeps and, as early as I thought decent, I zipped up my bag, declined Frau Mittel's offer of breakfast, and made a very quick trip to the bathroom on my way out, where I saw the saddest thing of all – a small plastic folding seat which, due to her bad hip, Frau Mittel must have to sit on each day as she showered. It damn near killed me seeing that.

'It's a very comfortable bed, *Danke*,' I told her as I made my way to the door of the apartment, because I figured she'd want to hear that sort of compliment even if she couldn't understand it. *Very warm and comfortable. The dolls are lovely and nothing Satanic happened. Thank you very much for having me.*

Frau Mittel smiled at my small linguistic gesture, limped to the door and shook my hand. '*Auf Wiedersehen*,' she said, and I tried not to burst into tears as the weight of this woman's lonely life smothered me all over again.

'So what's your place like?' I asked Anthony as we took a walk around the city.

'Oh marvellous. Warm, friendly. There are children, though, so there's a bit of noise.'

'Huh. This isn't a very pretty city, is it?'

'That's because Arthur Harris bombed the crap out of it in the war. Needlessly, I should add – the man was an egomaniacal, homicidal prick. And post-war reconstruction in many German cities has been a process of . . .'

We had lunch at an *über*-German restaurant by the *Hauptbahnhof* (five bratwurst for me – *small* ones – and a Wiener schnitzel for him; very Teutonic of us) and soon after I was on the train, heading home. I enjoyed my quick trip to northern Germany entirely because of Anthony, who, in the two and a half years since I'd seen him, had lost none of his generosity of spirit and intellect, to say nothing of his dazzling erudition, charm, affability and height. Before I left I gave him my watch because he liked it so much and did not himself have a watch. Apart from the fact that Anthony has many important appointments to keep and I myself have few, if not none, he is my friend and I felt it was the least I could do. I was very glad I did – long before I reached Amsterdam Centraal Station, I began to miss him.

No matter where I have been I am always very grateful to get back to Amsterdam, especially when I'm returning from large, polluted, crowded and ceaselessly noisy cities like London, Paris and New York, or just plain depressing joints like Düsseldorf and Hannover. Amsterdam feels like it's the perfect weight and density, and the city's quietness, the sedate calm of the canals, has an almost narcotic effect on my jangled nerves. There's even a comforting familiarity about hearing the Dutch language again (although this wears off after about a minute). And as I sit on a tram or in a cab, ticking off landmarks on my route home, I think about how I will soon be taking out my keys and unlocking the door to the flat, unpacking then putting the suitcase back up on top of the wardrobe, breathing slowly and deeply. And even though I am not actually there yet – I'm just anticipating it – I feel as though I have truly come home.

NEWS ITEM, APRIL 31ST, 2001: Queen's Day celebrations were marred by rioting in Amsterdam today. Around 700,000 people visited the city, many of whom were stranded for several hours when trains ceased operations because people were on the tracks. Police used tear gas to disperse a violent crowd at Central Station. Thirty-two people were arrested and more than twenty police officers injured. Officials estimate the damage to property to be as high as one million guilders.

I missed the fun of throwing rocks at glass and being tear-gassed, but my third Queen's Day was not without its own highlights: Joey came back from Poland for the weekend and talked incessantly about his girlfriend Elvira (which, because her name was Elvira, I quite enjoyed); I was offered Viagra by a street vendor in the Nieuwmarkt (I declined); and I had my first *broodje croquette* that evening. A popular Dutch snack, the *broodje croquette* is a baby-soft white roll inside which is a deeply fried croquette containing meat strands and glue-like gravy. It is a thing I will also decline in the future. Indeed, I hope to decline the whole *nachtmerrie* of *Koninginnedag* in the future. Many Amsterdammers share my feeling that Queen's Day is a meagre excuse for tens of thousands of people to wander the streets drinking booze and buying bits of second-hand junk, but nobody can seem to find it in them to actually leave the city on the day. Just in case we miss something like a ten cent television or a riot.

The sound I'd been waiting for all day – Sally's keys in the front door. I bounded out of the small room in which I spend my days typing and gave her a kiss, saying, 'Welcome home from work, you cheese bitch.'

'What?'

'Welcome back, cheese bitch.'

'You can stop calling me that now,' Sally said, removing her coat and hanging it on the rack in the hall. 'Why are you calling me a cheese bitch? Which you'd better stop doing.'

'Well, I'm glad you asked because there's quite an interesting reason behind it.'

'Great – another of your tales.' This was said sarcastically, not with genuine enthusiasm.

I followed her into our bedroom and, while she changed from work clothes into home clothes, I lay down and told her what I'd read in the paper that day. Linda de Mol, younger sister of my semi-enemy John de Mol, is the presenter of a 'Who Wants to be a Millionaire?' type game show prosaically named 'Chase for the Millions' which is broadcast in the Netherlands and Germany. After one of the show's contestants, who was in line to win ten million guilders, incorrectly identified the composer of the German national anthem, Ms de Mol, apparently in an effort to console the guy, said that it was a 'rotten melody' anyway. She later apologised and claimed that she had meant to say that it was a 'rotten question' (the words *melody* [*melodie*] and *question* [*vraag*] being so similar in Nederlandse). But the apology wasn't enough for one Gotthilf Fischer, conductor of the internationally unknown Fischer Choir, who remarked, 'Who does she think she is? The German anthem is one of the most famous in the world. Linda de Mol should ask herself if she can still work for German television with that attitude . . . The cheese bitch should stay in Holland.'

'He called her a "cheese bitch"?' Sally said, in black stockings.

'That's right – a cheese bitch.'

Sally laughed loudly. 'What the hell's a cheese bitch?'

'Any Dutch female who badmouths the German national anthem, I presume.'

'And what did the guy end up winning?'

'A million guilders.'

'Fiendish.' She took off her shirt. 'And who was responsible for the German national anthem?'

'Oh come on, it's one of the most famous anthems in the world. You must know.'

'*Who?*'

'I'm sure you don't need me to tell you.'

'Come on you cheese bitch, who *was* it?'

If we were a TV sitcom couple, Sally, wearing nothing but stockings and a bra, would have leaped onto the bed and begun tickling me until, through great hyperventilations of lusty laughter, I would give up the name, but as we are real people, I simply told her. 'Haydn,' I said, then followed her into the kitchen to help prepare dinner.

It is spring and, inspired by the change in weather to cloudless days of mild heat and long light, I seem to be trying to turn our balcony into what looks like the set of a 1960s TV sci-fi series where the ship's crew has landed on some cheap foreign planet. It's working: there are shiny glaucous leaves that look like they're made of some polymer prototype; there are low brown stumps that have sprouted hair; there are bulbous pink and purple things, quietly photosynthesising. Excited by my progress (and perhaps a new career as either a set-dresser or gardener), I invite Ray to come home with Sally after work to celebrate my plant purchases. Upon inspection he is nonplussed. 'What's gonna happen to them in winter, Connie?' he wants to know.

'What do you mean?'

'You can't leave 'em out here in winter, they'll die. You'll have to take them inside. Your place'll turn all Dutch. Don't get too involved in this. Keep it at fad level.'

'Are you saying this because you're about to become a father, Ray? Are you sublimating?'

He cracks a beer and laughs. 'I'm ready as I'll ever be for fatherhood, Connie. But you and vegetation, I dunno. D'you know a good plant-sitter?'

I change the subject ('So how's issue number one coming along?') and in their enthusiasm for explaining the cover photograph they've lined up – the great Japanese director Takeshi Kitano shooting himself in the head with his fingers – Ray and Sally forget all about my new hobby.

I ignore Ray's advice and the very next day I buy still more plants because doing so gives me pleasure. Even though the fact that I derive enjoyment from this particular source makes me feel quite miserable.

May 15th, 2001

Douglas Adams died a few days ago. He was only forty-nine. He died of a heart attack. From what I can gather, he was somewhat fatter than me but he didn't look like a smoker. And he died at the gym, so he was obviously fitter than me. In a way. A heart attack at forty-nine, for God's sake. That's so awful. And yet I continue to smoke like an idiot but begin the habit of chewing aspirin every day in a sad and deluded effort to evade the heart attack I know and fear is coming. *Every* day.

Days pass as I worry about my health and life and future and plants and general self-worth. I begin to wonder if I would feel better being the recent Manchester United FC purchase Ruud van Nistelrooy – the Dutchman earned a whopping (there's no other word for it) 19 million pound transfer fee. I probably would feel better if I was him although I'd like to keep my own hair. Still and all, I find it very difficult to take myself and my existence seriously, what with its easy hours, lack of boss (except Failure) and nonexistent health plan. I worry that I may actually be a clinically depressed person. But then I think, who isn't these days? Clinical depression is almost hip.

Sally comes home swearingly pissed off with life as a travellin' (three hours each day), workin' (five days a week) gal (born that way). Deciding that my emotional state has had more than enough attention for the day, I struggle to find ways of making her happy and, after introducing her to the latest additions to the balcony, suggest that we go out for dinner to NOA (Noodles of Amsterdam) with temporarily single woman, Darcy. (Simeon is once again away shooting an adidas commercial.) Darcy works in 'career placement' and, in light of my current career worries, I seek her advice freely and in detail. It is a long night, but with Darcy's help I have eliminated employment options including (but not limited to): cool hunter, anything in marketing (except the marketing of fine literary works), PR flack, celebrity chef and former child star. For the moment, I remain, a writer.

'I love your books, Sean,' Darcy says around two in the morning and I decide that she is very good at her job.

The next day Sally and I wander the west and chance upon what passes for a schoolyard fete in this city (or is it the whole country that doesn't get it? Maybe all of Europe?) and suddenly yearn for an Aussie school fair – snags* in white bread, old Ideal board games, parked cars ringed around the oval. Instead it's old people in clogs (which I admit is rather nice) and bizarre concession-stand games involving goats and upside-down bowling pins.

There is no more beautiful city on earth than the centre of Amsterdam when the weather's right and due to the fact that the weather is very, very right that afternoon we take wine and cheese to the dappled light of Vondelpark with Boom Chicagoans Jessika and Drew. Jessika is the promotions manager at Boom and Drew is the bar manager/dj; being friends with both of them means that Sally and I get invited to lots of parties where we drink for free. Drew was born and raised in Evanston, Illinois, and claims to know everyone famous who grew up near there – Vince Vaughan,

*Australian for *sausage*.

Dave Eggers and . . . that's about it. 'No, wait a minute, I forgot John Cusack. I know John Cusack,' he adds.

'What about Joan Cusack?' I ask, as we spread a rug not too far from the Blauwe Theehuis. 'D'you know her?'

'Sure, even her, too.'

Jessika, the most mature and serious young person (under twenty-five) I've ever met, grew up in Long Island so the only famous people she knows are mobsters and she's not allowed to mention who they are. Later, the four of us go and see Mark Eitzel, formerly of the American Music Club, at the Paradiso. He's a very sensitive performer who, understandably, doesn't like people talking loudly while he plays, so I march around and personally tell various Dutch strangers to shut up. Nevertheless, Mr E stops the show several times and has to be gently coaxed back on stage by his fans and managers.

On Sunday we go to various *tuin* shops (*tuin* means 'garden' in Dutch which is, linguistically speaking, highly ironic in that it's pronounced *town*, towns being more or less the opposite of gardens). Various visible neighbours seem to finally be according Sally and I some small measure of respect and friendliness due to our spectacular reinvention of the balcony. '*Mooie, buurmen*,' they say ('Nice, neighbours'). But I wish that they'd say it without the comma, thereby embracing *us*, rather than merely our balcony.

In the evening, Sally and I watch *High Fidelity*. I find it much better than I expected and start to wish I was John Cusack, before realising, with some atrabiliousness, that even being Joan Cusack would be better than being me.

Late that night I begin to wonder – what *will* become of all my greenery and herbs and flowers come winter? Will they die?* Can I save them? *How* will I save them? Is there a life-saving aspirin-type product for plants? Did I use the word *atrabiliousness* correctly? Should I have said *Weltschmerz*?

---

*The answer, by the end of the following winter, is yes.

Me and EU

My friends David, Peter, Sam and Jenny are lawyers. My sisters Leith and Julie are lawyers. My friend Chris Burns is a biotechnologist. Our mutual friend David is a winemaker. Anthony invents. James edits movie dialogue. Darcy's a head-hunter. Simeon, Damian, Larry and Laen are all in advertising. Michael used to be in advertising but now earns his living as an illustrator. Sonia is a journalist. Jeroen runs his own IT company. His sister Yolanda's in HR. My brother-in-law is a banker. My wife is a magazine editor.

Compared to all these people I feel like some sort of rootless career drifter, almost sinister in my lack of ambition, drive and commitment, the shady, self-taught handyman who'd kill you for your pay cheque. It's been this way forever. All my adult life I have glanced at dozens of different jobs without any clear view of the future, and I've interspersed those jobs with long periods of staring, indolence and mastering the art of inexpensive sandwich construction. I tried to go to university twice but did not last even an entire term at either institution, partly because the haircuts I preferred back then made me instantly – and deservedly – unpopular and partly because I lack the will, confidence and basic intelligence to be a successful graduate. In high school I was an uninterested, unmotivated, antisocial and profoundly stupid student; I don't remember too much about primary school but I dare say I was an idiot there, too; my mother didn't even bother to send me to kindergarten; and before kindergarten age I did a lot of inconsequential dribbling and sleeping.

One afternoon in June I pulled out my old laptop, which I'd not used since I was in Melbourne almost three years before, and

I was stunned by what the computer's contents revealed, the state of my life back then. In amongst the half-finished short stories, simple-minded book reviews, frivolous columns and a large chunk of novel, there was: a letter seeking the job of marketing manager for a publishing company (a position to which I would be as ill-suited as that of guidebook writer for the same company); another letter of wanton supplication to a film and television producer I'd been working for on and off for the previous year begging for any form of script-writing hackery; an application to the Australian Film Television and Radio School for entry into a short course; another application for a travel and writing grant from a charity foundation; and an insanely chatty letter to the CEO of Saatchi & Saatchi, written because I'd seen an interview with him on television and thought that the view from his office looked pretty good and that I'd quite like to live in Manhattan on a fat ad salary.

Looking at that collection of tics and jolts of shapeless desire and misguided inclination made me feel a little sad; however, for just a moment, I let myself believe that I'd left the person who wrote those dim, confused letters behind in Melbourne. But the truth was, I hadn't at all: only a short while ago I'd made that crazed attempt to become a television scheduler – of *Dutch* television, for God's sake, where they take scheduling and programming about as seriously as a Zimbabwean election; shortly before that I'd been loping through London covertly filming receptionists. And while I wasn't precisely unhappy about where my life had led me (or where, perhaps, I'd led my life), I wasn't particularly thrilled by it either – certainly there was no way I was going to win an Oscar doing what I was doing.

The problem was that I wasn't exactly sure of what I was doing. While I don't believe that a person is completely defined by their job (although with many people, especially lawyers, that is precisely the case), *having* one is certainly a good way of evading and postponing that difficult question of who you are. I had tried a great many things in an effort to give my life meaning and purpose, but I believed that I'd failed, that my life, apart from what I had with Sally, was amorphous and without base. I felt like the dust of a dandelion – I could wind up following whatever breezy notion captured me at any particular time.* But I didn't feel sorry for myself because I realised that, of course, it was the very absence of any great sense of career or ambition that had allowed me to pack up my life and move to Amsterdam in the first place. I realised that I was – and remain – part of a great spirit of adventure, Man's ineluctable desire to light out for parts new and unknown in search of destiny, fortune and a place for himself in the world. And if part of the pursuit of my particular destiny meant that I led the kind of life where I spent many mornings each week waiting to be served in a *slagerij* and being pushed around by a gaggle of silver-haired old Dutch women buying sneezed-on meat for their working husbands, and that apart from waiting for service in Holland's shops, I didn't know what I'd be doing from one day to the next – from one moment to the next, really – then so be it. Things could be a lot worse.

'Oh that's true, Sean,' I said out loud (because it was during the week, and it gets lonely during week). 'That's very true, but things could also be a hell of a lot better.' And an hour later, in pursuit of Sally's and my great dream of living in a land of freedom, opportunity and reliable television scheduling, I'd sent off two entries into the annual Green Card lottery run by the US State Department.

While I waited for America to get back to me (the results were months away and even in the unlikely event that we were selected, we would not be eligible for entry into the US until late 2003), I took some solace in the fact that if I felt my own life to be one of confusion and uncertainty, as long as I was living in the European Union, at least I was in the right place. The EU lacks unity and therefore authority and any strong sense of purpose: according to recent polls less than half of the EU's citizens think that membership is a good thing. The English position on any and all matters seems to consist of three words, 'remember the war' (whether the war referred to is the cold one, the second world one or the Malaya emergency one is not clear), except in regard to the euro, whereby

*Sally had recently expressed hope that I wouldn't suffer from 'wet leaves' syndrome. 'That's what they say happens to Japanese men who lose their jobs. They become very involved in their wives' lives, hanging around them all the time. Like wet leaves stuck to their shoes. Don't get it, baby. I have nice shoes.' How could the Japanese be so elegant and poetic about something so dismal, I wondered.

its policy is 'remember the pound'. The union has negligible influence over the United States; there's a constant battle between France and Germany about which of the two countries is 'the leader' of Europe; nobody trusts Berlusconi (because he's personally richer than some of the member countries); nobody can remember if Finland's in or out; few people know anything about Estonia; no one knows who the prime minister or president or king or queen of Denmark is . . . More than that, nobody knows very much about the EU itself. Here, I will try to bring some clarity (but not meaning) to the EU with a brief outline of its history.

1946. Winston Churchill recommends a 'kind of United States of Europe' in a speech delivered at Zurich University. Does not add 'except without the Hun' but notion is widely felt to be implied.

1948. The International Coordination of Movements for the Unification of Europe Committee meets in The Hague to discuss truncation of committee's name. Presided over by Winston Churchill and attended by 800 delegates, the meeting calls for the creation of a European Deliberative Assembly and a European Special Council, to oversee preparation of political and economic integration of European countries. It also proposes the adoption of a Human Rights Charter and a Court of Justice. Finally it requests further supplies of water and mints because 'Germany has annexed them'.

1951. A meeting to consider the creation of a European Community of Defence is held in Paris. Belgium, France, Italy, Luxembourg and Germany attend, as well as five observer countries – the United States, United Kingdom, Canada, Denmark and the Netherlands. Although perhaps too reliant on cream-based dishes, the catering is generally thought to be excellent.

1955. The Council of Europe adopts pretty but largely meaningless emblem of blue flag with twelve golden stars on it.

1957. Treaties establishing the European Economic Community (EEC) and the European Atomic Energy Community (Euratom) are signed by Belgium, France, Germany, Italy, Luxembourg and Netherlands (BFGILN) in Rome (R). From then on referred to as the 'Treaty of Rome' (TOR), which becomes the foundation stone of the modern-day European Union (EU).

1962. The Council of Europe adopts its first directive, establishing the EEC global foodstuff regulation by clarifying which colourants can be added to food. The Netherlands objects to all 'flavourants'.

1963. Euro-prescient French president General Charles de Gaulle is doubtful of the United Kingdom's political commitment to joining the community and says *non* to UK membership of the EC.

1967. The United Kingdom re-applies to join the community, followed by Ireland and Denmark. General de Gaulle still reluctant to accept the British, accurately predicting the spectacular failure of Marks & Spencer on the continent more than thirty years later.

1970. Member states approve the Davignon Report on political cooperation, the objective of which is for Europe to speak with a single voice on all major international issues; what language that single voice will be spoken in is a whole other can of worms.

1972. With de Gaulle conveniently dead, the United Kingdom signs the treaty of accession to the European Community.

1975. At a meeting of the European Council in Rome, ministers decide to establish a European Parliament elected by 'universal suffering', almost immediately amended to 'universal suffrage'.

1991. European Council Summit meeting in Maastricht reaches agreement on a draft treaty on European monetary union. British PM John Major successfully arranges a British opt-out. Charles de Gaulle, contacted by Ouija board says, 'I told you so.'

1997. The European Council meets in Amsterdam and outlines draft treaties for a new phase of economic and monetary union then adopts a resolution on growth and employment. With that out of the way, the council wanders the red-light district, drinking and making loud, stupid remarks.

1999. The single currency, the euro, launched on January 1st. Eleven member states adopt the new currency; however, three countries – Denmark, Sweden and, predictably, the United Kingdom – decide to defer a decision. In its first year, the new currency is not a great success – falling by 30 per cent in value in relation to other leading currencies. The United Kingdom, contacted by telephone, says, 'We told you so.' Following a report claiming widespread corruption and mismanagement in the European Commission, all twenty commissioners are forced to step down. Chaos descends upon the union.

2001. Usual confusion and disunity. Still no decent sausages available in Holland. 'When will this damned pork crisis end?' the people wonder.

Early in June posters appeared all over town announcing an event of unparalleled significance: Unilever's venerable cleaning product Jif would henceforth be known around the world by *de nieuwe internationaal naam* 'Cif'. (I presumed the old semi-international name was first coined as a snappy truncation of 'jiffy' – as in quick or quickly – and immediately adopted the new international phrase, 'I'll be there in a ciffy!') Under no circumstances would it be known as 'Gif', which in Dutch means poison.

I'm not kidding about it being a significant event: I think international name changes are a good thing and it's about time they did the same with Oil of Olay*, Oil of Olaz[†], Oil of Ulay[‡], Oil of Olé![§], Oil of Olas[||], Oil of Olive[#] and Oil of Ulan**, which are all the same product operating under different names[††] in various parts of the globe, a bit like spies. If this is truly going to be one world, here is where it will begin: we must be led by the cosmetic manufacturers.

We're certainly not going to be led by the European Union, which is still dithering over whether or not to accept English as its official language. Naturally there are fierce objections from everywhere, especially those bits of everywhere called France and Germany. I'm no cultural imperialist but it does seem inevitable that English will soon become the lingua franca (oh, the irony!) of official EU business, thus creating a glut of unemployed translators. The popular debate over this matter is, like so many popular debates, fuelled by ignorance, fear and suspicion, basically because most people believe that the adoption of an official EU language means that everyone living in the EU will have to speak it. This is not the case (not yet, anyway); all it means is that EU meetings, reports, treaties and catering menus will be written and conducted in English. But try to explain that to 300 million people in fifty different languages, even one of

*Australia and United States. [†]Austria, France Germany and the Netherlands. [‡]United Kingdom. [§]Spain. [||]Belgium. [#]Italy. **Elsewhere. [††]Except Spain and Italy, which I simply invented.

the multitude of Germanic-/Latin-/Greek-based ones with tons of words borrowed from French, by which I mean English.

Like everyone else in Europe, the Dutch are fond of their own language and have caressed and shaped it into something that suits their own particular needs and tongues. Part of this means having many slang words for their money – *piek*, *bal*, *pegels* and *pop* (all for the *f*1 coin); *knaak* and *Rijksdaalder* (*f*2.50 coin); *kwartje* (25 cent coin); *dubbeltje* (10 cent coin); and *stuiver* (5 cent coin). In just a few months' time, however, some of these words will no longer have an active place in the language; they will begin to disappear and die. And while the names are not nearly as imaginative or interesting as, for instance, the welter of slang words the English have for their mighty currency, it still seems sad – in much the same sad way as the co-joining of 'Sean' and 'Condon' will one day fall out of popular use.

But of course a new Euro slang will emerge in Holland (from school children, no doubt, because they did such a great job designing Dutch pastries, which mainly consist of cream and custard topped with pink and yellow icing, or anything green). The Austrians already refer to the new banknotes as 'Kalinas', after the graphic artist Robert Kalina who did such a remarkably unremarkable job of designing them. However, like so many things Austrian, this is unlikely to make much of an impression in Europe.* Whatever happens, the slang terms will differ from country to country and pretty soon we'll be back where we started – nobody knowing what the hell anybody's talking about when it comes to pan-European change – and we'll have to adopt an EU-wide official slang to be introduced on New Year's Day, 2020, to the distress and confusion of millions, especially shopkeepers, school children and petty criminals.

Increasingly, the mail makes my blood run cold. One day I opened the box downstairs and plucked out a letter from the Foreign Police regarding Sally's work/residency permit. It was full of long, negative-looking words, extremely Germanic in their sternness.

*Notable exceptions to this sweeping generalisation include the Hapsburgs, Lippizaner horses and Hitler. Proof lies in zither music.

I became very alarmed, unable to concentrate on anything other than being thrown out of the country, and decided to fax it to Sally at work. She then showed it to the appropriate authorities (i.e. anyone who speaks Dutch) and called five minutes later to tell me that contrary to what I'd thought, the application had been approved – in fact it had been *so* approved that she didn't even have to endure the usual tedium of an interview. I was so relieved that I bought a bottle of Moët. Sally, on the other hand, had for no reason at all bought me a lovely light blue Hugo Boss shirt. It was a good day for me – and, I like to think, Holland.

That night we went out for dinner with Ray and Sonia and their nice new baby Archie* to Moeder's (now that Sonia is one, it seemed appropriate) to celebrate fine weather and semi-legitimate residency (I still had to apply, yet again, as Sally's other half), two things I had not formerly associated too closely with my time in the Netherlands.

One thing that many culturally aware people do associate with Amsterdam is that it is a truly exciting, vibrant and edgy city renowned the world over for its devotion to all forms and aspects of the arts: almost every two weeks there is a festival, celebration, parade, concert, exhibition or cultural shindig. The biggest and most popular of these happens in June with the Holland Festival, an Amsterdam-based month of innovative music, theatre and dance productions from around the globe. Highlights of the 2001 program included: the Colombian Teatro de los Sentidos with 'the mysterious journey through the senses *Oraculos*'; avant-garde Polish director Krzysztof Warlikowski's interpretation of *Hamlet*; the Argentinian puppet and object theatre group El Periférico de Objetos with *Zooedipus*, their take on the Oedipus story; an absurd comedy by Richard Foreman entitled *Now That Communism is Dead, My Life Feels Empty*; Giorgio Battistelli's '*musique concrète*' composition 'Experimentum Mundi'; two days devoted to the music of modern Iceland; and Uri Caine presenting compositions based on Mahler, Bach, Schumann and pop.

For obvious reasons, Sally and I planned on seeing none of it.

*Named after Ray's uncle, the comic-book character.

June 11th, 2001

As Timothy McVeigh was being 'put to sleep' today I was returning a video. Right at the exact moment. And not even a very good
video. A terrible one, in fact (Dick Maas's Amsterdam-set *Do Not
Disturb*, if you must know). When I left the house he was alive
and when I returned twenty minutes later, he was dead. Amazing.
I wrote an email to Sally which said,

> Dear Sally,
> By the time you read this, I will be dead.
> Yours sincerely,
> Timothy McVeigh

She was very unimpressed with my pointless morbidity and,
upon reflection, I was too. What *was* I thinking? On the other
hand, Amsterdam itself has its own long, grim history of public
executions. The space in front of the town hall (now 'palace')
was the sight of dozens of beheadings, hangings, garrottings,
burnings at the stake and 'breaking' of various people on the
wheel. The condemned were murderers, sibyls, simoniacs and
heretics: early in the sixteenth century rebelling Anabaptists who
had sought to establish a Kingdom of Zion in the city had their
hearts 'cut from their living bodies and thrown in their faces';
several Lutherans were decapitated; and a couple of Mennonites
were tied to ladders and thrown face first into a pyre. Every so
often, as a change of pace, a woman thought to be a witch would
be sewn into a sack then tossed into the Ij River at a designated
place where Centraal Station now stands. Executionally, we've
come a long way since then.

**NEWS ITEM, JUNE 25TH, 2001: A Dutch department store
is trying to improve people's manners by displaying
scenes of good behaviour in its display windows. At the
moment de Bijenkorf's Rotterdam store windows feature
someone picking up litter and putting it into a bin. It also
plans to show children offering seats to old people, and
dog owners picking up after their pets.**

This act of arch retail hypocrisy made me want to place pictures of friendly, efficient store workers on top of litter bins throughout Amsterdam. And I probably would have, too, were it not for the fact that such pictures were absolutely impossible to find.

I received a message from Simco at 180 saying that he wanted to speak with me. My immediate thought was that I was in some sort of trouble and I began to feel a little watery. I called back and he asked if I'd be interested in some freelance work on the World Cup 2002 campaign for adidas. I said yes, but could not help wondering if this too would lead to some sort of trouble somewhere down the track. You never know with a person like me.

NEWS ITEM, JULY 16TH, 2001: Vincent Van Gogh had his ear sliced off in a booze-fuelled fight with his flatmate, historian Rita Wildegans has claimed. Paul Gauguin sliced Vincent's lobe off when his temper snapped after drinking too much absinthe, the historian says, and Gauguin feared admitting to the crime as he may have faced the guillotine. '[Gauguin] was a reckless and unpredictable daredevil,' Wildegans argues. She also believes that Van Gogh lent his ear to his favourite prostitute for 'safe keeping' and later told police he was too drunk to remember what had happened.

Which makes it all the more surprising that I still have both my own ears.

Sally and I were woken early one Sunday by a skanky red-haired lady *junk* (junkie) trying to kick down the ground-level door of the dealer who lives on the third floor of the apartment opposite our bedroom window. After long, dawn-stretched minutes of screaming and swaying on her tiny feet and thin legs, then scrabbling in the dirt in an attempt to find rocks she could throw up at the window, followed by more very loud kicking, the door was opened by a wiry guy around fifty wearing a pair of tiny black briefs. '*Ga weg!*' he shouted at her a few times ('Go away!'), before she attempted to suddenly run past him and into the doorway. The man grabbed the *junk* and started punching her. She seemed not to feel it. He shoved her back on to the sidewalk then slammed the door which, amazingly, she immediately began trying to kick open again. On the sidewalk, more punching and wrestling between the two of them followed until once again she made it into the entrance. He pushed her out yet again and closed the door. The whole time a fat guy with a moustache was standing about ten feet away just watching everything. By now the woman was covered in blood, still screaming. Somebody in a nearby window shouted out (in English), 'It's time to change!' I could guess what the person meant by that, but it was a strange, mild and somehow inelegant expression, more suited to a corporate workshop than inspiration for a desperate junkie. Sally and I just knelt on our bed, staring out the window at this grim, pathetic scene. And I wondered, if we had called the police, for whose benefit would it have been? I have to be honest and say that I really don't have too much sympathy for junkies, or for dealers who give away their home addresses.*

A short while later, as I tried to sleep, I thought back to what Joep! had said in Venlo that afternoon years before. Amsterdam may indeed not be Holland, but it certainly is Amsterdam.

Almost every morning the first thing I do – after I've done the preliminary things like showering, preparing a coffee, checking the weather outside and kissing Sally goodbye as she goes off to face another day of toil in Leiden – is fire up the computer and check out the *Age* website. The *Age* is a Melbourne broadsheet with a fine reputation, particularly for either ignoring my books or giving them poor reviews. I don't know why I am so compulsively drawn

---

*Several months later police would finally arrest the occupant of the flat, an event I watched from the window with quite some pleasure. Two things were notable about the operation. First was the fact that it took about an hour and a half for the five cops to get into the building because the guy they wanted to arrest wouldn't buzz them in and the police locksmith took forever to arrive. What particularly surprised me was that the cops just stood outside in the late December cold, rain and dark, laughing and joking with each other. The capacity of Dutch people to simply *wait* for things is absolutely astonishing. The second remarkable aspect of the arrest was that the staring Turkish girl could see none of it because it was all unfolding on her side of the street, right below her. She misses everything interesting – except watching me type.

to the paper, although I suppose if I thought about it for more than three seconds I'd have a pretty good idea.

Same day – slightly more than three seconds later

It's because, in the increasing absence of letters, packages, phone calls and emails from friends and family back in Melbourne, the *Age* is the best source of news from, and connection to, my former home. But why exactly do I care about what's happening back there? That the Australian government is shamefully refusing to let four hundred Afghan asylum-seekers into territorial waters? That some C-grade Australian TV star has been killed in a grisly air accident? (The frequency with which this sort of incident is occurring at the moment is quite remarkable.) Or that an Australian Olympic track star sometimes feels 'lonely and depressed'? That interest rates are climbing/slumping? That drivers are evading tolls when driving through the no-longer-new-but-nonexistent-when-I-was-last-there tunnel? That fog is causing air-traffic delays and road-traffic accidents? That homicide squad detectives seek mother of murdered six-year-old Frankston boy? That the time to buy a home in Sandringham has never been better/worse?

Naturally, I used to read the paper every day when I lived in Melbourne, to keep in touch with current events and the emotional torments of athletes, but I never made it my business to find out what was happening *elsewhere* in the world at the same level of banality – in Amsterdam or New York or Bombay – for the obvious reason that I wasn't living in any of those places. Now, though, I feel sort of domestically bi-hemispherical: I need to know what's going on here *and* there. Not that I really *do* know what's actually going on here because my Dutch is so poor. And because of my constant feeling of being on the verge of expulsion, I can't allow myself to become too involved with local politics or royalty. And the fact is that I don't really know, or at least I don't really *feel,* the effect of what's actually going on back in Melbourne – because merely reading about it on the Internet is not really knowing; I'm not involved, I'm just stopping by. In both cases, it's a little bit like having a mistress; it's enjoyable but you can't afford to commit because you've got a wife. I wonder, though, in this tortured analogy, what's the equivalent of my wife? Is it Melbourne or Amsterdam? Or is it Sally, my actual wife? Or is there no equivalent: am I unwed to both places now?

The end of August saw the grand unveiling in Munich (HQ of the European Central Bank) of the euro – or as we say in anti-mellifluous Dutch, *de oohro*. There was much talk about what a bonanza this would mean for counterfeiters on January 1st, 2002, because no one would have seen or touched the actual notes before (making me think that an interesting new career opportunity might be opening up for me).

While counterfeiters were rejoicing, vending-machine-dependent industries such as cigarette, condom and tiny-emergency-tooth-brush manufacturers were in slot-based despair because they hadn't been allowed access to samples of the new coins and therefore could not make the changes necessary for their machines to accept euros and reject roubles and dinars and whatever else was on the way out. It caused many headaches – not least in my own small head as I pretty much failed to grasp the whole concept. All I knew was that I'd have even fewer figures in my bank account after the end of the year than I did now. And this is never a good thing.

I wished I was a doddering old guy (instead of a doddering young one) who could shake his walking stick at retailers, Ray Milland-style, and growl, 'I won't spend the euro! I won't! I'll stick with me old money, thanks very much, if you don't mind!' Sure, I appreciated that we would all be one currency, but did that mean we'd be propping up each others' economies? That Germany would be a soft touch for a loan? And what the hell was I gonna do with that enormous tin bucket of tiny Dutch coins – especially those stupid microscopic tens, which didn't seem to be minted so much as cultivated in Petri dishes? Shouldn't there be a van with a speaker on the roof crying out 'Bring out your change!'? And if a smart, young (under thirty-six) fellow like me was still grappling with the euro concept, people in remote villages all over euro-land were gonna have a very tough time.

'And there are thirty million of us in that land,' I said to Sally, as I leafed through a euro information booklet. 'It's going to be chaos.'

'That's wrong,' she said. 'There are three *hundred* million people in the zone, man. It's going to be worse than chaos.'

'Or like it was on January 1st, 2000, when everybody, me included, thought that planes were going to fall from the skies, that banks would collapse and we'd all be left moneyless, hungry, dodging falling pieces of fuselage and waiting for Satan to show up and close down all the bars and theme parks. That was bad, but I tell you, things will be a lot worse when the *real* millennium starts in 2007.'

From what I could see in the booklet, the paper euros were a pretty unremarkable collection of notes. I have been fortunate enough to live in two countries where they take money design seriously. Both Australia and the Netherlands have beautiful, bright folding currency; the sunflower yellow of the fifty-guilder note is glorious and will be missed by the man who likes the contents of his wallet to have style as well as substance, as was the old Aussie twenty buck note (known as a 'lobster' because of its rich orange colour and smell). The euros looked too stern of design and anaemic of colour, probably like what a German mark looked like back in the 1930s when it was worth less than a peso, and a peso was worth less than sand. I wasn't happy, but at least I was unhappy in a non-vending-machine-dependent way . . .

None of the buildings, doorways, arches and stained-glass windows depicted on the euro notes actually exist. This design decision was taken so that none of the euro-zone countries with inferior buildings and monuments (such as Belgium) would take offence if they went unrepresented (which they most certainly would have been) and that countries with a plenitude of impressive structures (like France) would not be over-represented (which they most certainly would have been because people just can't get enough of the Eiffel Tower). Though in deference to the Netherlands it would have been nice to see a tulip somewhere on at least one bill. A tulip or a prostitute.

The boss euro is the five hundred, a bill I never expect to own as it's worth over *f*1000. I don't really mind, because it's lavender and I think that's an unacceptable shade for currency. Next is the two hundred, which is the sort of lemon yellow you often see on bottles of washing detergent. Again, this is unseemly in money, except for laundering purposes. Moving on down to a denomination that I have a slightly better chance of owning, although not for more than a day – the one hundred – we have a grass green note with a made-up portcullis on it, which will no doubt be popular in Italy and Greece. Then there's the peach-coloured fifty which looks almost edible, but should not be taken internally as it would make a very expensive and non-nutritious meal. The twenty is a sort of icy blue and looks more like actual money than its brothers, and will therefore be most likely to be counterfeited – and well. The ten euro is a strange pink that hovers somewhere between old salmon and the red of Mars. Maybe it's what salmon looks like on Mars. Whatever it is, it doesn't look like you should be spending it on anything other than Monopoly property. Finally there's the grey and dull five, the bleak tone of which is a shame because I'm sure that when I have folding money in my wallet it will be mostly made up of this very unimpressive bill.

Sally has tried to explain to me what the single currency means, but I'm a bit like England: even though it's just around the corner, it's inevitable and I simply have to accept it, I just don't get it. But at least *I* have the excuse of being one simple-minded man – those pound-lovers are an entire nation of knuckle-heads with apparently economically intelligent people to advise them on the matter. But they will have none of it. It's a wonder they ever let go of the tuppence and the ha'penny. Still, at least they're metric . . . or *are* they?

NEWS ITEM, SEPTEMBER 6TH, 2001: **The Dutch government has paid more than ƒ685,000 in disability payments to a convicted murderer for the time he spent in prison for kidnapping and killing a businessman in September 1987. The convict, identified only as Ferdi E., reportedly received the sum upon release from prison last month.**

After he had sent a severed finger to the family of Gert Jan Heijn – owners of the Albert Heijn chain of grocery stores – Ferdi E. was paid more than ƒ610,000 in cash and over ƒ10 million in diamonds in ransom demands. It was later discovered that Mr Heijn had been killed thirteen hours after the kidnap. Ferdi E. was subsequently captured and sentenced to twenty years in prison.

Using an obscure Dutch law, the kidnapper claimed *f* 50,000 in disability payments plus interest for each year spent behind bars, arguing that his mental condition, debilitated by his time in prison, prevented him from doing any work. A civil court in Groningen found in his favour.

August 27th, 2001

Sally was a ballet dancer for ten years, up until she was about sixteen. She was devoted to the art and for many years dreamed of becoming a professional ballerina, but unfortunately her Dutch heritage put paid to that dream by making her a too-tall teenager. Spending many years standing on tippy-toes ('It's on point, not tippy-toes, you fool') has left her with a few varicose veins which she has decided to have removed.

So here I am in Wing 4B of the Saint Lucas Andreas *ziekenhuis* (the charming Dutch word for 'hospital') awaiting Sally's return from routine surgery.

'We're doing the right leg, *ja*?' asked the confidence-sapping surgeon, after examining both of Sally's legs and drawing lines in green felt pen up and down both of them. The place is full of orderlies in Rasta hats and every time one of them wheels an empty bed back from the OR (or OK – *operatie kamer*), I wonder if my wife should be on it . . .

Several hours later, back home, Sally develops an intense headache. Various calls to various evasive doctors ('Oh, I t'ink you should talk to someone else') reveal that this is a common, although unpleasant, side effect of having a spinal anaesthetic. When she reaches the surgeon who'd performed the operation, he tells her to take some paracetamol ('I've had about a million,' she says. 'Oh my, dat's a lot,' he says) and to lie down frequently, although not constantly, and that she may have internal spinal leakage which, if the pain is still there in a week, might have to be cured by another spinal injection – this time of her own blood! This conversation leads to a 'leaking spine' jag.

In the bathroom: 'I couldn't get all the washing out of the machine because my spine leaked all over it.'

Pointing to the suitcase I'm taking down from on top of the

closet: 'What if my spines leaks when I'm in Tokyo? You have to pay off doctors there. They won't be used to a leaking spine. All they're used to is honoraria.'

Lying down (not constantly): 'Excuse me, Sean, is my spine leaking on the bed?'

The Next Day

Summer sure is over; it finished like a curtain coming down on a theatre stage. All of a sudden it's raining again, like the rest of the year. In a few days from now I will have been here for three years exactly. Three years. Good lord. I can hardly believe it. This time next week Sally will be in Tokyo with Ray shilling for the magazine, in the Okura Hotel on the company dime. I will be alone. I hate being alone, without Sally: it makes me more frightened of everything, mostly that for one reason or another, I'll never see her again.

But that's not all; among plenty of other things, I am very frightened of Satanic possession. It's unlikely that I will ever be a victim of it (I think) but it is nonetheless quite a scary prospect. Sometimes I can't even listen to the song 'The Jezebel Spirit' (from *My Life in the Bush of Ghosts* by Brian Eno and David Byrne) on my own, I'm that scared. And that new version of *The Exorcist* – forget it. I've been intrigued about the lost 'spider-walking' scene for years but the few times I caught even the trailer in the cinema I had to run out with my hands over my ears so as not to even *hear* any of the movie. The strange thing is that I don't even believe in the Devil. Not in any Catholic sense, anyway.

Same day. 3.30 p.m.

After picking up the ingredients for dinner (vegetarian tacos, if you must know) just now, I popped into the local wine and beer merchant Gall & Gall, at which I am a regular (and presumably valued) customer, in search of a reasonably priced wine accompaniment to vegetarian tacos. After selecting a bottle of French merlot (f18.99*) I took it up to the counter and exchanged the usual pleasantries with

*The actual price was f12.99 but I didn't want to seem cheap . . . and now I just seem like a liar.

Maarten, the tiny law-school flunk-out who has been working there full-time ever since the previous manager had a 'breakdown' after one too many youths stole one too many bottles of Bacardi Breezer six months ago (ah, good old Dutch social security).

'Well,' Maarten said, smiling up at me like an unshaven puppet. 'It's the middle of the afternoon on a Tuesday, so why aren't you at work?'

'I, uh, well, as a writer I sort of work from home,' I told him.

'Dat must be nice!' he suggested.

'It has its good points,' I said. 'And its crappy ones.'

'Like what?'

Like answering this same fucking question every time I buy a bottle of fucking booze or get my fucking hair cut! was what I wanted to say, but 'Well, there's no free stationery, for one thing,' was what I actually said. And seizing the opportunity to escape, I said, 'Okay, well, it was nice buying wine from you Maarten. I gotta get back now and . . . um . . . you now, work. From home. *Tot ziens*!

Then I slunk off home, bags filled with lettuce, beans, taco shells, cheese and that damn bottle of wine that led to all those difficult questions I prefer not to face in the middle of the afternoon. On a Tuesday.

A Very Long Way Away

Like too few other people, I'm fascinated by writers. (I'm fighting the urge to say 'other writers' but I won't because I can't stand writers who refer to writers as 'other writers', and do not wish to become one.) I'm fascinated because, for the most part writers are timid, poorly dressed, frequently bearded non-celebrities who rarely make so much as a dent in the popular consciousness due to the fact that they mutter and shuffle rather than stride about spitting out chaw and easily digested sound bites, like actors or politicians.

But every so often some writer – a Truman Capote, a Tom Wolfe or a Salman Rushdie – will break through and become '*that* writer' instead of merely '*a* writer', sometimes even with their name attached. (In the cases I mentioned, this celebrity status was based on their notable headgear – straw Stetson, white Milan and protective helmet respectively – as well as their literary talent.) My chance to become a 'literati' has passed me by, as much for my non-photogenic face and age (over thirty) as for my lack of literary stature; however, I still enjoy being around famous authors, getting books signed and asking interesting questions such as, 'Why aren't you wearing a hat?'

Which is why I decided to go and see 'that writer' Michael Chabon one night early in September. He was here in Amsterdam as a guest of the John Adams Institute, an institute named after America's second president (John Adams) and first ambassador to the Netherlands (John Adams), established to promote and maintain healthy literary relations between the two superpowers. At thirty-seven, Mr Chabon was just two years older than me; however, as winner of the 2001 Pulitzer Prize for fiction for his novel *The Amazing Adventures of Kavalier and Clay*, he was quite a bit more talented and successful.

I'd read a terrific short story by Mr Chabon called *The God of Dark Laughter*, but none of his books. Sally had told me *Wonder Boys* was 'long and stupid'* and I'd taken her word for it; on the other hand, almost a year ago a friend had told me that *Kavalier and Clay* was excellent and that I should pick it up immediately. Which I immediately did not do. In an effort to quickly familiarise myself with more of his work I hopped on to Mr Chabon's website and spent a morning reading his rejected TV series pilot, called 'House of Gold', which he'd posted there. It was a pleasant piece about several generations of a family living in Pittsburgh – no Emmy winner, but nice enough. Which just goes to show that a Pulitzer is all very well, but television is where *really* good writing counts.

I couldn't help wishing that I'd be the only one to show up to the lecture and, given the lowly status of the writer on the pop-cultural ladder, I figured there was a pretty good chance that I would be. I wasn't. In fact, there were about two hundred smartly dressed sophisticates gathered at West Indisch Huis, an elegant old building off Haarlemmerstraat with a fountain in the courtyard and expensive catering all over the place. As I sipped on a *genever*, I asked a Dutch woman what had brought her to the event – was she a fan of Chabon's? 'No, I've never read anything by him,' she told me. 'I just like to see the authors and take notes about them. Then I buy the books and later, if I want something to read, I look up the notes to remember if I liked the writer.' This struck me as either very brilliant or very insane. 'Have you read anything by him?' she asked me.

'Oh God yes, everything,' I said. 'Even his television scripts.'

The lecture itself was great, and, while not as well-dressed as most members of the audience (especially myself), Mr Chabon was very charming and amusing and self-deprecating. He talked about the inspiration for *Kavalier and Clay*, about Prague and golems and the under-appreciated art of the comic book medium; he read from his book in a pleasant, well-modulated voice then answered questions from the audience. Unfortunately, somebody

*In December of 2001, however, and only halfway through it, Sally pronounces *The Amazing Adventures of Kavalier and Clay* one of the best books she has ever read.

else beat me to it with the always entertaining, 'Where do you get your ideas from?' and the session ended before I could ask why he wasn't wearing a hat. But I took plenty of notes and based on those, I myself may well read one of his books one day.

September 26th, 2001

The staring girl across the way is back from her annual holiday break from doing nothing for a year.

Sally is back from Japan, where things went very well; she and Ray have developed and consolidated a number of relationships with contributing writers for the magazine. The first issue arrived from the printers just before they left for Tokyo and boy, it looked great. No wonder the response to the magazine in the country it was named after was so good.

I myself am just generally back – and proud.

October 8th, 2001

What a day. Last night the United States and Britain launched airstrikes against Afghanistan (part of America and CNN's 'War on Terror'); first thing this morning a Scandinavian jet crashes into a German Cessna in Milan; the *Kursk* is raised from the floor of the Barents Sea by a Dutch submarine-raising consortium; and by six o'clock there are renewed attacks on Afghanistan. In an act of stupefying generosity and law-abidement, a man suspected of planning terrorist attacks against American targets in Europe is released from Dutch custody and given almost f3000 compensation when a court in Haarlem rules that his rights have been violated because he had not been before a judge within the four-day time limit required under Dutch law.

NEWS ITEM, OCTOBER 8TH, 2001: That already wealthy writer Salman Rushdie was paid over f90,000 by the Dutch government to whip up a novel for its annual Book Week in March of this year, when over 700,000 copies were given away before it went on sale. The Dutch people were outraged that the extremely lucrative deal went to a foreigner rather than to a home-grown talent such as ... well, a home-grown talent. In Rushdie's book, *Fury*, the

main protagonist, Malik Solanka, visits Amsterdam and
the Rijksmuseum where he carries on a lot about the dis-
plays of doll's houses and is inspired to create a doll that
turns him into a star. Even in New York, where most of
the story takes place (although, curiously, it is understood
Mr Rushdie was not paid by the US government to locate
parts of his novel there), Solanka watches Holland play
'sublime football' and hangs out on Amsterdam Avenue
in Manhattan – perhaps wearing clogs and smoking a
joint, but this is not explicitly stated. Product placement
is of course well-established in movies; however, literature has always drawn a line at this sort of crass, blunt
commercialism. But thanks to Mr Rushdie and to
another already wealthy writer, Fay Weldon (who was
recently paid 'an undisclosed sum' by a jewellery firm to
incorporate its name and products into a novel), that line
appears to be blurring.

Allow me to blur it just a bit more. Coke. Or Pepsi.

October 30th, 2001
Dear Kitty,

After what seems like – and in fact, is – years, I have finally visited Amsterdam's number one tourist attraction. Not the Heineken
Free Beer Tour, not the Rijksmuseum or the Hashish Museum or
the Sex Museum or the Torture Museum; it's nothing tulip-related
and it's not a prostitute. It is, of course, the Anne Frank house/
museum/café/gift shop. The reason that I've never been before is
because every time I've passed it there's been a very long queue
all the way to the end of the block and snaking around the corner,
right down to a South American-themed cocktail bar (which I
have been to several times). But today I woke with that *I have to
see the inside of Anne Frank's house* feeling and there wasn't a
damned thing I could do about it.

The building where the families Frank and Van Pels lived in
hiding was a warehouse/office for the Opekta company, which
sold pectin used in the manufacture of jam. Otto Frank, Anne's
father and sometimes overzealous guardian of her memory,

worked for the company and it was his decision to turn the rear of the top two floors into secret dwellings. I mention this because early on in the experience there are quite a few colourful old posters for jam and, if you're unaware of Mr Frank's work history, this can be somewhat confusing. Heading further into the building, you come to assistant jam manager Victor Kugler's office, where there is more jam-related memorabilia such as tins of jam, jars of jam and lids of jars of jam.

The prescribed path is pretty winding, doubles back on itself and goes up and down a few sets of stairs, so it isn't long before I lose track of where I am, but at some point the jam theme wanes and I find myself in front of a bookcase pulled out at a forty-five degree angle, behind which is a doorway. And I know now that I've hit Anne Frank pay dirt. The doorway, through which you have to crouch (unless you're a midget; if you're a midget you just stroll on in), leads to a room wallpapered in a stale shade of brown and wood painted nausea green. It isn't clear what the families exactly did in this room, but it sure wasn't decorate. Of course, the blackout curtains account for a lot of why the room is so depressing (plus it *is* part of the Anne Frankhuis, so nobody's expecting a laff riot), and very quickly it is easy to see how grim and oppressive life here must have been. Still, I do my best to have a good time.

Unfortunately, the very next room is Anne's bedroom which is also kind of bleak. I don't start sniffling and weeping or anything, but seeing the cutouts of Simeon's old pal Ray Milland and Greta Garbo she'd stuck up on her wall in an attempt to brighten up the place does get to me. I mean Ray Milland – come on! Didn't Tyrone Power have *any* presence in wartime Amsterdam? The bedroom was where Anne did most of her writing, and while small, it is not nearly as small as the room where I do most of mine. And while I realise that, unlike young Anne, I am free to stomp around, use the phone and come and go as I please, her writing/living-in-silence-and-fear-for-more-than-two-years room has a much better view, albeit one that was obscured by heavy black curtain.

Up on the fourth floor is the communal living room, which at night was the Van Pels' bedroom. Despite the blackout curtains this is quite a cheery and sunny place; indeed Anne herself

described the room as 'large and bright'. Your own cheery disposition doesn't last though, because the next room, the front of the
top floor, is now given over to a visual account of the last months
of Anne Frank's life, following the families' betrayal, arrest and
deportation to concentration camps. It's not known who betrayed
the Franks and the Van Pels but, given my experience with them,
it is hard for me not to think it was a *makelaar* with an eye on
Prinsengracht 263.

There is a glass case containing many of the different editions
of Anne's *dagboek, diario, journal, dziennik*, which, it is frequently pointed out, has been translated into over sixty languages,
including the one where *dziennik* means 'diary'. Most of the
books have very solemn covers, except for the one issued in the
jaunty tartan that covered her actual diary, which strikes me as
appropriate. Except from a book-jacket-design point of view when
it strikes me as simply garish. (My apologies to Scotland.)

Way back downstairs is an excellent interactive CD-ROM that
covers everything you ever wanted to know about Anne Frank but
were afraid to ask in case you upset somebody. Revealed in the
section 'Day-to-Day Life', subsection 'Weekends', designation
'Sunday', paragraph '9 p.m. – 10 p.m.', is the fact that Anne used
this time alone in the bathroom to bleach the occasional dark hair
she discovered on her upper lip. Oddly, I find this tiny, intimate
fact more moving than anything I'd experienced while standing in
any of the actual rooms in the house, for which I blame a lamentable combination of my own insensitivity and the Internet. There
is also a section devoted to all the people who lived in the hidden
rooms. They appear on the screen like dossiers, containing dates
of birth and death, occupations and a category identified as
'Relationship to Anne Frank'. Such as:

'Otto Frank managed to raise his daughter with sensitivity and
love.'

'Edith had difficulties raising her daughter. Anne was extremely
rebellious toward her mother.'

'Anne Frank thought that Mrs Van Pels was stupid. She, in turn,
found Anne rude. Nevertheless, they did their best to get
along.'

'Sean Condon visited Anne's house more than half a century

after her death. Anne probably had no idea that he would be one of millions of such visitors. Then again, she may have had her suspicions.'

'Pfeffer was Anne's roommate, not voluntarily. He was often annoyed by her restless character.'

Mr Pfeffer, a dentist, comes in for further criticism in the 'Day-to-Day Life' section where they make much of the fact that when four o'clock came and it was his turn at the desk, he would loom over the scribbling Anne and assume his position at the very minute the time changed. Then they stick it to him again by pointing out that while everyone else went to bed at ten, Pfeffer chose to retire at eleven-thirty, disturbing Anne by putting away 'one of the many food parcels that his wife had sent to him'. Poor guy; if he'd known that his activities were going to be diarised and consumed all over the world for decades to come, I'm sure there would have been a lot less looming and paper-crinkling going on.

Skipping the café (because it's hard to be hungry after all that) there is the book store and gift shop, a tasteful and well-lit place where you can buy postcards, copies of the book and the afore-mentioned CD-ROM in case you forget what the Franks and Van Pels used to do between 12.30 and 1 p.m. on weekdays (vacuuming). And you can, like me, grab yourself a copy of *Anne Frank* magazine which contains, among other things, 'the only photo of Anne Frank on ice skates'.

October 31st, 2001

Went to an interview this morning for some freelance work at Wieden + Kennedy, the holy grail of advertising agencies (and arch foes of 180). The interview was with a nice fella called Glenn Cole who wore a pair of large, green, geeky spectacles, whether ironically or seriously I was unable to tell as they looked both terrible and quite excellent at the same time. I almost hyperventilated trying to be all charming and fun and interesting. Seemed to work though.

A city ordinance was passed today that allows condoms to be sold by taxi drivers in Amsterdam from next Thursday. Drivers have been asked to install vending machines in their vehicles. The first condom will be sold to Dutch soap star and presenter Winston

Gerstanowitz, whom I presume is quite the stud, despite being named Winston.

I also learned today that, according to the Study Center for Snacks and Sweets in Zeist, the Dutch are the biggest snackers in the world. But I'm not sure which fact I was more amazed by – the prodigious capacity of the Dutch to eat crap, or the fact that there was such a thing as a Study Center for Snacks and Sweets. The Netherlands boasts 15,000 different snack-type articles, provided by 250 producers and importers, and available at 75,000 sales points all over the country. And they call Australia the Lucky Country . . .

Australia is out of the World Cup. The Netherlands, too. Football supportingly, this leaves me without a nation. I need to be put in some sort of supporter's refugee camp.

BRUSHOFF WITH FAME NO. 6:
JACK RUBY

Chris Whitley is playing at the Paradiso (upstairs in the *kliene zaal*). So I make my way there with my camera and a copy of *Sean & David's Long Drive*, a book I came very close to actually dedicating to Mr Whitley, so moved and uplifted were David and I by his music, which travelled with us on that trip around Australia. After the show, accompanied by a tall, imposing Norwegian Wieden colleague named Thomas, I make my way backstage where Mr Whitley is eagerly trying to escape from the sweaty throng thrusting CD covers at him in the hope of an autograph. Just as the elevator door is about to fully close, Thomas shoves his arm into the gap and forces it open, saying, 'My friend has something he wants to give you.' As I thrust a grabbing hand into my bag, bone thin and sunken-eyed Whitley looks positively terrified, coming across as we must like tubby Jack Ruby (me) and his huge Euro-minder (Thomas). I pull my hand out of the bag, certain that Mr Whitley expects to see the black lump of his doom, and shove the book at him, explaining that he is mentioned all the way through it and that he is great and that I want to give him something of my own in return for all the moments of joy he's given me. Once he's absorbed the contents of my babbling, Whitley holds out his hand, which I just stare at. 'Thanks, man,' he says, smiling. 'That's so great. Thank you so much. And congratulations.'

'What for?' I ask.

'For, y'know, having a book published, man. That's really great.'

If you knew just how brilliant a musician – singer, guitarist, lyricist – Chris Whitley was, you'd have been struck dumb by him congratulating me for anything, too.

I can't sleep for hours after that brief meeting, an incident I'd been playing out in my head for many years before and will be replaying for years to come. And only in my head as there was not time to snap a photo of me and my musical hero.

November 30th, 2001

My neighbour Arnout once said that one thing he really disliked about this neighbourhood, possibly the entire city, was 'how deep underground you have to go just to get fuckin' milk'. I agree. In Australia, where I used to live, we have these things called 'milk bars' which are basically corner shops, more often than not run by quite unfriendly people, where you can buy a range of goods at slightly inflated prices which you don't mind paying because it means you don't have to line up for forty-five minutes to purchase, say, a box of matches or a button. In fact, you're often *glad* to pay the extra because you won't get hypertension from standing in a queue listening to people idle away the morning with some loud, dreary chat about pets or sore feet or how everyone in Amsterdam was a member of the resistance during the Second World War, just because you need milk in your coffee. They have milk bar equivalents in Amsterdam, called *nachtwinkels* or 'night shops'; however, as the name implies, they only open at night and even though night has completely draped by five these days, the Dutch retail definition of night means seven-thirty or eight. And it was due to these extremely vexing milk-purchasing circumstances that, upon returning from a relatively brief sojourn (twenty-five minutes) into the morning fluoro-gloom of the Dirk van den Broek half an hour ago, I was blocked at the entrance to our apartment block by Jaap the bus driver and his two small but very wide dogs.

'*Hoi* John,' he said. 'How are you?'

'Fine. You?'

'*Mooie dag, eh?*'

I nodded. It was (and still is) a gorgeous morning – very cold but bright, a warm-coloured sun burnishing the red brick of our large apartment block. Overnight most of the trees had lost their remaining leaves and those that had clung on for the past few weeks of winter were now scattered all over the Mercatorplein and the sidewalks. Long, pure white contrails of planes cut into the crisp blue in seven different directions. 'Yes,' I said. 'It really is.' I started to step around one of his leash-straining dogs but a medicine ball of fur and muscle hopped into my path.

'Vhere you been at?'

'Getting milk at the Dirk.'

'I know *dat* – vhere you been at for de past month? I not see you so much sinds November second.'

November second – was he keeping a record? And just how did he know I'd been getting milk at the Dirk? As much as I wanted answers to both these questions, I really didn't feel like being sucked into the conversational quagmire of chatting with Jaap; the Dutch have a seemingly inexhaustible supply of material in constant reserve for emergency weekday chatting. I had to think fast. I pointed downward. 'What breed are these dogs? They're very muscly.'

'De pitbull terrier.'

'Of course.'

'So, vhere you been at?'

'Well, Jaap, it's like this . . .' And so, against my better judgement and without actually wanting to, but either hypnotised or enervated by his insistence, boldness and curiosity, or maybe because I was just lonely, I told Jaap what I'd been doing since he last saw me. Sally and I went to Paris for a few days on or around November second, where we had a marvellous time generally wandering around the eighth arrondissement and pretending to be fancy and wealthy. As soon as we returned I had to start working at Wieden + Kennedy, on a project for Nike. Coincidentally it was more or less the very same project I'd recently had to work on for adidas at 180 – thinking of ideas for the sneaker people's World Cup 2002 website. It was a difficult but astonishingly well-paid three weeks and now that it's over I cannot help expecting a call from Puma or Reebok to see if I'm available to assist them with their WC '02 on-line plans. At W+K I worked with two Norwegian fellas, a Polish woman and a guy from the über-cool Tomato design firm in London, who drank cup-a-soup and had a terrible case of piles which he more or less constantly attended to, the soup thing probably leading to the ass thing. Wieden was an amazing contrast to 180 – almost five times the size and about five times as disorganised. One day I saw film director Terry Gilliam in the lunch room playing *fussball* and wearing an unbelievably horrible jumper. (I'd have chatted with him except for two things: I don't particularly like any of his films and I am already personal friends with Francis Coppola and one famous film director buddy is all a person really needs.) The project ended yesterday and I am confident – perhaps even relieved – that it will not be picked up by Nike and therefore never see the light of day. I hate having to prostitute myself and my few gifts to advertising, but unfortunately I must. Plus the money is just irresistible.

During those three weeks a number of notable things happened. A United Airlines plane crashed in Queens, killing about two hundred and sixty-five people; a Russian civilian airplane crashed north-east of Moscow, killing twenty-four people; two men died of smoke inhalation when their Lear jet smashed into a fence on takeoff in Salinas, California; a Crossair plane crashed in Switzerland, also killing twenty-four (including two members of the partially Dutch pop group Passion Fruit, as well as a young German/American soul singer named Melanie Thornton [who was promoting her new album entitled *Ready to Fly** – ouch], which reminded me of the fact that another young American soul singer, Aaliyah, was killed in a plane crash in the Bahamas in August,

---

*I received no payment from Ms Thornton's record company to mention the name of her album – it just seemed appropriate.

which, in turn, could not help but remind me of the many other American singers – of soul and otherwise – who have been killed in plane crashes: Buddy Holly, Patsy Cline and the real Michael Jackson to name but three); the Concorde resumed passenger flights after more than fifteen months on the ground following a crash which killed one hundred and thirteen people. Also, I explained, I was working on a book.

'You writing a book?' Jaap asked, smack-patting one of his dogs' rumps.

'Sort of. Yeah, I guess.'

'Vhat is he about?' In an expression of rich canine pleasure that made me almost embarrassed to witness, the dog's tongue drooped out of its mouth while his eyes rolled up into his head. 'Plane crashes?'

'No, he's about my life in Amsterdam for the past three years. The things that have happened to me since I came here.'

Jaap's hand started massaging the dog's behind. 'Vill I be in him?' he asked up at me.

'Oh, I wouldn't think so, Jaap,' I told him. 'But there may be an appearance by your dogs.'

Later. After a coffee – the wrong way

I have to go to the dentist this afternoon. (Why do people refer to *the* dentist and *the* doctor when there are more than one?) I have to go to a dentist this afternoon because I have a strange condition in my mouth called pain. The condition – or pain – occurs whenever something touches certain teeth: liquid, food, my tongue, air. They all cause the condition. Also there is a hole on the outside of one tooth up the back on the right near a dark, knotty collection of fillings from the 1970s.

Everything I've heard about Dutch dentists disinclines me toward visiting one. A former Boom colleague of Sally's went to a Dutch dentist a few years ago, had the wrong tooth removed then later in the day discovered that the guy had left a needle behind in her gum. She went back to have the needle extracted and the correct tooth removed – only half the procedure went correctly. A friend of my friend Stephan's had a nerve cut in his jaw when he was twelve and ever since, his mouth hangs open as though he's had a stroke. The dentist I called was recommended by Arnout who told me that he, the dentist, was 'fast'.

'I don't care about speed, Arnout. I'm after technique. Painless technique.' Arnout explained that what he meant was not how quickly the guy worked but how soon one was able to secure an appointment for this apparently rare and exclusive service. By fast, Arnout meant less than two or three weeks after calling, which made me think that perhaps I was right to call him *the* dentist; maybe there *was* only one in Amsterdam. I called six days ago and asked the woman who answered the phone whether it was the doctor's practice to use nitrous oxide.

'*Wat zeg je?*'

'Do you use nitrous oxide – laughing gas? I have very sensitive teeth. It hurts if a dentist just looks at them. I need nitrous oxide.'*

'I never heard of him,' the woman said. '*Momentje.*' There followed some conversation between her and the doctor, both of whom soon broke into hearty dental laughter. 'I t'ink maybe you go the university.'

What did she mean by this? That *I* went to the university and was pulling some non-humorous practical joke? That the only place in Amsterdam likely to have laughing gas was the university? If so, why? Was its use still in the experimental phase in this country? If that's the reason, some drug capital this turned out to be . . . Nevertheless, I have an appointment for today at two o'clock.

Killing time while I wait for D-hour, I call Sally at work to tell her that George Harrison has died. 'Two down, two to go,' she says. Sally is not, it may be gleaned from this comment, much of a Beatles fan. I, on the other hand, find it rather sad news. Apart from being the dishiest Beatle (especially in cartoon form), Harrison produced *Withnail & I* and *Mona Lisa*, two outstanding films. Plus he generally seemed to be a nice guy. He died of cancer, like everybody.

---

*While I am aware that there is some evidence that excessive or prolonged use of nitrous can damage the bone marrow and nervous system by interfering with the action of vitamin B-12, and that breathing it directly from pressurised tanks is dangerous because it is cold enough to cause frostbite of the nose, lips and vocal cords, I had nitrous oxide last time I was at a dentist – in Australia – and very much enjoyed it.

12.20 p.m.

It is with a mixture of relief and shame that I have to report that moments ago I cancelled my dental appointment. Apart from the no NO$_2$, the reason was simple: Arnout neglected to inform me that the reason it was possible to see this doctor so 'soon' is because his office is miles and miles away from where anyone lives, especially me. His main clients are probably cows.

Meanwhile I live with the pain, facing a future where the only thing I can be certain of is that it will always be difficult to get milk between nine and five.

The Dutch drinkers were clutching their *fluitjes* of beer, staring at us and the empty bottles that littered our table. It was three and a quarter years after we arrived in Amsterdam, and Ray, Sally, Sonia and I had gathered in a small bar on a crooked, nervous alley in the Jordaan to drink champagne* in celebration of this and the second issue of *Japan*. Like the first issue, it was a very impressive piece of work: intelligent, sophisticated, relevant, original and altogether worthwhile. It was everything most other magazines aren't. My tooth was still bothering me (investigative work by my busy tongue had deepened and widened the hole) and although I spoke somewhat strangely (like a teamster in urgent need of a dentist), I meant everything I said. 'Picture yourselves back in the dark, waning months of 1998, my friends,' I commanded. 'A night when our fortunes came undone in a most spectacular and dramatic fashion; when our reasons for being in this city were suddenly no longer. When our lives appeared to be without hope, purpose or meaning – like so many TV stars who tried to break into film. Imagine yourselves back in the sorry depths of that bleak night and then look at where we are now.'

'Stop talking like that, you foppish fop,' Sally ordered, holding her champagne glass up to the light, counting bubbles.

'My point being that back then none of us could have imagined that things would be the way they are now.'

---

*Final negotiations between my representatives and those of the champagne manufacturer are still pending so it is with regret that I cannot mention the brand.

'It's amazing,' Sonia said. 'Nowhere to live, no magazine, no work . . . It's a wonder that we're still here.'

'It *is* amazing and none of it could have happened if we were still living in Melbourne.' By this time I was a little drunk, becoming confident and certain of my assertions.

'And is that a good thing or a bad thing?'

'Oh, it's a good thing, Ray,' I asserted with a slight but certain slur. 'I'm sure of it. Everything is completely different for all of us. Everything that's happened since we came here has added up to very different lives than we possibly could have led in Australia, and taken us to a very different place. Which obviously I mean more than just literally. You guys wouldn't be responsible for this great new magazine, I'd never have met Coppola and Roger Moore and all those other people, Archie might have been born with different hair. This is all very specifically northern hemisphere stuff. It's the happening hemisphere.' I thought for a moment about what exactly I meant by this. 'Events unfold *live* up here. Before your very eyes.'

Sally agreed. 'It's true. Like when they were bombing Kosovo and we could see the B-52s flying over us.'

'Exactly. You feel much closer to events.'

'It's a shame so many of them are terrible events.' As a journalist, Sonia had covered the Lockerbie trial and hearings at the War Crimes Tribunal in The Hague: she was closer to these events than staring up at the sky or at the television.

'But terrible or wonderful, we're closer to them,' I said. 'We're right in the thrilling proximity of history.'

'You'd think it'd be different in the electronic age,' Ray said. 'That you wouldn't feel so far away in the southern hemisphere.'

'You would. But it's not. North is still north and south feels a very long way away.'

'So I guess that means we're staying up here,' Sally said. 'Europe. Or America if the Green Card lottery comes through.'

'Where else would we go?' I said. 'Provence? Tuscany?' Both Sally and Sonia sighed with approval at these destinations. 'We're too young to live in those places,' I said. 'Too young and too poor.'

'The food, though,' Sally said. 'My God, the food . . .'

'So what are you gonna do now, Connie?'

'The usual – write, worry about stuff. Try to become *that* writer instead of *a* writer.'

'What's that supposed to mean?'

'Something I've been thinking about, to do with dreams and success. How you wish things were, as opposed to how they actually are. But I guess that gap is what makes life interesting – reality colliding with your dreams.'

'Yeah. If only there was less collision and more collusion,' Ray said, opening the bar's one remaining bottle of champagne. I agreed. But then I wondered, if there was more collusion, less collision, where would I be then? And soon, much sooner than any of us wished or expected, the barman called last drinks and it was time for us to leave, to go home.

Epilogue: Collision

Weeks later there's still just a nasty space of jagged outcrops and splinters where my tooth used to be. My dental neglect has resulted in the ulceration of my tongue and mouth – it is a warm, moist moonscape of pain in there, and I also have a flu that makes me boil and shiver and not be able to eat or walk much; my thoughts are feverish, Stockhausenesque in their discord. In a few days, Sally and I are flying back to Melbourne for the first time in three and a half years. We are excited and nervous, dreading the inevitable changes we'll have to face – in our friends and family, in the city, in ourselves – and curious about what we will see, what's been happening while we've been gone.

Sally and Ray have been working like madmen – until midnight for ten days straight – preparing the third issue of *Japan* for printing. They're both exhausted but thrilled; it's the best one yet. They've finally got the magazine looking exactly the way they want. They're proud but almost too tired to feel it. I keep thinking about my suitcase, how it's empty and how I'll need Sally's help to pack it because I'm too faint to properly embrace the concept that is summer clothing – to fold it and pack it, to imagine wearing it later this week.

Much earlier than I expect I hear keys in the front door, warming to my weakened heart. 'Hi honey, you're home,' I yell from the living room where I am lying on the floor, but it sounds flat, feeble because of my flu and lumpen tongue. The keys are dropped on the table in the hallway, followed by a sad sniffle. 'What's up? Is it the euro, baby? Are you still having trouble with how the coins all look the same?' Sally comes into the living room. I look up at her and can see tears in her eyes; I can tell that she has been crying for some time. 'What is it?'

'The magazine's folded. The whole company's bankrupt.'

For a moment my mind empties, then, like an upended hour-glass, very slowly begins to fill with tiny, inadequate words. 'Oh, no . . .'

'Everybody's . . . we've all lost our jobs.' I get up off the floor and put my arms around my wife's heaving shoulders. 'They're saying it's because of September 11th. Part of it, anyway. That it was a bad time to launch and . . .' I can hardly believe what's happened, the palindromatic nature of our life over the last three years; how we left Australia for Amsterdam because of a magazine which collapsed shortly after we arrived, and how another magazine collapses shortly before we leave Amsterdam for Australia. It's incredible, but it's true. 'It's just . . . it's not fair.'

'I know, baby.' And she's right; it is not fair. Ray and Sally are both extremely intelligent, talented editors who worked hard to produce something good in the world, and who have both had a dream collide harshly with reality, seeing their hard work and dedication come to nothing. I feel awful waves of sympathy for them both, so powerful that I'm unsteady on my feet. The dissolution of the magazine also means that Sally's and my residency status is, yet again, imperilled. 'How's Ray?'

Sally sobs as she tells me that he and Sonia are already talking about moving to Italy. 'They've had it with this place.'

They're not the only ones: Simeon and Darcy have recently been thinking seriously of heading back to New York City; Arnout and Diana are planning to live in Biarritz; our friends Michelle and Stephan are going to work in Australia; Joey never made it back from Warsaw; Keith is still here – but only because the Dutch government doesn't know it. Perhaps there's something wrong with Amsterdam, or something wrong with people like us trying to live in Amsterdam. Or perhaps it's simply that none of us are rich, whimsical retirees and this is not Provence. Whatever it is, this city has failed us somehow, or we it. It makes me melancholy to recall the naive, foolish hopes I'd had for our new lives in a new city; that few of anybody's dreams and expectations really came to pass. But at the same time I don't regret for a moment our decision to move to Europe, because the great chasm between desire and reality truly is what makes life interesting.

Because that gap has made my damn life – if not particularly satisfying or enriching or valuable or adventuresome or even very
brutal and difficult – interesting. Sort of.

Two days later, as we sit on the plane taking us back to the place
where we used to live, Sally and I talk about our deep and great
hopes for that Green Card, but in the meantime, no matter what
happens to us or where we end up, wherever Sally is, I will be
home. I reach across the seat, take my wife's hand in mine and tell
her that everything will be all right, that I love her. 'Not on the
plane, baby,' she says. 'It's embarrassing.'